Teachers for the
New Millennium

Association of Teacher Educators

The National Congress on Teacher Education was sponsored by ATE in cooperation with the American Association of Colleges for Teacher Education and supported in part by the United States Department of Education, Office of Educational Research and Improvement. Other supporters of the congress were the College of Education, National-Louis University; the College of Education, University of Houston; the College of Education, University of South Carolina; the College of Education, Wayne State University; and IDS Financial Services. The National Congress on Teacher Education was held in Washington, D.C., December 10–12, 1995. The opinions, conclusions, and recommendations expressed by the contributors to this book do not necessarily reflect the views or the opinions of ATE, AACTE, or the United States Department of Education. None of the organizations supporting the congress endorse or warrant the content. Readers must evaluate and use the content in light of their unique circumstances.

Teachers for the New Millennium

Aligning Teacher Development, National Goals, and High Standards for All Students

Editors
Leonard Kaplan
Roy A. Edelfelt

CORWIN PRESS, INC.
A Sage Publications Company
Thousand Oaks, California

For information address:

Corwin Press, Inc.
A Sage Publications Company
2455 Teller Road
Thousand Oaks, California 91320
e-mail: order@corwin.sagepub.com

SAGE Publications Ltd.
6 Bonhill Street
London EC2A 4PU
United Kingdom

SAGE Publications India Pvt. Ltd.
M-32 Market
Greater Kailash I
New Delhi 110 048 India

Printed in the United States of America

Library of Congress Cataloging-in-Publication Data

Teachers for the new millennium : aligning teacher development,
    national goals, and high standards for all students / [edited by]
    Leonard Kaplan, Roy A. Edelfelt.
        p.   cm.
    A selection of papers presented at the National Congress on
Teacher Education, held Dec. 10-12, 1995, in Washington, D.C.
    Includes bibliographical references.
    ISBN 0-8039-6468-4 (cloth : alk. paper). — ISBN 0-8039-6469-2
(paper : alk. paper)
    1. Teachers—Training of—United States—Congresses. 2. Teachers—
Training of—Standards—United States—Congresses.   I. Kaplan,
Leonard, 1935-   . II. Edelfelt, Roy A.   III. National Congress on
Teacher Education (1995 : Washington, D.C.)
LB1715.T427   1996
370,71'0973—dc20   96-19928

This book is printed on acid-free paper.

96 97 98 99 00 10 9 8 7 6 5 4 3 2

Corwin Press Production Editor: S. Marlene Head

Contents

Foreword

American education faces significant challenges in responding to the talents and the needs of a growing and increasingly diverse student population. Today's and tomorrow's students will have to prepare themselves for what Linda Darling-Hammond calls the "thinking work" of information-age, global economies. Equally important, if American society is to flourish, its education system must join with parents, families, communities, and others in emphasizing the importance of personal and civic responsibility, strong character, hard work, and cooperation, as well as respect and caring for the cultures, the ideas, and the worth of others.

Much is happening in American education to meet these challenges. Higher standards for what students need to know and be able to do, more rigorous curricula and more authentic assessments, better use of technology, and restructured schools and classrooms are just a few examples of the essential changes under way.

The heart of the matter, though, is the day-to-day interaction of teachers and students. Without competent, creative, and caring teachers who expect and demand the best from themselves and from all their students, other changes will have little effect. Teachers must model the content mastery, the inquiry skills, the responsibility, the character, and the excitement for learning that they expect of their students. In turn, those who educate teachers must be models of exemplary practice. Research on both student and teacher learning strongly suggests that the way one is taught is a much stronger influence on learning than what is said.

Teachers must also have the support of other educators, families, and communities to help create rigorous, relevant, and safe learning environments for both students and teachers. A well-supported teacher workforce of excellence that is also reflective of and responsive to the diversity of students is imperative.

The National Congress on Teacher Education focused on how to recruit, prepare, license, induct, and continuously develop and support such a workforce. The Association of Teacher Educators, in cooperation with the American Association of Colleges for Teacher Education and with support from the U.S. Department of Education, brought together a wide range of education stakeholders to examine what is known and what needs to be done at many levels of the system to improve teacher development and teaching. The emphasis was on cross-role, small-group sessions in which participants focused on specific issues and developed research-based, practically grounded action plans for addressing those issues. Among the questions that guided discussions were these:

- What changes in policy, practice, and research are necessary to ensure that teachers can meet the needs of all students striving to reach high standards?
- What partnerships and strategies will be needed among stakeholders to garner and to use effectively the resources necessary to support those changes?

This book describes the deliberations on those questions, and their results. Although a major focus is on how to improve the content and the strategies of teacher preparation, considerable attention goes to what needs to happen before and after teacher preparation. The roles and the responsibilities of higher education institutions, local education agencies, state officials, the federal government, other human service professions, foundations, parents, communities, and business are prominent subjects of discussion.

In all likelihood, the reader will find views with which to agree and disagree, for discussions were wide ranging and opinions varied. The sponsoring agencies made no attempt to suppress viewpoints or to demand consensus. The intent was to invite diverse perspectives, air differences, and seek common ground on which to build.

The congress is an early step in what will be a long journey. Unless the participants in the congress and the readers of this volume take ideas and strategies of merit from the deliberations and act on them at home, the congress will not have served its purpose. Many participants have indicated that they will do so. I hope that readers will discover stimulating ideas and specific strategies that will motivate them to reflect, adapt, integrate, and improve on what is here, and to strengthen their own efforts. Teachers, students, and the nation will be the beneficiaries.

JOSEPH C. VAUGHAN
Special Advisor for Professional Development
Office of Educational Research and Improvement
U.S. Department of Education

Preface and Acknowledgments

Not long ago, I visited a kindergarten class in Detroit. The children were drawing pictures. I asked one 5-year-old, who supposedly came from a dysfunctional family, about her picture. "I'm drawing God," she said. "That's interesting," I remarked, "particularly because no one really knows what God looks like." Without hesitation she replied, "People will know what God looks like just as soon as I finish my picture." An awesome child. Is she unusual? I think not. Children who believe in the possible may not attain the notoriety of children who are angry, frightened, and unmotivated, but they are in America's homes and schools, in abundance.

Who are these children? They come from two-parent, one-parent, and no-parent homes. They are well fed, poorly fed, and not fed. They are in excellent health and in substandard health. Clearly, not all children come to school ready to learn; however, they come to school. America has declared a goal that by the year 2000, all children will come to school ready to learn. Many suggest that in light of the myriad problems facing America's communities and schools, this goal is unattainable. Maybe so. A more important, more realistic issue is whether schools will be ready to receive the nation's awesome children.

It is commonplace today to hear that schools are in varying degrees of disrepair. Supposedly, SAT scores are down, other standardized tests indicate a general decline in student achievement, and a general malaise has fallen over the schools. Those who believe what is suggested in *The Manufactured Crisis* (Berliner & Biddle, 1995) may be more optimistic. Of course, 1996 is an election year, so debate is likely to continue and even to increase. From this persistent dialogue will come calls for schools of choice, vouchers, charter schools, privatization, home schooling, change, and reform. What will not come is a call for no schools. Some place called school will continue to exist, and some form of human will be called on to teach in it. This raises myriad questions, particularly in light of America's constantly changing society. What do these new realities mean for how the nation educates its students? What will a society that cannot agree on basic values demand of its teachers? What kinds of partnerships will be necessary among schools, higher education institutions, families and communities, government agencies, and others to do the job? Will technology replace Mr. Peepers, Our Miss Brooks, Jaime Escalante, Tom Fleming, Louanne Johnson, and Terry Dozier? There are many questions and, for each, literally dozens of answers.

In 1993, the Association of Teacher Educators (ATE) created five new commissions and charged them to grapple with these and other questions directly influencing present and future directions in teacher education. The commissions, which continue to function, are Gender Equity in Education, Interprofessional Human Services in Teacher Education, Quality Standards and Teacher Education, Teachers in Urban Settings, and Teacher Education. Each group responded in its own way to its mandate. The Commission on Teacher Education coordinated much of the input from each of the other commissions. after 2 years of planning, the group put together a central theme, a National Congress on Teacher Education. A dream was in motion.

ATE and the American Association of Colleges for Teacher Education (AACTE), supported in part by the U.S. Department of Education's Office of Educational Research and Improvement, organized a congress that would bring together all the stakeholders in the preparation of the American teaching force. The philosophy behind this concept was simple: Those who teach America's children must view them as a societal concern, and even though professional teacher educators have much invested, all citizens benefit from an enlightened and sensitive teaching force.

Congress organizers commissioned five papers to serve as stimuli for dialogue and debate. Participants in the congress received the papers in advance. The papers appear in this volume as Chapters 2–6, each accompanied by a response.

Mary E. Diez, in "Who Will Prepare the Next Generation of Teachers?" raises five critical questions. She observes that many models of effective teaching are available, but not all meet six criteria that seem essential to successful teacher preparation. "Too few of the reform programs have addressed standards of performance and assessment as both a tool for development and a documentation of progress" (p. 34).

In "Right-Sizing Teacher Education: The Policy Imperative," Nancy L. Zimpher acknowledges a lack of leadership in the teacher education profession, thereby making it almost impossible for education schools to achieve professional status within the academy. Rather than speaking with one voice, teacher education speaks with many voices: those of large research-oriented universities, small colleges, and private, public, or religious institutions with diverse missions; those of various organizations; those of academic disciplines; and those of individuals. In her chapter, Zimpher identifies six conditions that not only balkanize the profession but may make it impossible to solidify philosophies and practices.

Carl A. Grant, in "The Influence of Agencies on Teacher Preparation: Social Justice in the New Millennium," asks teacher educators to reexamine what motivated them to enter the teaching profession. A commitment to social justice may be in conflict with a need to exert influence on education's policies and practices. He questions the profession's attention to the issues of equity and equality. "Without a new vision that 'revives debate and democracy internally and projects an inspiring social vision and agenda externally, we will fall short of the challenges before us' " ("Social Justice Unionism," 1994, as quoted in Grant, p. 96).

In "The Preparation of Teachers for a Diverse, Free Society," Martin J. Haberman contends that making university-based teacher education more multicultural would require a total reconstruction. Because of his skepticism, he suggests that alternative certification is the way to provide the number and the quality of teachers for schools in need of personnel for a diverse, free society. Haberman focuses on schools that attempt to serve the urban poor. However, his remarks are applicable to any setting that attempts to educate those whom American society has identified as the neediest.

Dean Corrigan, in "Teacher Education and Interprofessional Collaboration: Creation of Family-Centered, Community-Based Integrated Service Systems," argues that no single profession can assume the full responsibility for the nation's children. The problems facing youth today may be unparalleled and cannot be solved by a well-intended teacher, even though he or she is concerned with the whole child. All agencies concerned with young people—that is, social services, health, business, law, government, and especially families and communities—must learn to work together. Only through integrated services can America create an institution prepared to address the full development of its children.

The views on teacher education expressed in these chapters are controversial. However, the charge to the writers was to stimulate thinking. The 1990s are a time of skepticism and basic mistrust of most institutions. Schools that educate children and institutions that prepare teachers have not been excused or removed from the national debate.

Mary Hatwood Futrell, a former president of the National Education Association and currently the Dean of Education at George Washington University, and Richard W. Riley, the Secretary of Education, emphasize in their chapters the need for partnerships between the established profession and other constituencies, particularly families and communities. Both praise teaching as a career of value but also discuss the political, social, and economic strains on schools and teachers.

In this election year, it is imperative that educators reach consensus on issues such as certification, standards, national goals, staff development needs, and the role of the school in an ever-changing society. Sharon Robinson, Assistant Secretary of Education, suggests in her chapter that if educators cannot achieve consensus on these critical issues, the congress will not have lived up to its potential.

For many, collaboration among ATE, AACTE, and the Department of Education on a project as auspicious as the National Congress on Teacher Education is a beginning step toward consensus. ATE and AACTE represent individuals and institutions committed to effective teacher education policy and practice. Working toward consensus is a proactive stance, and a far cry from the reactive position frequently taken by professional organizations. Each organization seems prepared to reach out to its members for input into critical decision making. Even if the critics—and they are out there—continue to scoff, the profession can respond with a common set of beliefs. As Toffler (1980) advises, "We must do more than identify major trends. Difficult as it may be, we must resist the temptation to be seduced by straight lines." The ability to speak as one may be a tactic yet untested by teacher educators. I hope that *Teachers for the New Millennium* can help stimulate and focus dialogue.

Many friends and colleagues played significant roles in planning and implementing the National Congress on Teacher Education.

Much of the credit for conceptualizing the meeting goes to the ATE Commission on Teacher Education: Fred Sheheen, chair; Billy Dixon, Penny Early, Nancy Henzel, Richard Ishler, Leonard Kaplan, Ann Lydecker, John McIntyre, Judy Munn, Hans Olsen, Bill Peter, Robert Poch, and Betty Siegel.

We are very grateful to the more than 40 discussion leaders and facilitators who went through a rather strenuous training session ensuring commonality of purpose and who met before and after sessions to debrief and synthesize group discussions. Some of these people developed computer skills that they never realized they possessed.

A special acknowledgment goes to Sylvia Auton, Roy A. Edelfelt, Mary Ann Lecos, and Marilyn Scannell for their leadership. They orchestrated the activities, provided information and updates, and kept the congress on track.

The entire effort would not have been possible without the input, leadership, and good humor of Gloria Chernay, the executive director of ATE; David Imig, the chief executive officer of AACTE; and Joseph Vaughan, the project's program officer in the Office of Educational Research and Improvement. They and those with whom they work went the extra mile to ensure a successful and possibly historic conference.

Leonard Kaplan
Wayne State University
Chair, Planning Committee for the
National Congress on Teacher Education
and 1993–1994 President of ATE

References

Berliner, D. C., & Biddle, B. J. (1995). *The manufactured crisis.* Reading, MA: Addison-Wesley.

Social justice unionism: A working draft—A call to education unionists. (1994, Autumn). *Rethinking Schools, 9*(1), 12–13.

Toffler, A. (1980). *The third wave.* New York: Morrow.

About the Contributors

Barbara G. Burch is currently Vice President for Academic Affairs at Western Kentucky University. At the time she contributed to this book, she was Dean of the School of Education and Human Development at California State University, Fresno. She is the 1996–1997 president of AACTE and a past president of the Teacher Education Council of State Colleges and Universities. She has served on the Executive Committee of the Renaissance Group and on the Unit Accreditation Board, the Board of Examiners, and the Executive Council of the National Council for Accreditation of Teacher Education.

Dean Corrigan is Professor in the Department of Educational Administration at Texas A&M University and Director of Commitment to Education, a program that involves the university, the public schools, and the private sector. Earlier, he served as Dean of the university's College of Education. A past president of AACTE, he currently chairs ATE's National Commission on Leadership in Interprofessional Education to Create Family-Centered, Community-Based Education, Health, and Human Service Systems. He served on the editorial board of the first edition of ATE's *Handbook of Research on Teacher Education* and coauthored the chapter on the context of education with Martin J. Haberman. He authored the chapter on interprofessional education in the second edition.

Kathleen Densmore is Assistant Professor in the College of Education at San Jose State University in California. Sociology of education is one of her specializations. Currently, she coordinates a community service program for the university and surrounding communities. She also teaches in a bridge-to-college program for underrepresented high school students. Her research addresses the relationship between social change and educational change. She is bilingual and has taught and conducted research in three Latin American countries.

Mary E. Diez is Professor of Education and Dean of the School of Education at Alverno College in Milwaukee, Wisconsin. A 1995 winner of the McGraw Education Prize for her work in teacher education and a past president of AACTE, she serves on the National Board for Professional Teaching Standards, the Interstate New Teacher Assessment and Support Consortium, and the Board of Examiners of the National Council for Accreditation of Teacher Education. She was a member of the Alverno College faculty that pioneered an ability-based curriculum and a performance assessment program on the college level in the 1970s.

Edward R. Ducharme is the Ellis & Nelle Levitt Distinguished Professor of Education at Drake University in Des Moines, Iowa, where he has taught for the past 5 years. He is also a professor of education emeritus at the University of Vermont, where he taught and chaired academic departments for 19 years. He has published widely on teacher education, higher education faculty development, public education, and secondary teaching. Among his contributions are the chapter on needed research in teacher education in the second edition of ATE's *Handbook of Research on Teacher Education,* coauthored with Mary K. Ducharme, and the chapter on teacher education faculty in the *Teacher Educator's Handbook.* He and Mary K. Ducharme currently serve as coeditors of the *Journal of Teacher Education.*

Roy A. Edelfelt is Clinical Professor at the University of North Carolina at Chapel Hill and Adjunct Professor at North Carolina State University. He is also a partner in Edelfelt Johnson, a partnership specializing in consulting, writing, editing, and desktop publishing. Earlier, he served as Executive Secretary of the National Commission on Teacher Education and Professional Standards. Among his many publications are a chapter in the first edition of ATE's *Handbook of Research on Teacher Education,* coauthored with Ronald G. Corwin and William I. Burke, titled "The Impact of Federal Funding for Research and Demonstration on Teacher Education," and a book, *Careers in Education.* He is the managing editor of the *ATE Newsletter.*

Mary Hatwood Futrell is Dean of the Graduate School of Education and Human Development at George Washington University and Director of the school's Institute for Curriculum, Standards, and Technology. Through the institute, the university has taken a leadership role in implementing the voluntary certification process of the National Board for Professional Teaching Standards. She is a former president of the National Education Association and of the World Confederation of Organizations of the Teaching Profession and a member of the boards of the Carnegie Foundation for the Advancement of Teaching, the Kettering Foundation, the Newspaper Association of America, and the Institute for Educational Leadership.

Carl A. Grant is Hoefs-Bascom Professor of Teacher Education in the Department of Curriculum and Instruction and Professor in the Department of Afro-American Studies at the University of Wisconsin–Madison. In 1993, he became President of the National Association for Multicultural Education. In 1994, he was named Adams Visiting Distinguished Professor at Indiana State University. He has written or edited 15 books or monographs in multicultural education and teacher education, among them *Research and Multicultural Education* and *Making Choices for Multicultural Education* (with Christine E. Sleeter). He was a Fulbright Scholar in England in 1982–1983, researching and studying multicultural education. In 1990, ATE selected him as one of 70 leaders in teacher education.

Martin J. Haberman is Professor at the University of Wisconsin–Milwaukee. The most widely known of his contributions to teacher education over the past 30 years is the National Teacher Corps, which was based on his intern program in Milwaukee. He has conducted numerous research studies and published many articles and books. Also, he served as the editor of the *Journal of Teacher Education* for 6 years. He holds a Standard Oil Award for Excellence in Teaching and AACTE medals for the Hunt Lectureship and the Pomeroy Award (1990). The Wisconsin School Boards Association named him Teacher of the Year.

Leonard Kaplan is Professor of Education at Wayne State University in Michigan. He served as the 1993–1994 President of ATE and Chair of the Planning Committee for the National Congress on Teacher Education. Among his publications are *Education and the Family* and

Classrooms at the Crossroads. He teaches and writes in the general area of curriculum and instruction, with an emphasis on the role of the family in education and the relationship of affect to current issues of teaching and learning.

Richard W. Riley is the Secretary of Education. President Bill Clinton chose Riley for the post so that he could help work the same kind of education reform on a national scale that he had done as a two-term governor of South Carolina. A 1959 graduate of the University of South Carolina's law school, he served as legal counsel to the Judiciary Committee of the U.S. Senate in his early years out of law school. Later, he won election as state representative, then state senator, then governor. In the latter role, he spearheaded a comprehensive and highly successful reform of the state's school system by bringing together a coalition of groups, including businesspeople, educators, and parents.

Sharon Porter Robinson is Assistant Secretary for Educational Research and Improvement in the U.S. Department of Education. Before assuming that position, she served in various leadership positions at the National Education Association. She has also served as a consultant to the National Board for Professional Teaching Standards. A lifelong civil rights activist, she has waged a personal crusade to convince the education community of the economic necessity and the ethical responsibility to develop strategies to ensure that traditionally underserved student populations (e.g., minorities, students with disabilities, and students in both remote rural districts and beleaguered inner cities) receive an education that unleashes their potential.

Edward M. Wolpert is Dean of the School of Education at Georgia College. Before moving to the South, he spent 13 years at Ball State University as Professor of Elementary Education, the last 3 as chair of the department. He has written numerous articles on reading as well as other aspects of education and is the author of a college textbook, *Understanding Research in Education: A Consumer Guide to Critical Reading,* now in its third edition.

Nancy L. Zimpher is Dean of the College of Education at Ohio State University and Executive Dean of the Council of Professional College Deans. Her academic specialization is in teacher education and the continuing professional development of teachers. Among her many commitments, she serves on a national research team studying the perceptions by faculties, students, administrators, and other school personnel of teacher education programs. She is the recipient of the Ohio State University Alumni Distinguished Teaching Award and ATE's Distinguished Research Award. Also, ATE recognized her on its 70th anniversary as one of 70 distinguished educators.

1

The Courage to Change

MARY HATWOOD FUTRELL
George Washington University

My central thesis in this chapter is the courage to change. I use it to sketch my view of where teacher education is and to raise some challenges about where teacher education ought to be and what changes teacher educators ought to make.

I believe deeply that through education, individuals are better able to fulfill their roles and responsibilities in a democratic society. The education of the people must therefore be the first concern of a democratic state. This means that teacher educators must have the courage to change the education system. They must have the courage to insist that each generation receives the knowledge, the skills, and the training that will prepare children to help the nation fulfill its democratic mission and its mission of *e pluribus unum,* "one out of many."

I want to expound on the concept of courage to change by sharing an incident that occurred in the life of one of this nation's leaders. A little more than 32 years ago, a young man delivered what may have been the most remarkable speech of his brief and brilliant career. He spoke with passion and he spoke of peace:

> We are confronted primarily with a moral issue. It is as old as the scriptures and is as clear as the American Constitution. The heart of the question is whether all Americans are to be afforded equal rights and equal opportunities. ... Those who do nothing are inviting shame as well as violence. Those who act boldly are recognizing right as well as reality. (Kennedy, 1964, p. 469)

1

In that address, on June 11, 1963, President John F. Kennedy broke with his political past, discarding long-held and firmly held convictions.

This was a new Kennedy. This was a changed Kennedy, challenging Americans to accept the challenge of change. I invoke this quote, not because of the radiance of its rhetoric or the nobility of its sentiments, but because of its illumination of the direction in which individual teacher educators and teacher education institutions must move. On the day that Kennedy rebelled against his own most cherished convictions, he taught a lesson that has lost none of its relevance and none of its potency: There is more danger in complacency than in inconsistency.

As educators look to the future of education in the United States, they must see that this lesson drives their institutional agenda and shapes their educational priorities. The new world now in the making demands that all educators become brazen, bold, skeptical of the established order, and fearless in the face of a fearsome future. The world that is dawning demands above all a change in educators' attitude toward change.

Today's change confronts educators with a harsh choice: They can be either victims of change or agents of change. If they are not to be victimized, they must reexamine the convictions that bind them to the past. They must abandon what Secretary of Labor Robert Reich (1992) has called "vestigial thought" (p. 106), thought that stymies creativity and stifles innovation.

Should they fail to do this, education will lose forever the cutting-edge position that many have struggled for years to secure. Educators will violate the integrity of their profession. They will prove unworthy of public trust. They will break faith with those whom they teach: the men and the women who will play a vital role in determining the destiny of this democracy and the fate of the planet.

I refuse to believe that educators will permit this tragedy to unfold. However, this nation will not be prepared for the cataclysmic changes and colossal challenges of the 21st century unless teacher educators recommit themselves to finding more effective ways to prepare teachers to prepare future generations to address those changes and challenges.

The transformation that the profession now needs will occur only if teacher educators divest themselves of the assumption that the domain of education still neatly divides into the traditional triad.

Stated differently, teacher educators need to expose the foolishness of the dogma that it is still legitimate to talk of elementary school, secondary school, and postsecondary education as if they were three distinct domains existing in splendid isolation. As Ernest L. Boyer (1987) said in the foreword to the book *College,*

> All educational levels are related, and there is, we believe, an urgent need to bring colleges and universities more directly into the national debate about the purposes and goals of American education. If the push for educational excellence is to yield results, the nation's colleges and universities must ask hard questions about the quality of their own work. (p. xi)

Although *College* specifically addresses the undergraduate experience in America, it applies to all levels of education.

The traditional education triad is the Berlin wall of the education world. Educators ought to demolish it, for what becomes more obvious every day is that education is indivisible and that no part of education can prosper if any part hits bad times.

I shall express this more concretely: The fate of the schools and the colleges and universities in which teacher educators teach—in sum, the fate of the nation—depends on efforts to improve K–12 schools and colleges and universities and to improve the quality of life for the nation's citizens. The educational landscape has shifted. Old borders—borders that defined and divided educators—must be removed. Educators need a radical shift in their approach to the problems, the challenges, the opportunities that await them.

One last metaphor, which goes to the heart of the matter: Educators are all in the same boat.

Dean Corrigan says it well in Chapter 6: "The starting point in defining the purposes of integrated services, teacher education, and interprofessional development should be the actual needs, problems, and conditions of America's children and their families" (p. 146). He goes on to say this:

- Violence permeates the environments of families at all socioeconomic levels.
- Prejudice, racism, and polarization divide Americans.
- Family structures and roles are changing.

- Child care services are not available to help parents meet the enormous responsibilities of rearing a child while employed full-time, or to meet the needs of single-parent families.
- Homelessness is reaching epidemic proportions.
- Value systems are being transformed as children see materialistic rewards coming from dealing drugs and engaging in other illicit activities rather than from working at the kinds of jobs that can be obtained as a result of schooling. (pp. 146–148)

All educators—teachers, counselors, and administrators, whether at the preschool or postsecondary level—are affected by these conditions. The education community cannot single-handedly respond to them. Nor should it be expected to do so. Yet the profession and its clientele, the nation's children and youth, are being told to do more with less or to wait until things get better.

The children of America, regardless of ethnicity, race, gender, socioeconomic status, or exceptionality, cannot afford to wait. The type of education and support services that they receive today will determine not only their future but the nation's future in the new millennium.

To provide this nurturance and support means that all of education must join forces to create a vastly improved, more rigorous system of education for the nation's people, especially for America's children. The boundaries that once defined the domains of education must disappear. Interdependence defines the new reality. This fact will soon be impressed on all educators in a manner that will be decidedly unpleasant.

Public Perceptions of Education

The public's perception of education—all of education—is that the enterprise is still on the slippery slope of mediocrity. Following are a few examples:

A report from Public Agenda (Johnson, 1995), titled *Assignment Incomplete: The Unfinished Business of Education Reform,* states on the basis of extensive surveys and focus groups, "American support for public education is fragile and porous" (p. 5). According to this report, increasing numbers of Americans do not believe that public schools are safe, have high academic standards, or place enough emphasis on core values such as honesty, trustworthiness, and hard work. People want the public school system to provide an environment that is conducive to teaching and learning. Concomitantly, they strongly and consistently support higher academic standards for all children. However, the report emphasizes, if educators do not demonstrably change the public education system, parents, especially those in minority and low-income families, will turn to private schools.

Another recent example: The 26th annual Phi Delta Kappa/Gallup poll on education in the United States (Elam & Rose, 1994) shows that people give the school attended by their eldest child good grades: 70% give it an A or a B, 92% a passing grade. However, they give the nation's schools as a whole considerably lower grades: 22% an A or a B, 71% a passing grade. Most people polled do not believe that after 11 years of education reform, the schools in their community have improved, especially not in the past 5 years.

Two problems—the growth of fighting/violence/gangs and poor discipline—are by far the most serious ones that the public believes the schools are facing. This perception is vividly reflected and reinforced in the expanding voucher or educational choice movement. Although Americans reaffirmed their historical opposition to the government's providing financial support to those who choose non-public schools for their children's education, there is increasing support for educational choice programs.

Support for higher education, although still strong, has also begun to decline. Three recent reports from the American Council on Education (Harvey & Associates, 1994; Harvey & Immerwahr, 1995a, 1995b) indicate that the golden age of higher education is over. It is over in terms of finances, in terms of leaders' uncritical approbation of the work of the nation's colleges and universities, and possibly in terms of freedom from regulation.

Perceptions have severely damaged education's prestige, but the frontal assault on all of education is obviously still strong. The critical point here goes back to all my earlier comments: If educators are to reverse the crisis plaguing education, they must take proactive stances, they must implement systemic changes that enhance the quality of education for all students, and the changes must be comprehensive and courageous.

Educators should change, not because certain right-wing ideologies would like to use them as scapegoats for all the maladies that afflict the society, but because the challenges confronting America demand a probing reexamination of who educators are and what they are striving to become.

The pre-Socratic philosopher Heraclitus said, "A person cannot step into the same river twice, for the waters are forever flowing" (Bartlett, 1982, p. 70). The pace of change today tells people that not only can they not step into the same river twice, but sometimes they cannot step into the same river once.

Geopolitical changes such as the collapse of communism, the establishment of Western Europe as a unified political and economic market, the stunning economic surge of Japan and the Pacific Rim countries, and Congress's passage last year of the North American Free Trade Agreement all have tremendous implications for education and society. The fact that humans live in a world more at peace with itself—although admittedly a fragile peace—than at any period during this century is also testimony to the magnitude of the change occurring worldwide that affects all educators on their individual school and college campuses. It is therefore essential that educators engage in the self-reflection so essential to self-improvement.

Added to these developments are the far-reaching implications of sophisticated technologies such as satellites, computers, facsimile machines, robotics, lasers, and interactive video, which allow people to communicate anywhere in the world and to watch events as they unfold. Technologies are transforming the world, yet on too many campuses teachers and teacher educators are struggling to obtain adequate supplies of the most basic technologies—chalk and chalkboards on which to write.

Furthermore, the changing demographics in America have made its citizenry more diverse, more pluralistic, than ever before. I use the word diverse in its broadest sense, encompassing race, ethnicity, age, economic class, exceptionality, language, gender, sexual orientation, and religion. Again, these kaleidoscopic changes have had and are having a profound effect on the schools and on society in general.

Prerequisites of a Learning Culture

There are four prerequisites for educators to achieve if they are to lift all lives on a rising tide of learning, if they are to create a learning culture that spans the spectrum from preschool facilities to retirement communities.

Prerequisite 1

Educators must expand and tighten partnerships that will catapult them to the forefront of the effort to facilitate lifelong learning.

A first prerequisite is for educators to expand and tighten partnerships that will place them at the forefront of efforts to facilitate lifelong learning. To this end, they must launch a sustained and intensive outreach program to neighboring day care centers, the corporate community, parents, and religious and civic groups. In other words, they must help restore the sense of community that America desperately needs if education is to flourish in a context of hopefulness. A major part of that outreach must include colleges and universities' forming partnerships with area school districts. These partnerships could prove to be beneficial to all parties involved: School districts could benefit from the support and the expertise of college and university faculty, and college and university faculty could benefit from the practical day-to-day experiences of teachers, administrators, auxiliary school personnel, and other community groups. This is particularly true where efforts are being made to reform education and to restructure the organizational and governance paradigms of schools, be they elementary or postsecondary.

This need for allies is the pragmatic rationale for establishing closer ties within all segments of the education community. In all candor, uniting the education community will not be easy because, by and large, as the K–12 ranks took it on the chin, higher education kept its distance from the bloodshed. Higher education has yet to prove that it is prepared to offer practical (not theoretical) assistance to help solve the constellation of social, educational, and economic problems that schools and communities now confront.

An example: Last fall, I attended a meeting of staff development officials in the Virginia-Maryland-D.C. area. Staff development officials in two school districts said that their districts have designed yearlong programs to prepare new teachers to work in restructured school environments. They went on to say that teachers come to the district well prepared to teach the content of their discipline, but not prepared to teach in restructured classroom or school environments. These two districts can afford to provide extensive training to their new teachers. What happens to teachers who are employed in districts that cannot afford to provide this type of training?

Prerequisite 2

Educators must be cognizant of and responsive to the dramatic shifts that will determine enrollment trends, employment options, and public expectations of America's education system, preschool through graduate school.

A second prerequisite is that educators become cognizant of and responsive to the dramatic shifts that will determine enrollment trends, employment options, and public expectations of America's education system, preschool through graduate school. A specific example explains why this prerequisite is critical. During the 1980s, nine million people immigrated to the United States, three million of school age. Seven states—California, Florida, Texas, Virginia, and New Mexico among them—are now home to the vast majority of these people. Many of the youngsters had never been in a formal school before, and many more had lived their lives in abject poverty or in combat zones (some had actually served as soldiers). Others had been separated from their families for years. Still others have suffered from culture shock—the shock of being uprooted and moved to a foreign land where they are further isolated because they do not speak the language.

In Fairfax County, where I now live, the public schools are home to students from 127 national groups. In one Fairfax County elementary school, students were asked how many of them spoke a language at home other than English and what that language was. The staff counted 80 different languages.

Add to this the fact that 40% of the youth in the United States live in poverty, 75% of the youth will live in a single-parent home before they are 18 years old, and 60% of all children below the age of 6 come from families where mothers must work outside the home. All these factors affect the profession's ability to provide quality education for the nation's children and youth. Educators must succeed in their efforts to guarantee that each child receives the best education that he or she can acquire, because today these young people depend on their elders for education, nurturance, and survival but tomorrow their elders will depend on them for nurturance and survival.

On the point about minority and low-income students, I personally resent the commonly made argument that the only way in which prestigious schools can accommodate minority and low-income students is by diluting academic standards. At least five studies released during 1995 have found that when female, minority (especially African American and Hispanic), and low-income students enroll in rigorous academic courses such as geometry, trigonometry, physics, foreign languages, and advanced placement mathematics and English, increasingly higher percentages of them successfully complete the courses. Moreover, when this occurs, these students too have much higher ACT and SAT scores. Thus the message is that students can meet high academic standards when they have had opportunities to study the courses that prepare them to meet the standards.

If educators intensify their outreach to communities, if they clearly and publicly articulate admissions standards and work with schools and families to make sure that those standards are met, and if they act on the understanding that in the high-tech global marketplace, no student is dispensable, then they can blend the most resolute commitment for academic excellence with the ideal of educational equity. America as a nation cannot afford simply to educate 20% of its students well; it cannot afford to not educate, to miseducate, or to undereducate one single person. It must educate all its students to the best of America's and the students' own potential, and that potential is great.

Prerequisite 3

Educators must mobilize a national commitment to an education that prepares students to participate—and to thrive—in a democratic society and a global economy.

The third prerequisite for educators to forge a national learning community is that they mobilize a national commitment to an education that prepares students to participate—and to thrive—in a democratic society and a global economy. For the past two decades, educators and others have been trying to reform education in America. In 1989, they rightfully applauded President George Bush and the governors for establishing the six National Goals for Education. Educators should now support President Bill Clinton's efforts to implement Goals 2000: The Educate America Act, legislation that was passed by Congress in March 1994 enacting the national goals into law.

In passing Goals 2000, Congress added two new goals—parental involvement and teacher preparation and professional development—thus underscoring the critical role of parents and teachers in the achievement of education reform, restructured schools, and true academic excellence for all. The goal of teacher preparation and professional development clearly articulates that reform of elementary and secondary education cannot occur unless the nation has teachers and teacher educators capable of teaching in restructured classrooms, of teaching a very pluralistic student population, and of teaching that population to meet higher educational standards than any previous generation has met.

There have been and continue to be major criticisms of teacher education in the United States, cataloged by Boyer (1987), Goodlad, Soder, and Sirotnik (1990), the Holmes Group (1995), the Renaissance Group (1993), and Smith (1969), among others. Many claim that teacher education programs have not changed appreciably in the past 50 years. Some criticisms are justified, as noted by the comments I cited earlier. However, teacher education has also made significant progress. For example:

1. Teachers are better prepared than they have ever been. Since the 1950s, almost all teachers hold at least a bachelor's degree, and the vast majority master's degrees.

2. General education is much stronger and a greater part of teacher education than before.

3. Student teaching is almost universally full-time for 10 to 12 weeks in elementary and secondary schools. On this point, it is time for teacher educators to give serious thought to moving away from the traditional 2 1/2 to 3 months' student teaching practicum to an induction period during which prospective teachers work in schools with a highly successful experienced teacher for at least an

entire school year. This would give the prospective teacher a more realistic opportunity to be fully involved in the teaching-learning process.

4. Cooperating teachers are better prepared to work with student teachers than they used to be.

5. Many colleges and universities have developed close working relationships with public schools. In several instances, schools of education have supported and influenced school improvement through their collaboration with schools. This is particularly true as increasing numbers of professional development schools emerge across the country.

This, however, is not enough. As Mary E. Diez points out in Chapter 2, "One of the criticisms of teacher education as practiced for much of the past 50 years concerns the disjuncture between teacher preparation programs and the world of practice" (p. 28). Changes in prekindergarten through secondary education should occur simultaneously with and help guide changes in schools of education, and the changes that occur should reflect the reality of changes occurring in society in general. They should reflect the fact that demographically the United States is a vastly different nation than it was 50, 25, or even 10 years ago. For example, technology is transforming Americans' professional and personal lives. Teachers must educate students to understand that although they live in local and national communities, they are part of a global economy that will increasingly shape where and how they work, live, communicate, think, and play.

PROPOSALS AND INITIATIVES FOR REFORM IN TEACHER EDUCATION

Like K–12 education, teacher education has seen its share of reports advocating change: reports from the Holmes Group, the Renaissance Group, the Interstate New Teacher Assessment and Support Consortium, the National Council for Accreditation of Teacher Education, and the National Association of State Directors of Teacher Education and Certification; reports from foundations; and reports from government agencies. They contain many recommendations that would truly transform teacher education if implemented. Some specifically address teacher preparation programs; others focus on professional development. Four proposals represented in these reports—some of which are now initiatives—warrant discussion in this chapter: national certification of teachers, national subject-area standards, preparation for teaching diverse populations, and partnerships among higher education's schools and colleges.

National certification of teachers. The initiative with perhaps the most far-reaching potential to reconceptualize and restructure education is the assessment and certification process advocated by the National Board for Professional Teaching Standards (NBPTS). This process represents a conversation about professionalizing teaching that has broad implications for professional development of practicing teachers, teacher certification, and even initial teacher preparation. NBPTS is entering its third year of offering teachers the opportunity to become nationally certified. It is teacher educators' professional responsibility to support teachers in their efforts to attain this status. Teacher educators and teachers must be at the table in their state and local communities shaping policies and programs related to national certification. Teacher educators and teachers must work together to ensure that school administrators and the community in general understand what national certification is and how they can support teachers seeking it. Teacher educators must ensure that teachers who desire to become nationally certified have the knowledge, the skills, and the training to do so successfully. Teacher educators and teachers must also be involved in the design and the implementation of programs that help restructure K–12 and higher education classrooms and programs to use effectively the knowledge and the expertise of nationally certified teachers.

George Washington University and Norfolk State University have formed a partnership to support teachers in 18 districts in Maryland, Virginia, and Washington, D.C., who want to become nationally certified. The 18 districts are rural, suburban, and urban. They are also culturally diverse, ranging from several of the most affluent ones in the country to some with extremely limited resources. Teachers seeking national certification participate in a multifaceted assessment requiring them to demonstrate that they are exemplary teachers. Using portfolios, candidates evince knowledge of their subject matter, understanding of their students, and use of what they consider to be best practices in teaching. By writing case studies about their students, videotaping their classes, maintaining journals, and documenting professional service activities, these teachers provide further evidence of what they know and are able to do as teachers. The teachers are required to analyze their teaching, work collaboratively with other teachers, and demonstrate that they can teach culturally diverse groups of students.

Numerous teachers participating in the pilot phase of the assessment and certification process have commented that it is the most intensive, reflective professional development program in which they have been involved. Many have stated that it is the first time they have made an in-depth self-examination of how they teach and how students learn. Thus the NBPTS assessment and certification process has major implications for the professional development of practicing teachers and for the restructuring of the teaching profession (Baratz-Snowden, 1993; Futrell, 1994).

Preservice teacher education programs will also be affected. As more school districts and states recognize the NBPTS certificate as a sign of teaching excellence, they will expect future teachers to work toward a certificate. More important, they will expect teachers in their district to be able to model the skills and the knowledge that NBPTS-certified teachers exemplify. To ensure that their graduates are prepared to complete the national assessment and certification process or simply to model exemplary teaching, schools, colleges, and departments of education will have to radically rethink how they prepare teachers.

George Washington University and Norfolk State University are incorporating lessons learned from the NBPTS model into their teacher preparation programs. They are encouraging prospective teachers to model the reflective teaching strategies used in the project, demonstrate mastery of content, work collegially with peers, and demonstrate the ability to work effectively with diverse student populations.

National subject-area standards. A second initiative of consequence, the movement toward national subject-area standards, has already engaged at least 15 groups in developing national standards for their discipline. Many states are also involved in this process. If America's elementary and secondary schools are to rise to new standards, teachers and teacher educators must know what the standards are and how to teach to them. Yet too many schools of education are graduating teachers who have no knowledge of these standards or the National Education Goals, much less how to teach to them. Teacher educators must work with currently practicing teachers to ensure that they know about standards and the national goals that have been promulgated for their discipline, and strategies for teaching them. Neither teachers nor teacher educators will teach what they do not know or do not feel comfortable teaching.

Preparation for teaching diverse student populations. A third initiative is preparation of teachers to teach all students more effectively but especially those who are culturally diverse. Today, with 35% of all school-age children coming from minority racial or language groups, teacher educators can no longer refuse to be more responsive to these students' cultural needs. One state already has a majority "minority" student population, and at least five more states expect to have one by the year 2000 (Hodgkinson, 1991; McDonnell & Hill, 1993).

This means that teacher educators must teach all teachers, not just those from minority racial or language groups, to understand the critical role of culture and cultural diversity in the teaching-learning environment. It means that they must teach teachers to build on the cultural experiences that children bring to school, using those experiences to create moments of positive learning. It means that they must teach teachers to have high expectations for all students and to employ teaching strategies that help all students reach those expectations. Equally important, it means that they must model the strategies, the attitudes, the behaviors, and the expectations that they want teachers to model in classrooms.

Partnerships among higher education's schools and colleges. The fourth initiative recommended is partnerships in higher education. Other schools that comprise the nation's colleges and universities must join with schools of education in ensuring that higher education sends the best-prepared teachers into classrooms to work with children and youth. Schools and colleges such as arts and sciences, medicine, law, and business can no longer sit on the sidelines and complain about the quality of the students in their classes or cast aspersions on teacher educators. Preparing teachers for the new millennium requires the establishment of collaborative working relationships among the various schools on college and university campuses. It requires that the top administrators—the president, the provost, and all the vice presidents—support efforts to form such collaborative relationships. By doing so, they can help teacher educators build stronger content, research, and practice into teacher education programs. Through these types of collaborative arrangements, all can learn from one another and provide a stronger foundation of support for the children and youth of America.

Teacher educators should see teacher education as a continuum from early recruitment to careerlong professional development. This requires the development of better policies and strategies to ensure that all teachers are appropriately prepared and that they receive career-long support to help all students achieve the competence and the attitudes needed to live productive, satisfying lives. It also requires that administrators and boards of trustees stop treating schools of education like stepchildren and give them more support.

Today, despite the fact that states, local school districts, and colleges and universities are making slow but steady progress toward improving education, Congress stands on the threshold of eliminating all funds for the national goals and severely reducing funds for many other education programs. Leading the charge to eliminate funds for the national goals is the Republican leadership in Congress. This is ironic because education became a national issue and the National Education Goals originated under the leadership of Presidents Ronald Reagan and George Bush, respectively, both Republicans. By the way, in the Phi Delta Kappa/Gallup poll, the vast majority of respondents supported such Clinton administration initiatives as financial help with college expenses in return for public services; efforts to improve school-to-work transition programs; full funding of Head Start; and establishment of academic achievement goals for children, with financial help from the federal government so that states and districts can meet the goals.

It is absolutely imperative that all teacher educators become more involved in helping policymakers, school districts, schools, and individual teachers design and implement programs to ensure the realization of these reforms. Teacher educators must do more than simply inform the debate about the need to change the nation's educational ways. Teacher educators must be knowledgeable about the proposed reforms and fully understand the consequences of their implementation.

Teacher educators must be prepared to design curricula to ensure that all students can meet the new standards. Teacher educators cannot prepare students or school personnel for restructured schools or a redefined society unless they themselves have the courage to change, to explore new paradigms for schools and for teacher education.

Prerequisite 4

Educators must display steadfast devotion to their mission.

That statement brings me to the fourth prerequisite for transforming America into a learning community: Educators must display steadfast devotion to their mission, the mission that defines who they are, what they aspire to become, and what hopes they harbor for the America now in the making. All educators who believe that the mission of education transcends economics must teach the country and its leaders that the nations that will flourish in the 21st century will be those that give as much thought to ethics as to economics, to morality as to technology, and to standards as to the stock market.

The emphasis during the past decade has been on the restoration of a clear mission for America's schools and the establishment of high academic standards throughout the education system. Educators must instill in students the understanding that whether American democracy is able to reach maturity, whether America is able to move beyond the teenage years, depends on the ability of each generation to assume and to fulfill its responsibilities in a democratic society. Educators must help the nation's young people and the nation's old people see beyond the constraints, the fears, the alienations that keep them apart and destroy them as individuals—and thus the nation's potential. This is a mission that educators should remember as they consider how best to restructure education to facilitate the creation of a new educational order and a new domestic order that will combine the relentless quest for a more prosperous future with an abiding respect for the principles of justice and the dictates of conscience.

Finally, all these efforts are not enough. All of education and all of society must be willing to assess how they are serving the communities in which they live as well as the rest of America.

If teacher educators are to cast off the constraints on their efforts to transform the way in which they deliver education, they need leadership that understands not merely the violence of the waters, but the violence of the banks that encase the waters. For more than a decade, the public has kept its vision riveted on the raging waters, the problems infecting education, but it has been blind to the banks, the force that limits educators' ability to tame those problems. What teacher educators need above all else are resources to enable them to do the job that they were hired to do: to prepare the best cadre of teachers the world has ever known to educate all students, all citizens, to the best of their ability. Teacher educators need time to plan, implement, and evaluate programs designed to enable teachers and teacher educators to teach students to learn more effectively. Teachers and teacher educators need to be supported in their efforts to engage in research, especially research that will improve what and how they teach.

They cannot do the job alone. Efforts to provide quality education for all Americans—in environments that are not only safe and orderly but that engender a climate, an ethos, that encourages quality teaching and learning—require the support of the full university and the larger community. Educators need the public and university officials to understand that students' learning conditions and teachers' and teacher educators' working conditions are one and the same. These working conditions must be conducive to supporting teachers' and teacher educators' efforts to prepare future generations for a world far more complex and different than today's world.

The solution is threefold: educational, collaborative, and political. The solution is to make the case that if education remains the orphan of budgets—federal, state, or university—America will forfeit its preeminence in the world. Yet education is on the operating table. Politicians may perform radical surgery on the education budget, or they may recognize that an investment in education is an investment in the future of America. If they decide to make deep cuts in the education budget, the prognosis will be foreboding. Deep cuts will stunt the future of millions of Americans, especially children, for whom federal and state programs are the only hope of pulling themselves up by their bootstraps. Cuts in the education budget do not heal. They leave deep, permanent scars.

In the House of Representatives, it has been proposed that $3.5 billion be cut from last year's spending on education, across most programs. At the higher education level, Pell grants will be reduced by $500 million, Perkins loans by $156 million, and total student financial assistance by $735 million.

Educators must not sit by silently or passively. It is their moral and professional responsibility to speak out against efforts to reverse the progress that they are beginning to realize in reforming education. They must use every means within their power to say to America, especially to its elected and appointed officials, that to deny any child, any person, in America the right to a quality education is to deny the future of America. They must use their skills of persuasion and their votes to say no to those who would shortchange America by shortchanging education.

Conclusion

At the beginning of this chapter, I invoke the memory of President John F. Kennedy. I close with the words of one of education's own, Ernest L. Boyer, who spoke often, eloquently, and forcefully about the vital relationship between higher education and elementary and secondary schools. He said in 1985, "This nation's greatest strength is not its weapons, but its people. Our greatest hope is not technology but the potential of coming generations. Education is, as it has always been, an investment in the future of the nation" (p. 34). Today, Americans are once again living through a period of tremendous change and uncertainty about the future. America is a nation more diverse, more pluralistic, more complex than the young, fragmented country that put the statue of freedom on the U.S. Capitol's dome in 1865.

Also at the beginning of the chapter, I proclaim faith in democracy. I conclude with a call for faith in education. Nothing good was ever built by restraint on knowledge, inquiry, understanding, or the formation of expression of opinion. Truth and knowledge are the only possible sources from which, eventually, may flow the power to save humankind from catastrophe and kindle a hope, however faint, that tomorrow's sun may rise on a somewhat better world.

I believe, and have always believed, that the best way to protect and enjoy the freedoms that American government bestows—the best way to strengthen American democracy—is an educated citizenry. As the nation looks to the future, education will continue to ensure that the hope of democracy thrives for everyone. Educators must make sure that they are responsible and prepared enough to keep it!

That to me is what teacher education is all about.

References

Baratz-Snowden, J. (1993). *Opportunity to learn: The implications for professional development* (Background paper for the National Board for Professional Teaching Standards). Detroit, MI: National Board for Professional Teaching Standards.

Bartlett, J. (Ed.). (1982). *Bartlett's familiar quotations.* Boston: Little, Brown.

Boyer, E. L. (1985). Critical thoughts on education. *National Forum: Phi Kappa Phi Journal, 65*(1), 33–34.

Boyer, E. L. (1987). *College: The undergraduate experience in America.* New York: Harper & Row.

Elam, S. L., & Rose, L. C. (1994). The 26th annual Phi Delta Kappa/Gallup poll of the public's attitude toward the public schools. *Phi Delta Kappan, 76*(1), 41–56.

Futrell, M. H. (1994). Empowering teachers as learners and leaders. In R. W. Donovan (Ed.), *Teachers as leaders: Perspectives on the professional development of teachers* (pp. 119–137). Bloomington, IN: Phi Delta Kappa Educational Foundation.

Goodlad, J. I., Soder, R., & Sirotnik, K. A. (Eds.). (1990). *Places where teachers are taught.* San Francisco: Jossey-Bass.

Harvey, J., & Associates. (1994). *First impressions and second thoughts: Public support for higher education.* Washington, DC: American Council on Education.

Harvey, J., & Immerwahr, J. (1995a). *The fragile coalition.* Washington, DC: American Council on Education.

Harvey, J., & Immerwahr, J. (1995b). *Goodwill and growing worry: Public perceptions of higher education.* Washington, DC: American Council on Education.

Hodgkinson, H. L. (1991). Reforms vs. reality. *Phi Delta Kappan, 73*(1), 8–16.

Holmes Group. (1995). *Tomorrow's schools of education.* East Lansing, MI: Author.

Johnson, J. (1995). *Assignment incomplete: The unfinished business of education reform.* New York: Public Agenda.

Kennedy, J. F. (1964). Radio and TV report to the American people on civil rights, June 11, 1963. In *Public papers of the presidents of the United States: John F. Kennedy.* Washington, DC: U.S. Government Printing Office.

McDonnell, L. M., & Hill, P. T. (1993). *Newcomers in American schools: Meeting the educational needs of immigrant youths.* Santa Monica, CA: RAND.

Reich, R. B. (1992). *The work of nations: Preparing ourselves for 21st-century capitalism.* New York: Vintage.

Renaissance Group. (1993). *Teachers for the new world: A statement of principles.* Cedar Falls: University of Northern Iowa.

Smith, B. O. (1969). *Teachers for the real world.* Washington, DC: American Association of Colleges for Teacher Education.

2

Who Will Prepare the Next Generation of Teachers?

MARY E. DIEZ
Alverno College

We don't worry about teacher education—you're redundant.
LEADER OF A MAJOR STATE REFORM EFFORT
IN EDUCATION, 1993

Why don't we return to a 2-year normal school and let the school districts do the job?
DISTRICT SUPERINTENDENT ON A STATE TASK FORCE
ON TEACHER LICENSURE, 1994

We know what we should do to make teacher education effective, but the state won't let us.
TEACHER EDUCATOR IN A LARGE WESTERN STATE, 1994

Who will prepare the next generation of teachers? seems like a simple question at first, a matter of predicting the outcome of a marketplace struggle that has already begun between groups with competing visions of preparation. Today, a range of preparation models defines teacher education practice, from traditional teacher education and innovative reform efforts within colleges and universities to alternative programs mounted by school districts, states, and entrepreneurial agencies like Teach for America. Each of these models is linked to beliefs about teaching and learning to teach. Each is linked as well to political and economic realities and concepts of education reform. Thus several underlying questions must be addressed in making a case for the most appropriate setting for teacher education for the next generation of teachers. This chapter attempts to set out the underlying questions central to the future of teacher preparation, leading to a framework for responding to the main question, Who will prepare the next generation of teachers?

Underlying Question 1:
What Do Teachers Need to Know and Be Able to Do?

A question essential to the resolution of the future preparation of teachers is this: What do persons need to know and be able to do to fulfill the role of teacher? In the past 8 years, enormous efforts have addressed the need for a conceptualization of the knowledge, skills, and dispositions required for effective teaching. In 1987, the National Board for Professional Teaching Standards (NBPTS) set out to create not only a clear statement about expectations for the performance of accomplished teachers but also a means to recognize such performance through board certification. Its work has sparked continued discussion about the roles and responsibilities of teachers. For example, in 1990 the Interstate New Teacher Assessment and Support Consortium (INTASC) began work on a set of standards compatible with those of NBPTS to guide state licensure. INTASC represents another pioneering effort in the conceptualization of what teachers need to know and be able to do, focused on what should be in place when a teacher candidate is ready to take over a classroom as the teacher of record.

Similar work has been undertaken by state standards boards or special commissions, by the National Association of State Directors of Teacher Education and Certification (NASDTEC), and by the Educational Testing Service (ETS) in its development of Praxis III Performance Assessment Criteria. A chart recently developed to compare these varied efforts (Ingwerson, 1994) makes it fairly clear that consensus is emerging on what teachers need to know and be able to do.

The profession's need for a knowledge base—knowledge of both subject matter and educational frameworks—is also central to the redesigned standards of the National Council for Accreditation of Teacher Education (NCATE). The need for this knowledge base to be translated into what teachers are able to do is evident in NCATE's standards related to assessment of performance in classroom settings.

The answer to the question, What do teachers need to know and be able to do? is critical in determining who will prepare the next generation of teachers. In an incisive critique of Teach for America, Darling-Hammond (1994) summarizes a key assumption underlying the organization: Bright persons with degrees from prestigious institutions need little preparation beyond what is available through on-the-job experience. Indeed, a common myth is that "majoring in an academic subject satisfies the requirement for subject matter knowledge needed for teaching" (National Center for Research on Teacher Learning, 1993, p. 3). Principle 1 of the INTASC *Model Standards for Beginning Teacher Licensing and Development* (1992) offers another view: "The teacher understands the central concepts, tools of inquiry, and structures of the discipline(s) he or she teaches and *can create learning experiences that make these aspects of subject matter meaningful for students*" (p. 10; emphasis added).

Across the standards-writing movement, in the documents of NBPTS, INTASC, NASDTEC, and ETS, a clear requirement for teaching is the ability to link knowledge of subject area to knowledge of learners and the learning process. Indeed, learner-centered practice is at the heart of teaching ability as described by these documents (INTASC, 1994).

Underlying Question 2:
What Is the Purpose of Schooling?

Implicit in the emerging consensus on standards like those proposed by NBPTS, INTASC, NASDTEC, and ETS are beliefs about the purpose of schooling in a democracy and a multicultural society. Sinclair and Ghory (1990), drawing on the work of Goodlad (1990), address these purposes explicitly:

The fundamental mission of public schools in the United States is to provide quality, integrated education for all young people through age 16 and for any interested youth through grade 12. Not only are schools expected to develop a comprehensive program of studies and activities related to successful accomplishment of academic, vocational, social, and personal goals, but citizens and courts also expect affirmative action to reduce barriers for access to higher education or success in society that arise from economic, racial, gender, or cultural difference among students. (p. 127)

The expectation that teachers will be able to work effectively to provide quality education to all learners is a focus of NBPTS's standards, INTASC's principles, NASDTEC's standards, and NCATE's standards; concern with education to preserve a democratic society is explicit in Goodlad's work as well. In contrast, this issue has not been a strong focus in alternative licensure programs, such as Troops to Teachers and Teach for America.

These abstract and philosophical notions of quality and democracy need to be translated into the practice of teaching; that is, what does it look like for teachers to reflect on the purposes of schooling and to act on the requirements of teaching for democracy? Read from this perspective, INTASC (1992) principles like Principle 3, "The teacher understands how students differ in their approaches to learning and creates instructional opportunities that are adapted to diverse learners" (p. 14), become part of a belief system that must undergird the preparation process. The description of Principle 3 states that such a process must help potential teachers "understand how students' learning is influenced by . . . language, culture, family and community values" (p. 14). It must develop in potential teachers a sensitivity "to community and cultural norms" (p. 14). Furthermore, it must develop their ability to seek "to understand students' families, cultures and communities and [use] this information as a basis for connecting instruction to students' experiences (e.g., drawing explicit connections between subject matter and community matters, making assignments that can be related to students' experiences and cultures)" (p. 15).

Schools themselves are struggling with the challenge of making their practice more learner centered. Most notable is the shift from the perception that teaching is simply disseminating information to the recognition that teaching is developing learners. The myth that all a teacher needs is a subject-matter major was reinforced when teachers saw their role as providing clear lectures on the topics in the textbook. However, a renewed understanding of the nature of learning as constructing knowledge and connecting experiences to prior under-standings is leading to a more student-centered focus in the class-room. This in turn is challenging teachers to learn more about their students, as Principle 3 of INTASC describes.

The issue of collaborative leadership is also a shared challenge to make schools serve the democratic ideal. Schools and teachers en-gaged in reform or restructuring are recognizing the need to work collaboratively, not only with other school professionals but also with business and community persons, parents, and their students. They are challenged to work together in creating integrated curricula, in making links between the school and the workplace, and in develop-ing their ability to use technology as a resource for teaching and learning. They are challenged to recognize their own need for con-tinuing professional development and to seek opportunities for growth.

Underlying Question 3: Is Teaching a Profession?

Who will prepare the next generation of teachers may depend on perceptions of the role of teachers and their place in the society and the economy. Even as teaching struggles to become a profession in this country, policies in Great Britain and France appear to be moving toward exclusively field-based preparation of teachers (Judge, 1994). The most radical expression of this approach was the proposal for a "mommy brigade" to replace university-prepared elementary school teachers in Great Britain (William Taylor, personal communication, September 1993). The underlying message was clearly the reverse of the "all you need is content" argument; at least for the early grades, some believe that "all you need is caring."

The issue of teaching as a profession has been widely addressed in recent years. Among several excellent articles on this topic (Darling-Hammond, 1990; Duke, 1984; Sedlak & Schlossman, 1986), Darling-Hammond and Goodwin's (1993) discussion provides the major criteria for professional work:

- The nature of preparation
- Standards for entry
- The nature of the work

- The responsibilities assumed by members of the occupation for defining and enforcing professional practice
  (p. 19)

Two issues embedded in the struggle for professionalizing teaching may affect the answer to the question of who will prepare the next
generation of teachers. First, the unique context of teaching within
compulsory education for children to age 16 puts bureaucratic rules
and regulations in conflict with professional standards. The recently
emerging practice of establishing teacher-dominated standards
boards—both at the state level and at the national level (NBPTS)—is
a clear contrast to history, when state policies and local boards dominated decision making about teaching practice.

Second, much of the struggle for recognition of teaching as a
profession has been motivated by teachers' desire for two attributes
of most professions: respect and remuneration. Although these are
understandable issues for persons in what Goodlad (1990) terms "the
not-quite profession," they should not supplant the client-centered
focus that Darling-Hammond and Goodwin (1993) see as a central
aspect of the professional. Ironically, lack of primary focus on the
client (the children to be educated) in the context of economic or
political circumstances also marks a number of the alternative programs. How else can one explain the establishment of alternative
standards in many states that overproduce qualified teachers? These
routes are designed not to serve children, but to assist persons from
industries being downsized (from computers to the military) in trans-
lating their training into a well-paying job.

True professionalization of teaching will depend on the conceptualization of the complex abilities required for teaching and the
standards required for practice at entry and throughout a teacher's
career. Social, economic, and political forces, however, are likely to play
a role in determining who prepares the next generation of teachers.

Underlying Question 4:
What Does It Take to Develop Teaching Ability?

The INTASC (1995) model standards document describes each of
10 principles in terms of knowledge, dispositions, and performance
skills. As a member of the INTASC standards-writing committee, I

remember the discussions as the committee framed this approach. The committee saw teaching ability as a complex set of factors that involved cognitive understanding, values, and attitudes that guide action, and the translation of knowledge and dispositions into effective performance. Many states have adopted the knowledge-dispositions-performance structure to capture their expectations of teachers. If the abilities required of the teacher are complex and integrated, what can be inferred about their development?

The complexity of the principles suggests that learning to teach requires a coherent, developmental process focused on integrating knowing and doing, with critical reflection as an essential practice:

- *Coherent* because learning to teach requires more than serial presentation of chunks of information; all parts of learning must be integrally connected and mutually reinforcing.
- *Developmental* because the teacher must build understandings; learning to teach is a gradual process.
- *Integrative* because the nature of teaching requires connections between theory and practice; learning to teach is a process of integrating cognitive, affective, and performance modes.
- *Reflective* because teaching must be a thoughtful process; learning to teach (indeed lifelong learning as a teacher) is a process of critiquing one's performance.

What it takes to develop teaching ability can be addressed on levels other than the nature of preparation. Time and development are interwoven as a major issue of discussion. It makes little sense to argue that teacher education must take a particular amount of time: The point is not how long initial preparation should take, but whether initial preparation ensures that candidates develop the knowledge and the skill essential to practice and to continue to learn from experience. Furthermore, critics should be as disdainful of university-based programs made up of unconnected serial bits of preparation as they are of quick alternative routes. A serial program incorporating liberal arts or general education study unlinked to teacher education, and teacher education courses unlinked to clinical experiences—no matter how long that serial program takes—is unlikely to provide preparation that meets the INTASC model standards.

Obviously, some time is necessary to provide for development and integration. More time may be needed for some candidates and less for others; decisions must be made relative to the candidates' prior learning and already developed abilities. Perhaps the popularity of alternative routes results in part from traditional programs that function in a one-size-fits-all, lockstep manner. The role of assessment is critical in determining what skills candidates bring to their preparation and what they need to achieve the necessary performance. Policymakers and practitioners alike should be critical—and concerned—about the use of entry screening mechanisms (e.g., standardized test scores and increasingly higher grade-point averages) that may set up barriers to candidates who could develop the abilities of the teacher, particularly when these barriers appear to affect underrepresented groups. Policymakers and practitioners should ensure as well that persons who have developed understandings and skills through experience will be able to have those abilities recognized in program adaptations. Assessments used for decision making must be closely related to the performance sought.

Looking seriously at the answer to what it takes to develop teaching ability calls for rethinking teacher preparation from the ground up. That rethinking might well be guided by a standards-based approach. Standards for teacher performance like those developed by INTASC lead one to ask what standards should govern teacher preparation. In recent work, the INTASC standards-writing committee explored the interwoven nature of process and product standards. Not willing to assume only one approach, the committee used questions to describe necessary aspects of a program or a process that would prepare teachers. The following selections from that set of questions indicate critical aspects of teacher preparation:

- Is there appropriate/differential diagnosis of entering candidates?
- Does the process protect against unrealistic barriers to qualified candidates?
- Is the process of preparation coherent, with a sequential set of experiences?
- Does the process model the teaching expected of the candidate?
- Are there multiple and varied opportunities to develop and practice expected performance?

- Does the candidate have adequate opportunity to look at real student work, create exemplar answers, and design instruction to address weaknesses?
- Are assessment of the candidate's performance and feedback to the candidate guided by conceptual frameworks?

These and other questions generated by the INTASC group (and reflected in the NCATE standards as well) provide a useful framework for examining current and proposed teacher preparation approaches. Many programs—both traditional and alternative—would fall short in a review based on these questions, and this fact reinforces the critics quoted at the beginning of this chapter. There is need for a major rethinking of teacher preparation.

A final aspect of this important question must be addressed: the link between preparation and practice. One of the criticisms of teacher education as practiced for much of the past 50 years concerns the disjuncture between teacher preparation programs and the world of practice. This disjuncture is probably what makes the district superintendent whom I quoted earlier desire a return to the normal school approach. The issue has been addressed by Goodlad (1990) in his call for the "simultaneous renewal" of K–12 schooling and teacher education; by the Holmes Group (1991) in its design of professional development school models of teacher preparation; by NCATE (1992) in standards that require clinical experiences in schools with which the teacher preparation program maintains a relationship; and by INTASC (1994) in its description of an internship or residency year as the transition from initial preparation to induction into the profession.

The vision of a continuum of preparation, a "seamless" transition from initial preparation to teaching practice, is guiding reforms across the United States. The INTASC standards group (1994) sees the link as critical in answering the question, Who will prepare the next generation of teachers?

In the long run, teachers' and other educators' capacities for learner-centered practice and for collaborative leadership in school renewal can only be widely acquired by major rethinking of preparation programs and by restructuring of the systems by which states and school districts license, hire, induct, support, and provide for the continual learning and advancement of practitioners throughout their careers. (p. 3)

Rethinking of both teacher preparation and the organization of state and local systems is required to deal with the disjuncture between initial and continuing preparation. The focus of the change—teachers' capacities for learner-centered practice and collaborative leadership in school renewal—ought to guide that rethinking.

Underlying Question 5: How Does the Public Know That a Beginning Teacher Is Prepared for the Job?

Although the ability to assess teaching as knowledge, disposition, and performance is not fully developed, much is being learned from the work of NBPTS, INTASC, NASDTEC, and ETS, as well as from the efforts of institutions like Alverno College, which has pioneered performance assessment across the entire undergraduate curriculum for the past 20 years (Alverno College Faculty, 1994; Diez, 1994; Loacker, Cromwell, & O'Brien, 1986). If one accepts the emerging consensus of the various standards work groups that teaching requires a set of highly complex abilities, then the need to develop appropriate assessment processes for documenting the development of candidates is clear. Also evident is the need to stop using selection measures that set up barriers to candidates who could be successful teachers.

The INTASC group's questions highlight the importance of an integrated assessment process in which candidates practice the abilities that will be demanded of them as teachers and in which those responsible for preparation use assessment to help candidates develop, employing feedback to guide their growth. Assessment must be seen as integral to learning, with self-assessment or reflection as a tool for developing habits of lifelong learning. Screening is an important function, but assessment should be used first to provide opportunities to learn.

The issue of assessment is critical for another reason. One of the criticisms of traditional teacher preparation programs has been that they make no difference—hence the epithet "Mickey Mouse" applied to education courses. In the absence of evidence of a candidate's development, this criticism has led to the development of so-called alternative routes to licensure in over 40 states, to the imposition of caps on education requirements in states like Texas and Virginia, and to the emergence of "quickie" preparation schemes.

Yet the same criticism has led to serious teacher education reform efforts in states like Colorado, Vermont, and Wisconsin as well as to the major redesign effort that developed more rigorous standards for NCATE accreditation, implemented over the past 7 years. As many as 20 states are using the INTASC principles in the design of new requirements for teacher preparation; a coalition of states within INTASC is developing prototype assessments to guide states in developing their assessment process for licensure.

A puzzling anomaly exists in some states, where fairly rigorous requirements constrain college- and university-based teacher preparation programs while alternative routes allow easy entry into teaching jobs for persons with an undergraduate degree in another area. The position of the AACTE (1989) provides useful advice: There must be clear standards for the beginning teacher; although there should be alternative routes to meeting those standards, there should not be alternative standards.

Toward Criteria for the Preparation of Teachers

Whatever agencies prepare teachers for the next generation, America's future as a society depends on their preparing teachers who can meet the standards identified by INTASC (compatible with those articulated by the NBPTS, NASDTEC, and others): having the knowledge, the dispositions, and the performances needed to fulfill the purposes of schooling in a democratic, multicultural society. Can that be done outside a partnership between colleges/universities and schools/communities? Although doing so would not be impossible, it would be hard to develop and sustain without re-creating many of the aspects of this kind of partnership.

In spite of many efforts to create college/university–school/community partnerships—from the National Network for Educational Renewal, to the Holmes Group and the Renaissance Group, to many individual efforts by teacher preparation programs with their local schools and communities—there is no clear template for one. I believe that policymakers should seek not one model, but a set of criteria that could be met in varied ways, sensitive to the differences in local contexts. Before I address those criteria, let me suggest the following answer to the question, Who will prepare the next generation of teachers?

Preparation of a teacher first and foremost is the responsibility of the society itself. A potential teacher learns what it means to be a teacher from messages in the media, from decisions of voters in school board elections and bond issues, and from discussions among family and friends. The next generation of teachers is already being influenced through television, video, and commercial media dominated by violence, aggression, and uncollegial competition. Thus, to their peril, do policymakers and practitioners forget the influence of social forces on schools and education. How society views children, especially children living in poverty, is a central issue in the preparation of teachers.

Second, preparation of a teacher is the responsibility of those who model teaching when that future teacher is a student in K–12 and undergraduate settings. Much of what teachers learn about their role grows out of their images of their own teachers—for better or for worse. Goodlad's focus on the simultaneous renewal of K–12 schooling and teacher education (including undergraduate education) addresses the need to put energy into the improvement of teaching in all settings.

Third, formal preparation of a teacher is the joint responsibility of college and university teachers of liberal arts and sciences, college- and university-based teacher educators, teacher educators in local schools, and communities that support local schools. I have not separated these four because their contributions to the teacher's development must be integrated and collaborative.

Following are essential elements that agencies preparing teachers must address. My list is shorter than Goodlad's (1990) 19 postulates and less detailed than NCATE's (1992) 20 standards, but compatible with both formulations. I offer this shorter list to help examine some of the current models of teacher preparation. Whoever prepares the next generation of teachers must do the following:

1. *Understand the role of the teacher in society and the abilities needed to work effectively with all learners.* In the words of Goodlad's (1990) Postulate 5, they must "have a comprehensive understanding of the aims of education and the role of schools in our society and be fully committed to selecting and preparing teachers to assure the full range of educational responsibilities required" (p. 56). Many current traditional programs are not guided by clear concepts of the role of schools and teachers, nor do they ensure that candidates develop and demonstrate the complex abilities required of the teacher. Quick alternative

routes that send unprepared persons into classrooms—especially into classrooms of the neediest children—have not taken this responsibility seriously.

2. *Ground preparation in a conceptual framework that incorporates the knowledge bases for learner-centered education (including critical frameworks drawn from social, psychological, cultural, and philosophical studies).* The profession must develop and articulate knowledge bases for teaching. Although the role of the university has traditionally been the generation of knowledge, the university has too often implemented that role without respect for the knowledge sources available in professional practice. Thus many traditional programs do not take seriously the input of practicing teachers, and some alternative programs go too far in the other direction, ignoring resources in the college or university setting.

3. *Provide an experiential, developmental process that is designed to develop the knowledge, dispositions, and performances required for effective practice (using, e.g., the INTASC principles).* College- and university-based teacher preparation programs and alternative programs alike in school districts must deal with the disjuncture between the two sources of preparation. Essential to the preparation of the next generation of teachers is the establishment of collaborative working relationships, creating opportunities and the appropriate environment for developing the complex abilities of the teacher.

4. *Create experiences that model the kind of learning environment that policymakers and practitioners want the next generation of teachers to create for students.* Neither traditional programs nor alternatives based in school districts have fully achieved this goal. Goodlad's (1990) call in Postulate 10 must be extended to the full undergraduate liberal arts curriculum. All educational experiences—clinical training in K–12 sites, liberal arts course work, and professional education preparation—should model "in all respects the conditions for learning that future teachers are to establish in their own schools and classrooms" (p. 56).

5. *Provide a broad range of experiences in schools that model effective practice with diverse populations.* Too many programs focus on having candidates for teaching learn about diversity; they fail to recognize that in this area, knowing and doing are critically linked. Regardless of their type, preparation programs must find schools and teachers

who are working effectively with students who represent diversity, including racial and ethnic diversity, socioeconomic diversity, and ranges of learning styles and needs. College and university programs, again, should model effective supports for diversity in their own practice.

6. *Use assessment as a learning tool to provide feedback to candidates and to develop in them habits of lifelong reflection.* Assessment has the potential to be a powerful force in the development of teaching ability, providing diagnostic feedback to guide growth; self-assessment builds a base for the lifelong practice of reflection (Diez, 1994). Few college- or university-based programs currently use assessment effectively; even fewer alternative programs address the issue. Assessment practice should be addressed in K–12 settings as well—both the assessment of learner development and the continuing assessment of teacher performance. If initial preparation and continuing professional development are to be a connected and coherent process, then assessment must be standards based and improvement focused.

Many current models of college- or university-based teacher preparation have begun to address these six criteria, but I know of none that can present evidence of fully meeting them all. Some traditional programs are constrained by state limits on time and semester hours, as the western teacher educator whom I quoted earlier opines. Some others, I suggest, are constrained by their choice to let state requirements absolve them of the responsibility to develop a conceptual framework.

Alternative models typically fall short on a number of the criteria. Those that move candidates directly into full responsibility for a classroom after only a brief orientation can hardly ensure that those candidates meet the "full range of educational responsibilities" or that they have developed the knowledge, the dispositions, and the performance skills required for effective teaching. Of particular concern is the focus of some alternative programs on meeting the need of the candidate for a job—without much consideration of the needs of learners.

Teacher education reform efforts have not, to date, addressed the range of requirements outlined in the criteria that I propose. For example, even NCATE does not address the need for undergraduate liberal arts courses to model effective teaching; that requirement is placed on the teacher education unit. If teachers teach as they were taught, however—and the influence of modeling is powerful—then the reform of undergraduate education is critical in the preparation of the next generation of teachers.

Too few of the reform programs have addressed standards of performance and assessment as both a tool for development and a documentation of progress. Although they may give lip service to the complexity of teaching ability, too many college- or university-based programs resort to assessing what is most easily computed rather than developing evidence over time of a candidate's knowledge, dispositions, and performance.

Finally, although progress is being made in addressing the disjuncture between initial preparation and beginning practice, there is a long way to go. Even the promising approaches to creating professional development or partner schools are only in the early stages of development. Some concerns are emerging that indicate the difficulty of bringing two cultures together in a joint commitment to the preparation of teachers. Some in the K–12 setting will have to overcome years of suspicion bred by arrogance. Some in the college or university setting will have to learn the implications of constructivist approaches to the generation of knowledge, as well as try to change the reward structures to support new ways of working. All who identify themselves as teacher educators will have to learn to collaborate in creating processes that will ensure the development of teachers ready for the challenge. Moreover, concerted institutional efforts will be necessary to create structures that support simultaneous renewal.

The question that I have really answered is not, Who will prepare the next generation of teachers? but Who will best prepare them? The question is not, Who will win this latest skirmish? but How can all who are concerned with teacher education "win" support for effectively linking K–12 practice, liberal arts undergraduate education, and teacher education in a coherent design, united in a profession that puts the learner's need first?

References

Alverno College Faculty. (1994). *Student assessment-as-learning at Alverno College*. Milwaukee, WI: Alverno Productions.

American Association of Colleges for Teacher Education. (1989). *Alternative preparation for licensure: A policy statement*. Washington, DC: Author.

Darling-Hammond, L. (1990). Teacher professionalism: Why and how? In A. Lieberman (Ed.), *Schools as collaborative cultures: Creating the future now* (pp. 25–50). New York: Falmer.

Darling-Hammond, L. (1994). Who will speak for the children? How Teach for America hurts urban schools and students. *Phi Delta Kappan, 76*(1), 21–34.

Darling-Hammond, L., & Goodwin, A. L. (1993). Progress toward professionalism in teaching. In G. Cawelti (Ed.), *Challenges and achievements of American education* (pp. 19–52). 1993 yearbook of the Association for Supervision and Curriculum Development. Alexandria, VA: Association for Supervision and Curriculum Development.

Diez, M. E. (1994). Probing the meaning of assessment. In *Essays on emerging assessment issues* (pp. 5–11). Washington, DC: American Association of Colleges for Teacher Education.

Duke, D. L. (1984). *Teaching: The imperiled profession.* Albany: State University of New York Press.

Goodlad, J. I. (1990). *Teachers for our nation's schools.* San Francisco: Jossey-Bass.

Holmes Group. (1991). *Tomorrow's schools.* East Lansing, MI: Author.

Ingwerson, L. (1994). *A comparative view.* Princeton, NJ: Educational Testing Service.

Interstate New Teacher Assessment and Support Consortium. (1992). *Model standards for beginning teacher licensing and development: A resource for state dialogue.* Washington, DC: Author.

Interstate New Teacher Assessment and Support Consortium. (1994). *Moving toward performance-based licensing in teaching: Next steps* (Working draft). Washington, DC: Author.

Interstate New Teacher Assessment and Support Consortium. (1995). *Core elements of teacher preparation programs* (Working draft). Washington, DC: Author.

Judge, H. (1994, December 14). Teachers and universities: Vive la difference: The uncommonalities of teacher training in England, France, and the United States. *Education Week,* p. 56.

Loacker, G., Cromwell, L., & O'Brien, K. (1986). Assessment in higher education: To serve the learner. In C. Adelman (Ed)., *Assessment in higher education: Issues and contexts* (Report No. OR 86-301, pp. 47–62). Washington, DC: U.S. Department of Education.

National Center for Research on Teacher Learning. (1993). *An annotated bibliography: Findings on learning to teach.* East Lansing, MI: Author.

National Council for Accreditation of Teacher Education. (1992). *Standards, procedures, and policies for the accreditation of professional education units.* Washington, DC: Author.

Sedlak, M., & Schlossman, S. (1986). *Who will teach? Historical perspectives on the changing appeal of teaching as a profession* (R-3472). Santa Monica, CA: RAND.

Sinclair, R. L., & Ghory, W. J. (1990). Last things first: Realizing equality by improving conditions. In J. I. Goodlad & P. Keating (Eds.), *Access to knowledge: An agenda for our nation's schools* (pp. 125–157). New York: College Board.

A Response to Chapter 2,
"Who Will Prepare the Next Generation of Teachers?" by Mary E. Diez

EDWARD M. WOLPERT
Georgia College

Mary E. Diez's thoughtful, well-reasoned chapter is organized according to five "underlying questions" followed by six "criteria for the preparation of teachers." Teacher educators as well as others who have a keen interest in this area of endeavor will find little with which to take issue. However, some matters that are not stated should be addressed to render a more complete answer to the question posed by the title of the chapter.

Teachers' Characteristics

Diez's first underlying question, "What do teachers need to know and be able to do?" is perhaps the most basic question in the realm of teacher education. There is no quarrel with the notion that the profession must give careful consideration to what teachers need to know and be able to do. Certainly, teachers must know their subject matter, and certainly they must be able to do a variety of instructional and noninstructional tasks to meet their professional responsibilities.

However, the question omits a key element in asking what teachers must bring to the job. The profession must also know what teachers should be like; that is, what kinds of personality or behavioral traits they should have. The vision of NBPTS makes no mention of this, nor do the outcomes-based standards of NASDTEC, the standards of NCATE, or the 10 INTASC principles except perhaps implicitly. Yet in terms of a teacher successfully implementing an instruction program for students of any age, personality variables are crucial.

The literature is replete with research showing the personality traits of superior teachers. Professional educators themselves, who have been students for 16, 19, or more years, are aware of this from personal experience, so it seems appropriate to address this issue in a discussion of teacher characteristics.

At the root of this idea of what teachers should be like is the thought that teaching is vastly different from other professions, even the other helping professions. In teaching (the reference is to K–12 public school teaching, although many of these thoughts are appropriate for other teaching environments), the clients, students, are required by law to attend school whether or not they want to do so and whether or not they are ready to learn in terms of adequate nourishment, sleep, or background knowledge of the subjects being taught. In most other professions, clients come to the professional of their own volition with a sense of purpose. Discipline, motivation, and management of clients are rarely problems. Because of this difference, teaching is without a doubt the most difficult profession in which to engage successfully.

In some segments of American society, education and learning have been defamed. Many students come to school with low motivation; in addition, they are physically and emotionally unprepared to do schoolwork. This fact shows the importance of personality variables in the competence of teachers. Unlike most other professionals, teachers must stimulate and motivate their clients, and this requires certain kinds of personality traits often referred to as people skills. Teachers who have these skills are generally more effective than teachers who do not.

The importance of people skills to teaching cannot be overstated. A fundamental question is, What does the profession do with a teacher who has no people skills? It is instructive to contemplate other professions in this regard—for example, medicine, accounting, and law. A physician lacking a bedside manner can ply his or her trade as a pathologist, who handles only dead tissue, or an anesthesiologist, who has very limited exposure to conscious human beings. An accountant with a drab personality can work in the back office on tax audits while livelier colleagues meet with clients and engage in activities external to the office. A lawyer without people skills can take on research or other activities that do not require much social interaction. In the teaching profession, however, there is virtually nowhere at the entry level to put a person lacking people skills. Teaching is, by definition, working with people. Positions in administration or curriculum development exist, but persons who already have teaching experience generally fill them.

Accordingly, as a profession, teaching must consider screening preservice teachers for essential personality traits. This is not an easy task to accomplish. Whether people skills can be taught is debatable. Certainly, refining preexisting people skills is easier than teaching the skills to candidates who demonstrate no talent in this area. Some teacher preparation programs try to screen applicants using interviews. Others place teacher education students in settings where they work with young people and subject them to observation; those who do not show the necessary talent in working with young people are often counseled out. This screening does not seem to be employed widely, however, and many teachers who lack people skills are still recommended for certification. Without specific guidance from approval or accrediting agencies, this type of screening may never be employed to the degree that it should be, and teachers without the ability to motivate students will continue to be found in classrooms.

The Teach for America Controversy

Diez correctly states that teachers must know how to connect students with subject matter and that mere knowledge of the subject, albeit extensive knowledge, is insufficient to ensure success at teaching. In so doing, she refers to Darling-Hammond's piece on Teach for America, published in the September 1994 issue of *Phi Delta Kappan*. Diez characterizes the article as an "incisive critique" (p. 22). That it was, to be sure, but it was also one sided and prosecutorial. Darling-Hammond's exclusive focus on Teach for America's preservice preparation component suggests that she had incomplete information on the organization's program.

The Teach for America structure of teacher development includes recruitment, selection, preservice training, placement, and inservice training. In contrast, most traditional teacher education programs focus heavily on preservice training, almost to the exclusion of these other elements.

The weakest part of the Teach for America structure is the preservice training. Since its inception, Teach for America has experimented with several models, all of which are contained in a 7-week summer period. It started with a college course–type format using professors and classroom teachers for instructors. That has evolved into a field-based experience using Teach for America corpsmembers and staff. No doubt more experimentation will be forthcoming.

On the surface, this weakness in preservice preparation would appear to doom the corpsmembers to failure in the classroom. Some of them do indeed fail, although not in disproportion to other beginning teachers in the schools served by Teach for America. (In the November 16, 1995 issue of *Teacher Education Reports*, "Principals, Others, Rate Teach for America Corps Members in the Classroom" recounts the results of two independent surveys of school administrators and others. The respondents, in large part, view Teach for America corpsmembers quite favorably compared with other beginning teachers.) However, Teach for America has always recognized the limitations of its and others' preservice preparation and has included in its total program a focus on continued professional development. Teach for America's latest thrust is to form collaborative relationships with colleges and universities involved in ongoing professional preparation.

One question addressed by Teach for America but not often addressed by traditional teacher educators is, When is the best time to teach teachers the professional knowledge that they need, the ability to "create learning experiences that make these aspects of subject matter [the central concepts, tools of inquiry, and structures of the discipline] meaningful for students" (Principle 1, INTASC, 1992, p. 10)? Should it happen during the preservice phase or the inservice phase? If preservice preparation does not have a strong field component during which teaching methods can be tried and refined, can effective preparation indeed take place? In such a case, would it not be better to do this on the job, where there is an immediacy to teaching and learning and where the novice teacher is working with real children in a real school setting? On the other hand, should or can all this be done during the preservice phase of a program? Do the motivation, academic preparation, and people skills of the novice teachers make a difference?

These are important questions, the answers to which can have a profound effect on the structure of teacher education programs. The paradigm employed by most teacher preparation programs for decades has emphasized professional education during the preservice phase. Is this necessarily the best way to prepare a teacher? Teach for America has been challenging this and other assumptions as it seeks to find a workable paradigm that fits its philosophy. As a profession, teacher education should laud such interest and efforts and reserve summative judgment on the program itself until Teach for America settles on a model and a thorough evaluation is conducted.

Learner-Centered Teaching

The author refers to the challenge to schools "of making their practice more learner centered" (p. 23). As a group, elementary schools have responded to this challenge much more readily than secondary schools. Perhaps this trend will continue, but there is strong opposition from persons on the very far right of the political spectrum to learner-centered teaching and to outcomes-based education in general. The very name *outcomes-based education*—indeed, even the word *outcome*—incites anger and controversy among these persons. Educators who deal with the public are constantly scurrying to find synonymous words and phrases not laden with the emotion of outcomes-based education or outcomes. All the concepts associated with outcomes-based education—learning-centered instruction, whole-language approach, peer tutoring, cooperative learning, and other indexes of progressive education or a constructivist philosophy—are under severe attack from this group. They are angry, they are vocal, they are well funded, and they know how to act effectively within the political arena. Although the result of this group's activity is far from clear, as a profession, teacher education must educate preservice teachers in the best of practice while trying to educate the far right. It will not be easy. Almost 100 years after John Dewey espoused his views, people are still fussing about them.

Teaching as a Profession

Diez's view that the true professionalization of teaching depends on one's concept of abilities and standards for practice is well taken. K–12 teaching has always been a profession in its responsibilities, but never in its remuneration or respect.

Diez's observation (p. 25) that alternative standards "to assist persons from industries being downsized" (including the military) are not designed to serve children is also valid. The same standards should be applied, although different programs to deliver those standards may be appropriate for different kinds of people. The larger point to be considered is, How does the profession best provide meaningful preparation for persons who enter programs after having other careers, that is, nontraditional students? Such persons should be actively recruited into the teaching profession. Teachers have often been criticized for their lack of breadth and real-life experience. The programs from which they graduate are frequently viewed as narrow, parochial, and too focused on professional education. This explains, in part, the growing popularity of 5-year teacher preparation programs and the renaissance of the Master of Arts in Teaching. Former military and business personnel who become teachers can share a plethora of experiences and insights with their students in everyday interchange.

There is a great difference between the experiential base of 22-year-old college graduates and that of persons who have had other work experience before teaching. Principals generally recognize and appreciate the difference. The difference is apparent in the reception that K–12 students have given to many teachers who have participated in the Peace Corps Fellows/USA program, a program that places returned Peace Corps volunteers in classrooms while they pursue a master's degree. The public's response to these varied persons— former military and business people, returned Peace Corps volunteers, and others—may very well contain the message that the public wants a more broadly educated, experienced person in the classroom. That message, however, must be reconciled with the profession's desire for more, and more meaningful, professional education.

So Who Will Prepare the Next Generation of Teachers?

This leads to Diez's ultimate question, Who will prepare the next generation of teachers? Whoever does will do well to adhere to the standards of NCATE, NASDTEC, INTASC, and Goodlad, as suggested by Diez and as summarized in her six criteria. Moreover, her belief that "policymakers should seek not one model, but a set of criteria that could be met in varied ways, sensitive to the differences in local contexts" (p. 30) is precisely on target. There remains, however, the question of who will deliver these programs, by whatever model or configuration and in whatever context.

By and large, colleges and universities have had a virtual monopoly on teacher education—a regulated one, to be sure, but a monopoly nonetheless—and as with most monopolies, there have been abuses. The political context in which the United States has been operating in the past 15 years suggests that the days of monopolies are over. Whether one is speaking of airlines, electric utilities, telecommunications, or a host of other industries, deregulation, decentralization, competition, and opening of an endeavor to new players characterize the present time. Teacher education currently finds itself in this context.

Must colleges and universities necessarily do teacher education? Could the K–12 communities themselves do it, or the teachers unions? Could for-profit or not-for-profit private enterprises do it, such as Performance Learning Systems or Teach for America, respectively? Could any one of these entities by itself do teacher education best for all those who want to teach, or should some combination of players do it, different combinations for different people with differing backgrounds and needs? Could the pool of prospective teachers be segmented and various combinations of entities be assembled to provide preparation for different segments?

The best preparation of teachers will come from programs that are based on a sound philosophy and knowledge base, as articulated by Diez, and that meet the special needs of the particular groups of people at whom they are aimed. They will be delivered by various combinations of preparers, including colleges and universities and other professional and private entities in the field. The need is for teacher preparation programs that provide quality options and alternatives to the traditional college- or university-based programs. The implementation and the evaluation of these alternative programs as applied to the specific groups of prospective teachers for which they are intended will answer the question, Who will best prepare the next generation of teachers?

References

Darling-Hammond, L. (1994). Who will speak for the children? How Teach for America hurts urban schools and students. *Phi Delta Kappan, 76*(1), 21–34.

Interstate New Teacher Assessment and Support Consortium. (1992). *Model standards for beginning teacher licensing and development: A resource for state dialogue.* Washington, DC: Author.

Principals, others, rate Teach for America corps members in the classroom. (1995, November 16). *Teacher Education Reports,* pp. 7-8.

3

Right-Sizing Teacher Education: The Policy Imperative

NANCY L. ZIMPHER
Ohio State University

Threats to the integrity of teacher education abound. For example, at the federal level, professional development has found its way into the National Education Goals, but there is still little acknowledgment in the enabling language that schools, colleges, and departments of education (hereafter education schools) should be the agents of change. Rather, school districts are implored to intervene through enhanced teacher development. Because the National Education Goals are at risk in the Contract With America, the argument may be moot anyway. At the state level, seats at the policy table are rarely reserved for teacher education. As professional standards board models emerge in over a dozen states, there is a clear preference for boards on which teachers hold a majority of seats (which I strongly support). Teacher education may have a seat or two, but it will not wield the obvious influence of either the teachers organizations or the school board or administrator groups, which carry considerable clout at the state level.

In the university context, teacher education has been at risk literally since it left the confines of the normal school and joined the ranks of the academy. As Clifford and Guthrie (1988) observe,

> Schools of education, particularly those located on the campuses of prestigious research universities, have become ensnared improvidently in the academic and political cultures

of their institutions and have neglected their professional allegiances. They are like marginal men, aliens in their own world. They have seldom succeeded in satisfying the scholarly norms of their campus letters and science colleagues, and they are simultaneously estranged from their practicing professional peers. (p. 3)

The consequences of such role confusion have been the absence of a clear and purposeful focus, failed mission, lack of leadership, and certain internal and external forces that have mitigated against education schools achieving real professional status within the academy (Zimpher & Sherrill, 1996).

For example, it has been over a decade since Clark (1984) scolded the enterprise. The "charm" of teacher education, he opined, is that it is easily accessible, nonexclusive, easy to enter, easy to exit, and until very recently would result in a secure and relatively stable job placement. Today, several reform groups continue to call for the transformation of teacher education. The 19 postulates of Goodlad (1994) are an exhortation to collaborative reform, or "simultaneous renewal." The agenda of the Holmes Group, set forth in its trilogy *Tomorrow's Teachers* (1986), *Tomorrow's Schools* (1990), and *Tomorrow's Schools of Education* (1995), is a multidimensional proposal for the reform of teacher education. So is the Renaissance Group's agenda, apparently now embraced by the leadership of both the American Association of State Colleges and Universities and the National Association of State Universities and Land-Grant Colleges. Essentially, the collective call of these initiatives is for more professionalism in teacher education, *professionalism* being defined by Darling-Hammond and Berry (1988) as

the extent to which members of an occupation share a common body of knowledge and use shared standards of practice in exercising that knowledge on behalf of clients. It incorporates conditions of specialized knowledge, self-regulation, special attention to the unique needs of clients, autonomous performance, and a large dose of responsibility for child welfare. (p. 10)

According to Howey (1994), to meet these conditions, education schools must demonstrate that they can make direct contributions to improvements in K–12 schools, create a clinical faculty, develop a scientific knowledge base on teaching, demonstrate both pedagogical and content-specific knowledge, and create more coherent, inter-related, and potent programs of teacher preparation. Goodlad (1990) characterizes professional programs for teacher education as ideally reflecting

> a reasonably coherent body of necessary knowledge and skills; a considerable measure of "professional" control over admissions to teacher education programs and of autonomy with respect to determining the relevant knowledge, skills, and norms; a degree of homogeneity in groups of program candidates with respect to expectations and curricula; and rather clear borders demarcating qualified candidates from the unqualified, legitimate programs of preparation from the shoddy and entrepreneurial, and fads from innovation grounded in theory and research. With these conditions largely lacking, teacher education and the occupation of school-teaching have been at the mercy of supply and de-mand, pillages from without, and balkanization from within. Even today, teaching remains the not-quite profession. (pp. 70–71)

This chapter does not revisit in detail the challenges before the profession; rather, it addresses on a broad scale how the profession might meet them. First, it examines the configuration of teacher education. Goodlad is right: Teacher education has become highly balkanized. The cacophony at the 1995 town meeting of AACTE on a proposal to link AACTE membership to accreditation by the National Council for Accreditation of Teacher Education (NCATE) is ample testimony to that. People rose to speak not as teacher educators, but as representatives of Teacher Education Colleges in State Colleges and Universities (TECSCU); the Association of Independent Liberal Arts Colleges for Teacher Education (AILACTE); the Association of Colleges and Schools of Education in State Universities and Land Grant Colleges, and Affiliated Private Universities (ACSESULGC/ APU); NCATE-approved or NCATE-eschewing institutions; and even NCATE-boycotting institutions!

Why is teacher education so balkanized? In an attempt to address that question, this chapter reviews conditions that characterize teacher education: (a) the size and the diversity of teacher preparation institutions; (b) the accreditation profile of these institutions; (c) the organizational affiliations of these institutions; (d) issues of supply and demand that undergird the enterprise; (e) a profile of education school graduates and their expectations about employment; and (f) the competition, public and private agencies eager to do teacher education's work for it and without it.

The Symptoms

The Size and the Diversity of the Enterprise

How many education schools are there, offering just what types of degrees? Although some would view this question as relatively easy to answer, the enterprise is so big and the programs are tucked away in so many institutional configurations that the actual number and types are difficult to track at any given time. For instance, in Ohio the number of state-approved education schools just rose to 51 with the addition of a master's program in art education at the Art Academy of Cincinnati. In 1988, Clifford and Guthrie reported the enterprise to consist of 1,287 education schools, with 645 of them private institutions. In contrast, there were 202 accredited business schools, 243 engineering programs, 172 law schools, 127 medical schools, and 74 journalism and mass communication schools.

Beyond the sheer number of institutions, results from the AACTE-sponsored Research About Teacher Education (RATE) studies, drawing on an annual stratified random sample of education schools, indicate that enrollments are on the rise for all degree levels, with institutions granting only the baccalaureate experiencing a 44% increase. What minority enrollment there is, is found largely in the master's- and doctoral-level institutions. There has also been a general shift among institutions formerly offering the baccalaureate only, with many now offering master's-level programs as well (Howey, Arends, Galluzzo, Yarger, & Zimpher, 1995).

Institutions offering all degrees, including the doctorate, are significantly larger overall than those offering the master's as the highest degree and those offering the baccalaureate only. For instance, in the most recent RATE study, RATE VIII (Howey et al., 1995), the mean student enrollment in teacher education programs offering the baccalaureate only was 259; in programs offering the master's as the highest degree, 788; and in programs offering the doctorate as the highest degree, 1,424. The small institutions employed a mean of 20 full-time equivalent (FTE) faculty; the medium-size institutions, a mean of 73 FTE faculty; and the large institutions, a mean of 157 FTE faculty. Tenure density increased with the level of degree offered, 45% of all faculty being tenured at baccalaureate-only institutions, 57% at master's-level institutions, and 67% at doctoral-level institutions.

The Accreditation Profile

Of the 1,287 education schools in the United States (Clifford & Guthrie, 1988), over 500 are NCATE accredited (NCATE, 1994). By type, these 500-plus accredited institutions represent 72% of all doctoral-level education schools, 61% of all master's-level education schools, and 55% of all baccalaureate-only education schools (Howey et al., 1995). Of the accredited institutions, almost all (505) are members of AACTE (along with approximately 200 institutions that are not NCATE accredited).

During the 31-year history of NCATE, the standards and the review process (self-study and site visitation) have been the subjects of much debate. The redesign of both has been undertaken several times, most recently in 1987, culminating in new standards and review procedures. New variations of joint accreditation and program approval at the state level are emerging, including partnerships with state departments of education. Furthermore, a new cycle of standards revision has commenced.

In 1995, the immediate past president of AACTE, Richard Wisniewski, sparked a provocative debate about NCATE when he proposed that AACTE membership be linked to the accreditation status of an institution. His notion was that institutions should become approved by NCATE by July 1, 2001, to be full members of AACTE (Bradley, 1995). Those in favor of the resolution argued that education schools should unite behind a common set of standards to make teaching a true profession. Those opposed argued that the resolution represented an exclusionary stance for the organization; they suggested that instead, AACTE remain open to all education schools and help them improve their programs to become worthy of accreditation. Organizational opposition to the Wisniewski resolution came from AILACTE and TECSCU, opposing the move by a majority of their votes (over 700 members voting against the motion, some 200 in favor), and from ACSESULGC, favoring the move by only a handful of votes.

In contrast, the Holmes Group, an organization of deans, has agreed to an action item in its new report, *Tomorrow's Schools of Education* (1995), that calls for strengthening accreditation and partnering with NCATE to do so, to maintain accreditation as an institutional standard of excellence.

Organizational Affiliation

A host of umbrella organizations offer membership to teacher education schools, dividing institutional affiliation among them. The largest organization, and therefore the most common organizational affiliation for education schools, is AACTE, with membership for 1994 at over 700, including private, state, and municipal colleges and universities. Together, AACTE institutions graduate more than 85% of new school personnel entering the profession in the United States each year. A voluntary national organization of colleges and universities, AACTE (1994) is, by its own definition, "the major catalyst for initiative and innovation in teacher education" (p. 1).

Other institution-based teacher education organizations include AILACTE, ACSESULGC, and TECSCU. In addition, the national Holmes Group represents comprehensive research institutions housing teacher education, including a cluster of historically black colleges and universities. Membership in this group overlaps membership in the national land grant organization and AACTE. The Renaissance Group, like the Holmes Group, focuses its primary agenda on the reform of teacher education. Nineteen institutions held membership in the Renaissance Group initially; the organization has grown since the leadership of TECSCU and ACSESULGC decided to support expansion of institutional memberships. As active as the Holmes and Renaissance Groups is the Goodlad Network for Simultaneous Renewal, with a membership of 20 institutions organized in common support of Goodlad's 19 postulates for reform. All these organizations consist of institutions that for the most part also enjoy membership in AACTE. As well, AACTE has over 2,000 institutional representatives, many of whom are also, as individuals, members of ATE. In short, this profile reflects not only the diversity of organizational affiliations common in teacher education but also the array of competing reform agendas that currently exists.

Issues of Supply and Demand

Determining if the nation's schools will be well supplied with qualified teachers in the future has been and continues to be a troubling exercise. Darling-Hammond (1984) reports that during the 1980s, as more children of the baby boom generation entered the school system and fewer college graduates chose teaching as a career, concerns surfaced about the availability of enough teachers for these children. Furthermore, some worried that those who taught would be poorly prepared for their task. Although the study of teacher supply and demand is inexact, with several confounding variables, recent studies reveal that teacher attrition (one of the critical variables in the supply-demand formula) is actually at a low point, largely because of a more mature, stable teaching force, secondarily because of a drop in attrition rates among new teachers and women (National Center for Education Statistics, 1993). Although massive shortages in the next 10 years seem unlikely, the possibility of shifts in supply and demand by geographic location warrants vigilance, as does the trend toward lucrative teacher retirement buy-out programs.

Of particular relevance in studies of supply and demand are the variables considered in determining teacher supply: (a) continuing teachers, or stayers (those who are teaching in the school in which they taught the previous year); (b) immigrant teachers, or movers (those who have stayed in the profession, but have moved to a new academic subject, or to a new school, district, state, or country); (c) new, first-time teachers (new teacher education graduates and others who have never taught); and (d) re-entrants (former teachers who were not teaching in the previous year). Critically relevant to education schools are the data in these categories. For example, in an analysis completed for the 1987–1988 school year, only 2% of the teachers hired nationally for public schools were in fact new teachers, 98% coming from the ranks of movers or re-entrants (National Center for Education Statistics, 1993). Further affecting demand are regional and demographic variations. For instance, demand is greatest in large urban districts, which now and will increasingly serve populations in which minorities are a majority. This fact, juxtaposed with the demographic profile of exiting teacher graduates, suggests a particular type of employment challenge. Studies of the preferences of teacher graduates to remain near the institution from which they graduated and the communities of their childhood reveal another problem: a tight and highly competitive job market in surrounding suburban and small-town communities.

On the other side of the equation, supply of teachers in the states has been buffeted by demand contexts. When supply has been up, state policymakers have used this opportunity to stiffen entrance and licensure requirements. When supply has been low, they have made exceptions to established standards in the form of massive issuance of emergency licenses. Alternative routes to licensure have been advocated as a stopgap for certain shortages—for example, by the business community to provide more and better math and science teachers.

Supply-and-demand studies executed at the state level have been very controversial. Dilemmas about how to count graduates, how to predict vacancies, and how to juggle data on new hires with appropriate licenses against data on new hires without appropriate licenses have left consumers (i.e., education schools) confused. A study in Ohio (Bowers, 1989), for example, reflected a profile of overproduction, with education schools graduating eight teachers for every one job hire. In adjacent Michigan, the ratio of certificates issued to graduates hired was two to one, and schools were reporting an oversupply of job applicants in all fields (Scheetz, 1994).

Although many have challenged the inputs to the Ohio study, a subsequent study in more depth confirmed the market glut (Hedden, 1995). According to this study, from 1992 through 1994, 50 public and private institutions in Ohio generated 22,576 graduates. Over 50% were prepared in elementary education, whereas only about 9% were prepared in math or science education. Fewer than 4% were minorities. Although this study did not seek exact data on potential vacancies, it did survey superintendents about projected needs, given local knowledge about likely vacancies. Data from a representative sample of urban, rural, and small-town districts reflected high agreement on the overabundance of elementary-level beginning teachers (far exceeding the demand); some concern about the small number of potential new teachers in the high-shortage areas of math, science, special education, and computer science; and universal concern about the absence of diversity in the pool of future teachers.

Relative to vacancies, the study projected a fair degree of stability in Ohio's demand. Because superintendents reported that the greatest source of teacher vacancies was retirements, the likelihood of massive separations was calculated. Of the 102,933 sitting teachers with Ohio assignments for 1993–1994, the average age was 43, with 14.7 years of experience; only 10% were age 55 or over. Thus massive teacher turnover does not seem imminent in Ohio. This study also reports hiring preferences in local school districts for new teachers with some experience; with multiple teaching certificates, reflecting demographic diversity; and with areas of specialization in math, science, all types of special education, selected areas in vocational education, and foreign languages. These are not attributes of the majority of teacher candidates. There is an obvious mismatch between the supply and the demand sides of the ledger.

Institutional "Products"

In an age of product orientation in the business and corporate community, which is slowly creeping into the fabric of higher education, a discussion about clients and products seems appropriate. Best chronicled in the AACTE RATE project, cumulative data about teacher candidates (Howey et al., 1995; Zimpher, 1989) can be summarized as follows: The typical graduate of the American education school is female, is of Anglo descent, is about 21 years of age, speaks only English, travels less than 100 miles to attend college, was raised in a small town or a suburban or rural setting, and expects to teach in a school whose demographics are similar to her own. In fact, this typical prospective teacher does not seek to teach students out of the mainstream, or to serve in a school of innovative architecture or one organized around anything other than a traditional curriculum or facility.

Repeated cycles of RATE data reflect fewer than 8% minorities among education school graduates (mostly African American, with some Hispanic and Asian students), increasing to only 15% in institutions located in large urban areas. In seven iterations of RATE, the proportion of graduates who would seek teaching positions in urban settings never rose above 10% in general and rose to only 20% in the urban institutions. The RATE team also collected perceptions of these graduates and their professors, which suggest their possessing little knowledge of other cultures, experiencing limited travel, having a relatively closed circle of friends and acquaintances on campus, living in student housing with others of like demographics, attending church and social functions with the same friends, and admitting to limited interactions with persons of other cultures while on campus.

In spite of these rather common demographics, graduates' attitudes about teaching as a career are very positive. Their expressions of satisfaction with their career choice are high at the beginning of the teacher education program, and even higher on graduation. Students expect to spend up to 20 years in the career, find the salary adequate and the working conditions appealing, and feel very positive about their preparation for teaching, both from their campus experience and from their field experience and student teaching placements. Subsequent institutional follow-up studies, reflected in an annual study conducted at Ohio State University (Loadman, 1992), reveal graduates' concerns about limits in their preparation, as does the comprehensive study conducted by Veenman (1987), which documents reports from first-year teachers of deficiencies encountered on the job. However, the optimism of the new graduate does not foreshadow these early career frustrations.

Teacher education's response to the limited demographic profile has resulted in changes in the nature of initial preparation programs to include significant course work in multiculturalism, reemphasis in the NCATE standards relative to diversity, attempts to diversify the faculty profile (which to date resembles the teacher graduate profile, in ethnicity particularly), and a number of recruitment strategies to change the demographic profile of its programs. Among the latter is the creation of teaching academies at the high school level to attract more candidates early in the pipeline to careers in teaching.

Although all these remedies are employed to some degree across most education schools, with the exception of the teaching academy, they have not as yet changed the profile of teacher graduates. One of the most visible strategies has been the Holmes Scholar program, under which Holmes Group institutions appoint minority candidates in their master's and doctoral programs to participate in a national initiative that includes access to other Holmes Scholars and to career development. The ultimate intent is increased placement of underrepresented populations in the professoriate. This strategy, like the teaching academy, is fundamentally a long-term one. Such approaches, and even more radical measures, will be required before the profession significantly changes the demographic face of teacher education and the teacher candidates it produces.

Competing Agencies

A number of efforts have challenged traditional teacher preparation programs in recent years. Initially, variations focused on alternative routes to teacher licensure, widely fostered by the state of New Jersey's decision to legislate and fund such alternatives. Legislative provisions allow candidates with baccalaureates in teaching majors to enter the classroom after a 6-week summer preteaching seminar and then require them to take an additional 60 hours of on-the-job professional development during the first year of teaching. Researchers at the National Center for Research in Teacher Education are monitoring the program's capacity to attract and prepare beginning teachers as effectively or more so than traditional teacher education programs.

A more pervasive alternative for teacher preparation is Teach for America. Like candidates in regular alternative certification programs now offered in over 30 states, Teach for America candidates must have a baccalaureate in a teaching discipline but need not have previous pedagogical course work or school experience. They complete brief seminar work the summer before assuming the teacher position and engage in limited hours of inservice work while on the job. Teach for America was thoroughly analyzed after several years of implementation (Darling-Hammond, 1994), and considerable limitations with the model were cited.

The model currently under development by the National Board for Professional Teaching Standards (NBPTS; 1994) is not an alternative to initial teacher preparation but may ultimately be an alternative to continuing professional development—that is, to the master's degree as traditionally employed. Standing for NBPTS certification may someday lead to an NBC, a national board certificate. It is easy to imagine the NBC supplanting the MA as the model for advanced professional credentialing.

A fourth potent alternative to traditional teacher education is the action by several major school districts across the country to launch their own teacher preparation program. To date, probably the best known example is that of the Los Angeles City Public Schools. This model has led many representatives of California teacher preparation institutions to claim that they will be out of the initial teacher preparation business by the end of the century, if not sooner. The L.A. model suggests initial preteaching seminars and continuing "course work" throughout the early years of teaching, exclusively at the school site.

Will these alternatives ultimately result in the demise of initial teacher preparation as it exists today? More important, should they? Issues of reforming current practice among education schools as invoked by the multiple reform agendas of Goodlad, the Holmes Group, the Renaissance Group, and others may suggest an antidote to the competition. Significant school-based linkages like those that characterize professional development school initiatives (Holmes Group, 1990) may defuse these alternatives.

***

A profile of American teacher education emerges. Far from the roots of the normal school, over 1,200 programs of teacher education have evolved in every manner of institution, from the large publics to the church-affiliated privates. Not even half of these institutions are nationally accredited. They produce a student cohort that exceeds— some would say, far exceeds—the demand created by retirements or discontinuations in the current teaching force. They do not come close to producing a diverse teaching force reflective of the increasing minority student population in this country. The culminating RATE study, RATE VIII (Howey et al., 1995), characterizes the limitations in progress toward true reform of teacher education programs. Slow to make structural and programmatic changes, with faculty whom many believe are out of touch with the realities of the classroom, teacher education programs now face serious competitors, who have captured not only the policy window (i.e., the opening into policy circles) but a considerable amount of the foundation funding that might well have been invested in extant institutions had they proven their capacity to adapt to new and emerging needs. Having wrapped themselves in the advocacy mantle of various constituent organizations, they have created a veritable alphabet soup of acronyms and adversarial fiefdoms: the privates against the publics, the large state and land grants against the big-producing directionals (e.g., northeast state, western state), the accredited against the nonaccredited.

The imperative: The proliferation of teacher education programs must be addressed, squarely and honestly, and by the profession itself. The issue is not survival by institutional type—that is, the large institutions over the small ones, the privates over the publics, the currently nonaccredited over the accredited. Rather, the issue is the creation of a unified enterprise that generates for itself a common set of national standards to be attested to by peer review and upheld by institutions no matter what their size, locale, or affiliation.

Other national imperatives include the following:

- A close look at the regionalization of teacher education, strengthening capacity and coordination around targets of teacher supply and demand
- A national materials development effort, and dissemination and testing of program prototypes for use in teacher education programs
- A national strategy for recruitment of a more diverse cohort into the teaching profession, one that will ensure greater progress than the meager results of the past decade
- A feeder system of preeducation colleges, possibly including community colleges
- Wide-scale articulation of an agenda with elementary and secondary schools, supporting the critical linkage between teacher development and school reform
- Creation of a professional development continuum wherein teacher preparation is extended into the early years of teaching

This is the common and manifold agenda. The profession must develop it nationally to coordinate efforts toward unification. The profession must also pay serious attention to a series of action steps that will ensure success in meeting the parameters of unification.

The Diagnosis

Following is a set of strategic steps that must be considered in the creation of a unified teacher education enterprise. Although they can be debated individually, true articulation of the profession will probably come only if all elements of this strategy are considered collectively.

Accreditation 2001

Already on the table is the 1995 Wisniewski resolution, which gives AACTE 5 years to assist every teacher education institution member to pursue national voluntary accreditation through NCATE.

Although the motion to make membership in AACTE contingent on accreditation was defeated, sentiment remained to make the organization's commitment to standards a goal for 1995–1996. The goal could, of course, be revisited as an organizational imperative. To take on such a massive development process would require the assistance of nearly all currently accredited institutions, working jointly with one or more institutions, perhaps regionally, given that the ratio of nonaccredited to accredited institutions currently stands at one and a half to one.

The advantage to this strategy would be the clarity of the starting place: The scope of the task is known, the standards exist, and the activity could be viewed as the greatest educational experiment of its time. Considerable collective attention could be given to the refinement of the standards and an improved oversight function. The lessons to be learned are like the benefits that Pearson (1994) cites in assessing the value of the national standards initiative for K–12 schooling: First, focusing on standards and an improved NCATE will force a national conversation about what teacher educators value in teaching and learning and expose the profession's standards and thus its belief system to public scrutiny. Second, it could influence both public and professional investment of time and resources and create a healthy tension between commonality and diversity within the field, at the same time ensuring a thoughtful curriculum for teacher education. Third, it would create a relationship between standards and scholarship because the profession would be studying the effects of standards on all of the foregoing issues.

The disadvantage to this strategy would be that those not accredited would oppose it for the same reasons that the AACTE resolution was roundly defeated. Institutions oppose the fundamental nature of the standards and see the review process as flawed. They are, as well, undoubtedly threatened by such action, fearing that they will be left out of the business because of lack of resources and capacity to meet the standards, even with assistance at the program design level. In short, they simply do not have the number of faculty, the programmatic dollars, the contacts with schools, and the research connection to respond to the standards, and no amount of coaching will help them meet the mark, nor likely should it.

A Regionalized Profession

Another way to build capacity and to unify efforts is to regionalize teacher education. Ohio serves as a reasonable example of how this could be done. Already, professional development delivery systems have been regionalized into eight areas of the state through Regional Professional Development Centers. In all but one of these regions, the demographics are at once urban, suburban, and rural. Large and small, public and private institutions exist in each region, as do accredited and nonaccredited institutions. Their missions are diverse, as are their program emphases. One could envision enrollment caps being set for a region, including specified areas of certification, limits on gender, and targets on ethnicity. Institutions could engage collectively in program reform and redesign, and the sheer capacity of the total configuration by region could pull the enterprise up by its bootstraps into full functioning.

The advantage to this strategy would be the limits set on the proliferation of jobless teacher candidates, with targets set for areas of shortage. Institutions would receive a state mandate to work together, from which would surely come a strengthened teacher education.

The disadvantage to the strategy would be that people might view the regional model as threatening to the institutional autonomy that all enjoy and from which many profit. That is, some institutions are stronger than others and can corner not only teacher candidate recruitment but also the continuing professional development market. If they are asked to share that market, internal enrollments might fall. For state-supported institutions, this is suicide. For the privates, it is a lifeline. Either outcome spells doom. It also places teacher education at risk as the only program in the institution's portfolio whose fate is determined through alliances with other universities. Although this may very well be a viable postsecondary model of the future, it would be difficult for teacher education to have to swallow the pill first.

The Feeder System

The strategy of a feeder system has its antecedents in the early rhetoric of the Holmes Group. When the Holmes Group's model was first discussed, in *Tomorrow's Teachers* (1986), graduate preparation for teachers was assumed. With teaching candidates striving to meet the prerequisites of a well-rounded liberal arts program and a full major in the teaching discipline, time would simply run out at the undergraduate level for a robust pedagogical curriculum. The rigor of graduate education and the selectivity that accompanies it were also intended planks in the Holmes Group profile. Today, many Holmes Group members have stepped away from the plate, offering instead a redesigned undergraduate curriculum or the extension of teacher preparation into a fifth year, leading to graduate hours but not including the completion of a master's degree. Still others, fewer in number, have actually moved their entire program to the advanced level. Prospective students apply only after completing a liberal arts degree with a major in a teaching discipline and, it is hoped, some preliminary career exploration and field experiences in teaching, if not foundation course work in schools and society.

The feeder system would evolve in such a way that institutions would be designated as preeducation colleges and professional education schools. In other words, some and probably many institutions would be designated as accredited institutions for preeducation course work, including a bona fide preeducation minor of foundation courses, career exploration, and field experiences, along with a liberal arts sequence and a strong major in a teaching discipline. Although the focus in this strategy might very well be on building capacity among small liberal arts institutions, it could include linkages with community colleges as well. Graduates of these programs would then apply for admission to the graduate program, perhaps through some kind of consortium arrangement whereby admission would be competitive but enabled through previous institutional agreements.

The advantage to the strategy would be the limits set on fully functioning teacher education programs, without necessarily excluding any institution from participation in the enterprise. In Ohio, for instance, 85% of the graduates are already prepared in the state institutions (Hedden, 1995), which are mostly large institutions with graduate programs.

The disadvantage to the strategy would be that institutions would be robbed of their legitimate status as fully functioning teacher education programs. They would share in production, but not without affiliating with an approved licensure program.

The School-University Collaborative

This strategy, a variation on the several themes sounded earlier, factors in one more player, the schools. In this model, a consortium of teacher preparation institutions would align itself with a set of school districts, perhaps by region or even by certain other demographics (e.g., urban character). In some senses, this model exists as institutions increasingly become involved in the professional development school movement. It invokes support not only from school district administrators but also from teachers unions. The model would exact more contractual specificity in school-community relationships, including binding the school district to hire graduates from the affiliated programs.

The advantage to the strategy would be its codification of the relationship between teacher preparation and school practice, a relationship that continues to be difficult to execute across diverse cultures and uncommon agendas. Furthermore, it would calibrate institutional enrollments to school district demands.

The disadvantage, again as with other strategies, would be the forced institutional affiliations, the possible reduction in enrollments, and the challenge of determining collaboration boundaries.

The Minority Pipeline

None of the foregoing strategic steps adequately or specifically addresses the special need for teacher education to play a leading role in diversification of the future teaching force. Among the reasonable strategies to be pursued is a network among traditionally majority institutions and historically black colleges and universities. Although the former severely surpass the latter in number, creating contractual affiliations is possible, even on the basis of 10 traditionally majority institutions to 1 historically black college or university. Such arrangements would guarantee admission to advanced programs and enable exchanges at the undergraduate level, and institutional linkages could accommodate this network.

There are only advantages to this model in that a pipeline of minority students would begin to grow across all institutions. If the linkage of institutional type with large urban school districts were added to this, teacher education might finally have a recruitment intervention that works. One could envision increased access and awareness across historically black colleges and universities, majority institutions, urban school districts, and minority teaching academies through a network that literally spans the nation.

The Prescription

Working through the strategic actions just proposed, or others that could surely be generated, will not be easy; some will say that it is not even possible. On the contrary, focusing a national conversation on these issues is critically important because continuing discourse among professional constituents is necessary to negotiate the future of teacher education in America. Those invited to the table could include the heads (or chief negotiators) of the major teacher preparation organizations, including AACTE, TECSCU, AILACTE, ACSESULGC, ATE, the Holmes Group, the Renaissance Group, the Goodlad Network, NCATE, and NBPTS, all of which have direct connections and interests in teacher preparation. Beyond that, the profession should call to the table constituent groups that are in a sense the clients of teacher education: the American Federation of Teachers, the National Education Association, the American Association of School Administrators, the National School Boards Association, the Council of Chief State School Officers, the National Associations of Elementary and Secondary School Principals, and probably because of their interest in education, the Business Roundtable. In addition to sponsoring this national conversation, the profession should encourage state-level dialogue on these and other unification strategies as a template for subsequent state policy deliberation.

Because of the difficult issues that would be addressed, variations on a negotiated settlement might be framed around a win-win strategy. The result would be a collaborative problem-solving initiative, the outcome of which would be an improved product (i.e., a better education for teacher candidates), a shared resource base for teacher education institutions with more realistic and meetable goals, and a more satisfied constituency, including school districts, teachers, and states.

To make this model workable, certain assumptions must be operative (Herman & Megiveron, 1993):

1. Participants must achieve clarity about a common belief system for teacher education, in particular, about common goals.

2. Participants must view the enterprise as developmental, it being a significant new stage in progress toward professionalization.

3. Participants must achieve clarity about their constituent groups, determining whom they serve and how they can best serve those constituents collectively.

4. Participants must focus the discussion on how the various stakeholders in teacher education can work together more effectively.

5. Participants must agree on how to communicate during the course of national negotiations, including what to communicate when, how to caucus, and what to bring to the table.

6. Participants must determine what is discussible. For example, will there be mandated subjects, prohibited subjects, and permitted subjects? What will be binding, if anything?

Skill in guiding this summit will be a given, so agreeing in advance on a brokering organization will be as critical as deciding what is talked about and how. Finally, viewing the exercise as largely experimental and as only a template for state-level discussion should allow a degree of creativity and imagination that will help participants meet the critical teacher education imperative of right-sizing, and subsequently unifying, the enterprise.

References

American Association of Colleges for Teacher Education. (1994). *AACTE directory of members.* Washington, DC: Author.

Bowers, R. (1989). *Supply and demand of teachers for the State of Ohio.* Columbus: Ohio Department of Education.

Bradley, A. (1995, February 22). Teacher training group trounces NCATE mandate. *Education Week,* p. 1.

Clark, D. (1984). Transforming the structure for the professional preparation of teachers. In J. D. Raths & L. G. Katz (Eds.), *Advances in teacher education* (Vol. 2, pp. 1–18). Norwood, NJ: Ablex.

Clifford, G. J., & Guthrie, J. W. (1988). *Ed school: A brief for professional education.* Chicago: University of Chicago Press.

Darling-Hammond, L. (1984). *Beyond the commission reports: The coming crisis in teaching.* Santa Monica, CA: RAND.

Darling-Hammond, L. (1994). Who will speak for the children? How Teach for America hurts urban schools and students. *Phi Delta Kappan, 76*(1), 21–34.

Darling-Hammond, L., & Berry, B. (1988). *The evolution of teacher policy.* Santa Monica, CA: RAND.

Goodlad, J. I. (1990). *Teachers for our nation's schools.* San Francisco: Jossey-Bass.

Goodlad, J. I. (1994). *Educational renewal: Better teachers, better schools.* San Francisco: Jossey-Bass.

Hedden, I. (1995). *Teacher education: Supply, demand, quality, diversity, and their implications* (Technical Report to Ohio State University, College of Education, Policy Research for Ohio-Based Education). Dublin, OH: Paragon Communications.

Herman, J., & Megiveron, G. (1993). *Collective bargaining in education: Win/win, win/lose, lose/lose.* Lancaster, PA: Technomic.

Holmes Group. (1986). *Tomorrow's teachers: A report of the Holmes Group.* East Lansing, MI: Author.

Holmes Group. (1990). *Tomorrow's schools: Principles for the design of professional development schools.* East Lansing, MI: Author.

Holmes Group. (1995). *Tomorrow's schools of education.* East Lansing, MI: Author.

Howey, K. R. (1994). *Recent reform and restructuring initiatives in elementary and secondary schools: Implications for preservice teacher education.* Unpublished manuscript, Ohio State University, College of Education.

Howey, K. R., Arends, R., Galluzzo, G., Yarger, S., & Zimpher, N. L. (1995). *RATE VIII: Teaching teachers—Relationships with the world of practice.* Washington, DC: American Association of Colleges for Teacher Education.

Loadman, W. (1992). *Technical report: Instructional follow-up studies.* Columbus: Ohio State University, College of Education.

National Board for Professional Teaching Standards. (1994). *Toward high and rigorous standards for the teaching profession* (2nd ed.). Washington, DC: Author.

National Center for Education Statistics. (1993). [Data on supply and demand]. Washington, DC: Office of Educational Research and Improvement.

National Council for Accreditation of Teacher Education. (1994). *Annual list.* Washington, DC: Author.

Pearson, P. D. (1994). Standards and teacher education: A policy perspective. In M. E. Diez, V. Richardson, & P. D. Pearson (Eds.), *Setting standards and educating teachers* (Report from the Wingspread Conference, pp. 37–67). Washington, DC: American Association of Colleges for Teacher Education.

Scheetz, L. P. (1994). *Recruiting trends 1994–95: Education supplement.* East Lansing: Michigan State University, Collegiate Employment Research Institute.

Veenman, S. (1987). Perceived problems of beginning teachers. *Review of Educational Research, 54*(2), 143–178.

Zimpher, N. L. (1989). The RATE project: A profile of teacher education students. *Journal of Teacher Education, 40*(6), 27–31.

Zimpher, N. L., & Sherrill, J. (1996). Professors, teachers, and leaders in schools, colleges, and departments of education. In J. Sikula, T. J. Buttery, & E. Guyton (Eds.), *Handbook of research on teacher education* (2nd ed., pp. 279–305). New York: Macmillan.

A Response to Chapter 3,
"Right-Sizing Teacher Education:
The Policy Imperative," by Nancy L. Zimpher

EDWARD R. DUCHARME
Drake University

Nancy L. Zimpher raises a number of provocative points in Chapter 3. Few teacher educators would agree with all of them; even fewer would agree with none of them.

I begin by taking issue with an apparent distinction that Zimpher makes in her first paragraph, namely, that in the remainder of her chapter, she will use the term *education schools* rather than *schools, colleges, and departments of education*. Much is implicitly lost in the transition. Gone are the Grinnell and Smith colleges, the universities of New Hampshire, and many other quality producers of teachers that call themselves departments.

I have organized these remarks around the headings in Zimpher's section on symptoms, referring to other sections of her chapter along the way. I respond to all the headings except two, Organizational Affiliation and Competing Agencies. I agree with nearly all that Zimpher writes in these parts.

The Size and the Diversity of the Enterprise

On the subject of the size and the scope of teacher education, any response must begin with, "My goodness, there are a lot of programs!" There have been numerous countings of the number of institutions preparing teachers. Consensus settles on 1,250–1,300. Whether this range has anything to do with the number of law schools, business schools, medical schools, and so forth is beyond me.

I have five points to express on size and diversity:

1. Many institutions prepare teachers.
2. There appears to be no way of cutting the number.
3. The mission of preparing teachers remains a low priority in terms of commitment of resources, despite the pious platitudes in institutional accreditation and approval process reports.
4. In the main, teacher preparation programs make money for the institutions that sponsor them, first, by being low in cost and, second, by continuing to provide a career option for students who might otherwise leave.
5. Teacher education is not a primary activity of professors of education in schools, colleges, and departments of education, even for those for whom teacher education is a primary responsibility.

English educator Harry Judge (1982) commented on several schools of education in major American research universities after visiting them. In 1993, I observed,

> One of [Judge's] major points [is] the little value that such institutions, their faculties, and their administrations have for teacher preparation. He contends that the more distant education faculty are from teacher education, the better they feel about themselves. Ironically, it may be that when education faculty distance themselves from teacher education, they most resemble arts and sciences faculty, who, as Lanier and Little (1986) have pointed out, almost totally distance themselves from it. (Ducharme, 1993, p. 9)

Soder (1990) notes, "At major private institutions, 71.6% [of faculty] say that preparing teachers is of considerable importance, but only 11.9% see preparing teachers as essential for tenure" (p. 706). The RATE (AACTE, 1987, 1988, 1989, 1990, 1991) data repeatedly show that those who teach teachers are reluctant to identify themselves as teacher educators. In several years of the surveys, respondents had the opportunity to indicate how they identified themselves professionally. They never selected the title *teacher educator* more than 15% of the time. Judge, Lemosse, Paine, and Sedlak (1994) address the question of identity of teacher educators in their remarks on teacher education in America:

> The teachers of teachers wrestle with a twofold problem of identity. One is a question of allegiance: in many cases, it is their basic disciplines, rather than the training of teachers itself, which command their loyalty. This is true for teachers of foundations courses, whose primary interest is in the sociology, psychology, history, or philosophy of education. To them, the real teachers are those who teach the methods courses, but the latter in their turn tend to identify more readily with the school subject of their expertise. (p. 134)

I question whether, as Zimpher says, teacher education "left the confines of the normal school and joined the ranks of the academy" (p. 43) or whether the academy seized and seduced teacher education for, among possible reasons, its income-generating potential. Few institutions, including many in the Holmes Group, have abandoned undergraduate teacher preparation. As the several-year RATE studies point out, the dollar return on teacher education far exceeds that of more costly programs. Clifford and Guthrie (1988) note that universities

> launched their initially modest ventures in professional education because it directly served their own interests. . . . As some elite colleges and universities found it convenient to have a theological seminary as a token to quiet critics of their "godless materialism," they similarly found that educating a few teachers could project an image of contributing to the public weal. (p. 123)

Hence one could contend, and I do, that universities appropriated teacher education for its monetary and moral potentials and that the normal schools gladly sought the increased prestige of being in "legitimate" higher education environments.

In another section, Zimpher writes of the possibility of a "regionalized profession" (p. 56). The concept needs much more clarification before it can receive any serious discussion.

The Accreditation Profile

Regarding the profession's accreditation profile, 8 years have passed since the last full iteration of the NCATE standards and review processes. The total number of institutions preparing teachers remains about what it was 15 years ago. In addition, numerous groups not affiliated with institutions (e.g., Teach for America) and numerous preparation programs initiated by states outside the higher education framework (e.g., California and Texas) have emerged. In a chapter on needed research in teacher education, prepared for the *Handbook of Research on Teacher Education*, Mary Ducharme and I (1996) raise questions about accreditation that researchers should pursue:

> Are there differences that relate to teacher performance between teaching graduates of NCATE member institutions and graduates of nonmember institutions otherwise similar in size, type, and scope? Are there differences between NCATE member institutions and nonmember institutions otherwise similar in size, type, and scope? Chief claims for national accreditation in any profession are that standards for admission will be higher, the graduates will perform better in their work, and there will be a higher level of public trust. The contention is that the clients fare better when dealing with professionals from nationally accredited institutions. Little research exists either to demonstrate or disprove the contention. Katz and Raths asked a similar question in 1985: "Are graduates of NCATE-accredited institutions better teachers, on the average, than graduates from nonaccredited institutions? Is the content of NCATE-approved teacher education programs different from those which are not NCATE approved?" (p. 13). Despite nearly a decade of heightened attention to and development of accreditation practices and programs, Katz and Raths' questions remain unanswered. Wise (1993–1994) comments that "Graduation from an NCATE-accredited school equips a teacher with the tools he

or she needs to accept the challenges faced by educators today" (p. v).

What are the tools? Are graduates from nonaccredited schools not in possession of the same "tools"? The matter of the precise differences between those from accredited institutions and those from nonaccredited institutions remains vague. Are there discernible differences in content knowledge, rapport with students, social commitment, methods of instruction, and/or effectiveness in a multicultural setting? We suggest that researchers might study the effects of accreditation, not the perceived professional need. This would be an enormous but immensely valuable task. We suggest that researchers develop strategies and methods to study what, if any, results accrue to students in elementary and secondary schools that relate to their having been taught by individuals from either accredited or nonaccredited programs. Teacher education would also profit from analyses of the various accreditation processes of regional higher education reviews and profession-specific reviews. Realistic and rigorous cost analyses would also be helpful. Valuable research would move from the rhetoric of the asserted professional responsibility for institutional membership in much current literature (i.e., Gideonse et al., 1993) to the demonstrable value for teacher education graduates, the schools in which they teach, and the youth whom they teach. (Ducharme & Ducharme, 1996, p. 1043)

Issues of Supply and Demand

Issues of supply and demand remain enigmatic. Teacher education programs clearly graduate more candidates than there are positions. Supply and demand has been a contentious matter from my entry into teaching over three decades ago, when teachers were in such short supply that the main criteria appeared to be little more than being ambulatory and able to draw breath; through the 1970s and the 1980s, when positions were scarce; to the present, when the situation is somewhere between those two extremes depending on geographic area and area of specialization.

One thing is certain, however. As long as students can go to an adviser, say that they want to enroll in teacher education, and successfully meet program requirements, there will be a surplus of persons with teaching credentials. It continues to be ironic that although institutions produce an oversupply of teachers, states like New Jersey and others approve alternative certification programs with thus far little demonstrated efficacy.

The cities, however, need teachers. The New York City school-age population is increasing by 15,000 a year. At the same time, data from the RATE studies demonstrate that large cities are precisely where the vast majority of teacher education students do not want to go. Martin Haberman addresses this matter in Chapter 5. The issue needs the attention of all teacher educators. Most of America has abandoned the cities except for their museums, playhouses, and ballparks. Can teacher education abandon the children of the cities? What can and must teacher education do about the issues of thousands on thousands of children emerging from uneven years in school totally or nearly totally unequipped to deal with life? I have no answers, only questions. I suspect, however, that the necessary actions do not lie in meetings of the various associations and committees to which Zimpher refers in her chapter.

Institutional "Products"

Zimpher writes, "In an age of product orientation in the business and corporate community, which is slowly creeping into the fabric of higher education, a discussion about clients and products seems appropriate" (p. 51). True enough, business and corporate leaders are insidiously creeping into higher and lower education, but teacher educators do not have to use their language. Educators have already adopted too many of their mantras: *world-class* whatevers, *roundtables, total quality management, product control, global competition, marketplace,* and on and on. I, for one, do not see the students whom I teach as the products of my work, nor do I see the arena in which I work as the market. One of the marks of a true profession is the possession of its own language, neither arcane nor obtuse. A demiprofession like teacher education would do well to talk and write in its own language: *students, teachers, learning, schools, human development,* and so forth. In general, teacher educators would do well to talk of themselves in terms of themselves, not always in terms of someone else.

However, to the point of the students whom teacher educators recommend for graduation and certification: Indeed, they are largely white, politically conservative, place bound, suburban or rural, and provincial. What else would one expect, given the current class structure of the nation? The population of prospective teachers certainly does not reflect the nation that is evolving. Teacher education continues to recruit a small percentage of minority students into programs. Zimpher refers later in her chapter to a "feeder system" (p. 60) to attract minority students to teaching and retain them. This is a laudable idea to pursue, but even an unlikely increase of 100% in the number of minority students in teaching would leave the teaching force considerably short of the kind of diversity that the nation has and certainly will have.

The increases of around 40% that Zimpher reports in undergraduate teacher education's enrollment of largely white, politically conservative, place-bound, suburban or rural, and provincial students will only exacerbate the difference. Thus, although the matter of recruiting minority students remains critical, the issue of how to educate and prepare majority students so that they both wish to teach in diverse environments and know how to grow in knowledge and skill in teaching in these environments is also critical. More than 10 years of national, regional, and state accreditation and program approval visits have taught me that programs are doing well at providing the opportunity for students to learn about persons and cultures different from their own, but doing poorly at truly educating students and strongly influencing them to teach children from backgrounds vastly different from their own.

More than 90% of elementary school teacher education students are female; more than 50% of those who teach them in their preparation programs are male. Most of the teachers in the nation's elementary schools are female. The majority of elementary school principals are male. This is a serious problem that teacher education must address as it strives to prepare and develop strong, viable candidates for difficult, albeit fulfilling, lives as teachers. Teacher education faculty, both male and female, should provide prospective teachers with better models to confront a sometimes sexist professional world and a curriculum and a set of experiences that enlighten them and empower them to live and teach effectively.

Other Reactions and Comments

I wish to comment on a matter only indirectly present, if at all, in Zimpher's chapter. Teacher education is largely central to departments of education in small liberal arts colleges, if for no other reason than that teacher education is all they can do. When one considers schools and colleges of education, however, one often finds a blurred focus on teacher education. By this I mean that these institutions too often focus primarily on their doctoral programs, their grant programs, their educational administration programs, their counseling programs, and so forth. It is difficult to develop and maintain an emphasis on the preparation of elementary and secondary teachers with so scattered a focus. I always peruse the catalogs of the institutions that I visit as part of a national, regional, or state accreditation or program approval team. I note a generally higher percentage of full and associate professors in areas such as higher education, educational administration, policy studies (where the traditional foundations people often hide), and student affairs than I note in teacher education, however the institution defines it. I also note a generally higher percentage of female faculty in teacher education than in the other areas. Schools and colleges of education are not houses divided against themselves. Rather, they are high-rise apartments with private elevators leading to each unit, and teacher educators often live on the bottom floor. As part of addressing the many significant issues in Zimpher's chapter, teacher education must face this matter directly and decide what its place is and should be within schools and colleges of education.

Zimpher notes as one of her national imperatives the necessity to create "a professional development continuum wherein teacher preparation is extended into the early years of teaching" (p. 55). The concept is laudable but its implementation doubtful. I offer an addition to the imperative: Teacher educators should attempt to develop in students the notion that teaching is a lifelong activity requiring continuous growth, that collegial relationships with teachers and other educators are essential to this growth, and that responsibility for the growth is the teacher's own. I further recommend that teacher educators find ways to work with principals, superintendents, and department heads and help them understand that a new teacher is, in one sense, not a teacher but a person striving to become good at teaching and learning with young people. The experience in Iowa is that school administrators are increasingly happy with the people whom they are hiring. They must go beyond being happy, to providing those whom they hire with an environment for growth. That might even be a place for those in schools and colleges of education to work with professors in educational administration.

A Final Note

In her chapter, Zimpher makes a major contribution to what must be a dialogue about how teacher educators make better sense of their work. To repeat what I said at the beginning of this response: "Few teacher educators would agree with all of [the provocative points that Zimpher raises]; even fewer would agree with none of them." For Zimpher and me to agree or disagree on something is not new; we spent 6 wonderful and sometimes contentious years as colleagues on the RATE committee. Neither of us has altered the style in which we write certitudes about essentially ambiguous matters. I believe, however, that teacher education will grow and prosper when people with certitudes sit and talk and move toward new and more vital places.

References

American Association of Colleges for Teacher Education. (1987, 1988, 1989, 1990, 1991). *Teaching teachers: Facts and figures.* Washington, DC: Author.

Clifford, G. J., & Guthrie, J. W. (1988). *Ed school: A brief for professional education.* Chicago: University of Chicago Press.

Ducharme, E. (1993). *The lives of teacher educators.* New York: Teachers College Press.

Ducharme, E., & Ducharme, M. (1996). Needed research in teacher education. In J. Sikula, T. J. Buttery, & E. Guyton (Eds.), *Handbook of research on teacher education* (2nd ed., pp. 1030–1046). New York: Macmillan.

Gideonse, H., Ducharme, E., Ducharme, M., Gollnick, D., Lilly, S., Schelke, E. L., & Smith, P. (1993). *Capturing the vision: Reflections on NCATE's redesign five years after.* Washington, DC: American Association of Colleges for Teacher Education.

Judge, H. (1982). *American graduate schools of education: A view from abroad.* New York: Ford Foundation.

Judge, H., Lemosse, M., Paine, L., & Sedlak, M. (1994). *The university and the teachers: France, the United States, England: The Oxford Comparative Studies in Education* (Vol. 4). Oxfordshire, England: Triangle.

Katz, L., & Raths, J. (1985). A framework for research on teacher education programs. *Journal of Teacher Education, 36*(6), 9–15.

Lanier, J., & Little, J. (1986). Research in teacher education. In M. Wittrock (Ed.), *Handbook of research on teaching* (3rd ed., pp. 527–569). New York: Macmillan.

Soder, R. (1990). How faculty members feel when the reward structure changes. *Phi Delta Kappan, 71,* 702–709.

Wise, A. (1993–1994). Preface. In *Teacher education: A guide to NCATE-accredited colleges and institutions* (p. 1). Washington, DC: National Council for Accreditation of Teacher Education.

4

The Influence of Agencies on Teacher Preparation: Social Justice in the New Millennium

CARL A. GRANT
University of Wisconsin–Madison

The beginning of a new millennium is just a few years away. Teachers educators will take into the 21st century many of the questions that have haunted them during the past century—for example, questions about governance and the effectiveness of teacher education. This chapter addresses the issue of governance, specifically the question, What role will participating agencies play in teacher preparation? I have interpreted the question to mean, What influence will agencies have on teacher preparation? Also, I have taken a critical stance in examining the motivation of the agencies of influence.

It is important to recognize that the word *influence* conveys the concepts of power and control, which are often motivated by self-interest, public (altruistic) interest, or both. A statement on social justice unionism by 29 teacher union activists in a recent issue of *Rethinking Schools* ("Social Justice Unionism," 1994) addresses this point:

> The ideals that led us to organize our unions and fight for economic justice—indeed, that led many of us to enter teaching in the first place—are no less compelling than in the past: a desire to help children; hope for the future; service to community; and a conviction that public education is a cornerstone of society's commitment to opportunity, equity, and democratic participation. (p. 12)

These are the ideals that need to be revisited by all agencies that have an influence on education (including teacher education) as they develop and implement policies and practices. Currently, the majority of these agencies appear to be more motivated by their own self-interests than by the democratic ideals just cited.

The first section of this chapter examines the preservice teachers that the agencies influence and the way in which they are currently being prepared for their role as educators. The second section describes the schoolchildren that these preservice teachers will face and examines those children's social and school contexts. The third section describes the agencies and their influence on teacher education. It also discusses whether the agencies' motivation for their influence is based on self-interest or the ideals of social justice.

Teachers for the New Millennium
and Their Course Work

A Profile of Preservice Teachers

Currently, approximately 1,180 colleges and universities in the United States offer a teacher education program (AACTE, 1988). Of these institutions, 1,020 are predominantly white and 89 are historically black. The white student enrollment in schools of education is over 90% at the predominantly white universities. Most of the students are females from middle-class communities in small cities and suburban or rural areas (AACTE, 1990; Zimpher, 1989). Stone (1994) describes their upbringing as follows:

> They grew up in an American society that is, overall, multicultural and pluralistic, but they were raised in homes and neighborhoods generally more culturally homogeneous than heterogeneous. They inherited an informal legacy of white, middle-class cultural hegemony, of which they may not even be aware, that is difficult for them to loosen and shake off. (p. 13)

The white students' experiences with and understanding of people of color and their knowledge of causes and sites of oppression affecting people of color are limited. A majority of this cohort of future teachers are the "younger sisters" of a professional group that Dilworth (1990) describes as "well educated White women, dedicated to the [teaching] profession, but unfamiliar with the ethos of the major racial/ethnic culture of society" (p. 17).

Students of color entering teacher education make up approximately 10% of the preservice teacher population. They come mostly from blue-collar homes, low-income homes, or both (Dilworth, 1990). According to AACTE (1988), "The average college of education enrolls approximately 400 students. Of this number, only 22 students will be Black, 7 Hispanic, 3 Asian and 2 American Indian/Alaskan Native" (p. 22).

The personal experiences of nonwhite ethnic group members (e.g., African Americans or Mexican Americans) with other groups of color and their understanding of other groups of color are similar to those of their white counterparts—that is, very narrow and limited. For example, Marshall (1994) found that some African American students perceived multicultural education (i.e., the idea of including "all the groups") as an effort to restructure curricula to include, if not emphasize, contributions and perspectives of African Americans. Despite their professed concern about including all groups, students of color who share this misconception frequently fail to include other nonwhite groups. In addition, the experiences of students of color in analyzing sites of oppression and encouraging social change are usually limited to their own racial group.

Unfortunately, college events and activities offer students only limited opportunities to gain cross-cultural experiences (e.g., working with members of ethnic groups other than their own and listening to speakers of ethnic groups other than their own). In-depth cross-cultural experiences (e.g., living in an ethnic community different than their own or in a multicultural community) are rare (Grant, 1994). Many students seem hesitant to engage in cross-cultural experiences that challenge their beliefs unless they are required to do so by a program or instructed to do so by a professor as an assignment (Grant & Koskela, 1986). Although most of the teacher education programs require students to take ethnic studies or multicultural education classes, these courses are often so content driven that attitudes and behaviors of both white students and students of color are not examined, or the courses lack robust discussions, analyses, and critiques of race, class, and gender issues. Also, even when students take an excellent multicultural course, it alone is not sufficient to provide them with the necessary knowledge and skills for teaching in a culturally diverse nation (Ahlquist, 1991; Gomez, 1990; Ladson-Billings, 1991).

Preservice Course Work

The program of study for most future teachers is similar. During the first 2 years of college, they complete their liberal studies requirement and in some cases begin taking education courses. In the third year, most students planning to teach enter the education school and begin a professional sequence that leads to teacher certification. This professional sequence includes foundations of education, methods, special education, and educational psychology courses, as well as field experiences (e.g., practicums and student teaching).

In recent years, many predominantly white colleges have begun to address issues of diversity in their teacher education programs. Some universities require students to take a course in multicultural education. Others attempt to infuse multicultural education into the traditional curriculum. A few have developed master's degree programs in multicultural education. Most of these efforts are supplementary, limited, or repetitive: supplementary because they mainly involve requiring students to take one or two ethnic studies courses; limited because only a few instructors (other than the instructors of ethnic studies courses) systematically infuse study of diversity into their courses; or repetitive because similar activities or practices (e.g., analysis of textbooks for bias) appear in different courses (Grant, 1994; Grant & Koskela, 1986; Grant & Secada, 1990). In addition, according to Gollnick (1992),

> In only a few cases have courses identified by institutions as multicultural critically examined race and ethnicity, gender, and class and the interactions of these dynamics in schools and society. Issues of institutional discrimination, prejudice, power, and the cultural dominance of the curriculum have received minimal attention in most professional education courses. (p. 66)

Students at historically black colleges follow a similar curriculum as their peers at predominantly white colleges. They spend the freshman and sophomore years taking liberal arts courses, the junior and senior years in the professional sequence. Courses in multicultural education are limited (Mills & Buckley, 1992), and often there is debate over their importance. This debate occurs because students are required to take courses in African American history, and the belief exists (among a number of staff and students) that these courses satisfy the need for multicultural education. However, recent interviews that I informally conducted with students graduating from historically black colleges reveal that they have received only a limited amount of formal instruction in African American studies and that they have a limited understanding of multicultural education.

Preservice teachers now and in the 21st century need a variety of formal and informal intercultural experiences; they need to examine their own life experiences, including their privileges and oppression; they need to be advocates for democratic principles and social justice issues; and they must be able to prepare their students to be advocates as well. In addition, preservice teachers need formal course work that teaches them to identify and analyze the meanings and the causes of the different forms of oppression and to understand that schools are sites of power struggles and inequalities. They need, as well, course work that introduces them to the histories and the literature of diverse cultures and that provides them with a range of pedagogical knowledge and skills to teach diverse learners effectively.

Schoolchildren of the New Millennium and Their Needs

Many preservice teachers will be searching for jobs in small cities or in the suburbs of large cities, where they expect the students to be white, middle-class, or both. The possibility of finding such positions is not great because the major population growth is occurring among children of color who live in urban areas. Furthermore, many small cities and suburbs of large cities are becoming more racially and economically diverse. An examination of 1990 census data reveals that newly certified teachers are likely to encounter the following classroom profile: Of a total of 30 students (15 girls and 15 boys), 21 are whites, 5 are African Americans, 3 are Hispanics, 2 are Mexican Americans, 1 is a Cuban American, and 1 is a second-generation Asian American. Four white students, 2 African American students, and 1 Hispanic student are from upper-income homes. The students' families are largely nontraditional: 19 are two-parent families in which both parents hold or have recently held jobs at least part-time; 9 are single-parent families (6 of them below the poverty line); and only 2 are two-parent families in which one parent, the father, works outside the home. Most of the students have grown up speaking English, but 2 of the Hispanic students speak Spanish at home, and 1 white student speaks French at home. Five of the students are not in the mainstream of academic skills: Two spend part of the day in a learning disabilities class, 1 is in a class for the mentally retarded, 1 is in a gifted program, and 1 is in a speech therapy program (National Center for Education Statistics, personal communication, 1991).

Also, even small-town USA has a growing population of students of color. In Verona, Wisconsin, with a general population of 5,374 (Bureau of the Census, 1990) and a student population of 2,918 (pre-kindergarten through Grade 12), 172 (5.9%) of the students are students of color. Although this population is small, it is diverse, with 79 African Americans, 46 Asian Americans, 29 Hispanics, and 18 Native Americans (Wisconsin Department of Public Instruction, 1992).

In both urban and small-town settings, students need a culturally responsive curriculum that includes knowledge about their own ethnic history and culture as well as those of other ethnic group members. They need skills and strategies in how to control their life circumstances and how to participate effectively in democratic decision making. They need a school climate that is caring and supportive while inspiring high expectations. In addition, they need knowledge and experiences in how to accept and affirm one another's cultural groups. Studies over the past decade have reported that the United States is increasingly becoming a two-class society, that is, haves and have-nots (Harrington, 1984). Students need to be educated in why this social and economic separation is occurring, what the social justice implications of such a separation are, and what they can do to stop the separation.

The preceding sections have described preservice teachers and schoolchildren and painted a picture of their educational experiences and their socioeconomic backgrounds. Their educational experiences have been guided predominantly by standards and accountability, with little attention to social justice issues. It is therefore important to examine the agencies that influence teacher education and discuss how they exert their influence. Critical to this examination is how these agencies handle their self-interest and social justice concerns and whether they actually support "public education [as a] corner-stone of society's commitment to opportunity, equity, and democratic participation" ("Social Justice Unionism," 1994, p. 12).

Agencies and Their Influence on Teacher Education

A host of agencies and groups influence teacher education at both the preservice and the inservice level: federal and state governments, courts, foundations, corporations, unions, associations, scholars, and researchers. Spring (1988) provides an excellent framework for discussing them. According to Spring, they can be divided into three primary categories: major government actors, special interest groups, and the knowledge industry. "Within each of these three categories," Spring (1988) states, "individuals and organizations pursue a particular set of interests and goals" (p. 3). Table 4.1 shows (with modifications) the three categories and their subcategories.

Major Government Actors

THE FEDERAL GOVERNMENT

Although the U.S. Constitution does not refer directly to education or delegate power to the federal government in educational areas, the federal government does influence both education and teacher preparation. Kirst (1974) has identified six modes of federal influence:

1. [Give] general aid: provide "no strings" block grants to aid states and localities
2. Stimulate through differential funding: earmark categories of aid, specific services
3. Regulate: legally specify behavior, impose standards, enforce accountability procedures
4. Discover knowledge and make it available: have research conducted, data gathered, and results reported
5. Provide services: furnish technical assistance and consultants in specialized subjects or areas

TABLE 4.1 Major Political Groups in Education

Major Government Actors	Special Interest Groups	The Knowledge Industry
Federal government	Foundations	Funding agencies
State government	Business community/ corporate sector	Researchers
Politicians	Teacher unions	
Courts	Educational interest groups	

SOURCE: From *Conflict of Interests: The Politics of American Education* by Joel Spring. Copyright © 1988 by Longman Publishers. Reprinted with permission.

6. Exert moral suasion: develop vision and question educational assumptions through publications and through speeches by top officials (p. 450)

Although these six modes of influence do not directly specify teacher education as a target, they can and do have an effect on it. For example, with the passage of Public Law 94-142, teacher education programs added a special education course (e.g., Strategies for Inclusive Schooling) to their licensure program. Recent federal influence in teacher education, however, has mainly been in the area of moral suasion. As Clark and McNergney (1990) state, "The Department of Education has focused on exhortative tactics, encouraging states and institutions of higher education to raise standards of teacher preparation and local education agencies to use devices such as career ladders for teachers to improve teacher performance" (p. 102).

I agree with Clark and McNergney's assessment, but argue that the federal government's exertion of moral suasion has been weak or limited in promoting social justice but forceful in supporting the self-interests of the political party and the administration in power. *A Nation at Risk* (National Commission on Excellence in Education, 1983), which was sponsored by the Department of Education under the administration of Ronald Reagan, provides a classic example. With the release of *A Nation at Risk*, the federal government exerted moral suasion by "*develop[ing a] vision [of education] and question[ing] educational assumptions"* (Kirst, 1974, p. 450; emphasis added). The report claimed that America's public schools were failing. It cited low achievement scores, grade inflation, the assignment of less homework, the absence of a foreign language requirement, and the absence of a rigorous curriculum as part of the failure. The report also questioned the quality of teacher education, calling for changes that would include attracting persons who demonstrated an aptitude for teaching and competence in an academic discipline.

The vision proposed in *A Nation at Risk* possessed twin educational goals: equity and excellence. In the report's discussion of these goals, however, one can find the lack of attention to social justice issues and locate the interest of the government parties in power. The report acknowledges that

> the twin goals of equity and high-quality schooling have profound and practical meaning for our economy and society, and we cannot permit one to yield to the other in principle or practice. To do so would deny young people their chance to learn and live according to their aspiration and abilities. It would lead to a generalized accommodation of mediocrity in our society on the one hand or the creation of an undemocratic elitism on the other. (p. 13)

Other than this statement, there is very little attention to equity. The report's definition of *equity* seems to be synonymous with "equality," that is, "access equality" and "process equality." This definition is misleading. Secada's (1989) definition of equity stresses its essence, that is, social justice:

> The heart of equity lies in our ability to acknowledge that, even though our actions might be in accord with a set of rules, their results may be unjust. Equity goes beyond following those rules, even if we have agreed that they are intended to achieve justice. Equity gauges the results of actions directly against standards of justice, and it is used to decide whether or not what is being done is just. Educational equity, therefore, should be constructed as a check on the justice of specific actions that are carried out within the education arena and the arrangements that result from those actions. (p. 69)

A Nation at Risk is, on the other hand, very clear about what it means by *excellence*:

> We define "excellence" to mean several things. At the level of the *individual learner*, it means performing on the boundary of individual ability in ways that test and push back personal limits, in school and in the work place. Excellence characterizes a *school or college* that sets high expectations and goals for all learners, then tries every way possible to help students reach them. Excellence characterizes a *society* that has adopted these policies, for it will then be prepared through the education and skill of its people to respond to the challenges of a rapidly changing world. (p. 13; emphasis in original)

Although the report speaks of "high expectations" and "performing on the boundary of individual ability" as those ideas relate to students, it does not offer a vision of how they will be achieved in an educational system with savage financial inequalities and lack of social justice.

In the 21st century, the federal government will continue to offer a vision of education and to question educational assumptions. The vision and the questions, though, will be clothed in the politics of the party in power. The extent to which the vision will include social justice for marginalized people, and the extent to which the questions will challenge or illuminate inequalities and inequities, will depend on the person who occupies the White House and the people who control Congress.

STATE GOVERNMENT

Most scholars of the U.S. Constitution support the thesis that the governance of education is the states' responsibility. Correspondingly, most state constitutions give legal responsibility for education to the state. However, before the 1980s and especially up to the 1960s, the states' role in the governance of education was low key, almost silent, except in some special areas such as desegregation or integration of schools and universities. States invested their time and attention in collecting educational data, reporting on the social and financial welfare of schools and students, deciding on curriculum guidelines, and determining teacher certification and compulsory attendance policies.

State involvement in education began to increase in the 1960s with President Lyndon B. Johnson's War on Poverty. Federal money designated to help local school districts was funneled through state departments of education, leading to an expansion in their responsibility. However, it was during the administration of Ronald Reagan and with the publication of *A Nation at Risk* in 1983 (which advocated major education reform) that the states' role in the governance of education started to change dramatically. Reagan's policy was to send money back to the states as block grants so that educational decisions could be made at the state and local levels. Operating in concert with this policy was the reform movement, intended generally to improve the country's education system and specifically to improve the academic performance of students by giving more control of education governance to the states.

In 1989, President George Bush and the nation's governors further endorsed state control over education when they put forth the first National Education Goals. The purpose of the goals, according to Governor Roy Romer (1991), was to "capture the attention and resolve of Americans to restructure our schools and radically increase our expectations for student performance" (p. 1). In 1994, President Bill Clinton continued this effort when he signed Goals 2000 into law. Each state's progress toward the achievement of the goals is to be the indicator of the nation's response to reform.

Now, with the Republicans controlling Congress and driving pell-mell to increase state control of education, and with the Clinton administration championing systemic reform (including national content and performance standards to achieve world-class education), state governance of education has achieved a status never before seen.

Will high activity and high involvement on the part of the states, along with content and performance standards identified within the National Education Goals, lead to better education for diversity? Not necessarily. The state education agencies' support of education reform has not seriously considered issues of diversity in areas such as standards and challenging content. Standards (for resources, practice, and outcomes; see O'Day & Smith, 1993) are fundamental to state education agencies' increased involvement in the education reform movement. O'Day and Smith (1993) state, "Within the context of content-driven systemic reform, the purpose of school standards should be to provide operational specifications for assessing whether a school is giving its students the opportunity to learn the content and skills set out in the curriculum framework" (p. 274). Although the opportunity to which O'Day and Smith allude is supposed to be couched in the concept of equal opportunity, it can easily be interpreted as couched in a compensatory model of educational opportunity. For example, in discussing the importance of having language resources for students, O'Day and Smith leave unclear whether the resources are to aid students in their transition to English or to support students in becoming bilingual.

According to O'Day and Smith (1993), challenging content for all students is at the heart of content-based systemic reform. However, proponents of systemic reform ignore the serious debate about race, class, and gender issues in the curriculum occurring across the nation. In other words, discussions are lacking about whose knowledge and what knowledge will make up the challenging content.

In sum, educators and other specialists in charge of defining the character and the dimensions of reform, including the increasing state voice in education governance, have proceeded from a misconception of equity, mainly basing their view on an access or a compensatory model. In addition, there is an even greater separation between the ideals of equity and the practical involvement of state agencies. Analyzing Minnesota's reform efforts, Crumpton (1995) reports that the involvement of people of color has been the exception not the rule in the implementation of reform and that there has been little attention to policy that seriously deals with multicultural education.

A stronger state voice in educational matters can be useful to the people, but only if and when equity is understood as more than just equal access to institutions. There are issues of equity to be addressed after students enter education institutions. Equity means valuing students' cultural background, rather than erasing it and educating students for assimilation into the dominant culture. In addition, to meet the needs of people from diverse backgrounds adequately and appropriately, there must be representative involvement at all levels of reform.

POLITICIANS

Teacher education has increasingly become a political issue, and more and more politicians are courting professional education organizations (e.g., the National Education Association and the American

Federation of Teachers) for their votes. At the same time, politicians criticize educators and the educational system for not preparing students with the basic skills needed for living and competing in a global market where technology continues to advance at a rapid pace.

In national and local political campaigns, politicians often propose major changes in education. They use catchy statements such as "We should demand more from students," "We should demand more from teachers," and "We should demand more from administrators" (e.g., Bush, 1988; Bush & Wead, 1988). Often, their message is one of accountability. For example, as a presidential candidate in 1988, George Bush argued that to have better schools, America must emphasize accountability: setting goals, objectively measuring progress toward those goals, changing what does not work, and rewarding what does.

Rarely do politicians directly address teacher education. They may indirectly refer to teacher education, for example, by calling for competency tests for beginning teachers in the subjects they teach, or tests in speaking and listening proficiency. These ideas suggest more about the qualifications of an incoming teacher candidate than about the quality of a teacher preparation program. Absent from the politicians' discourse is attention to the compelling needs facing teacher education as American society becomes more racially diverse and divides into haves and have-nots, and as students bring more social and personal problems to school. Beyond supporting the recruitment of teachers of color and the selection of top teacher candidates, politicians pay little attention to the need for programs to prepare teacher candidates to be responsive to the race, class, gender, and social justice needs of K–12 students.

Self-interest and political advantage seem to be motivating factors behind much of what politicians do. For example, there is currently a heated debate in Wisconsin between three-term Republican Governor Tommy Thompson and independently elected Superintendent of the Department of Public Instruction (DPI) John Benson about the state agency that handles teacher licensure. The debate centers on the abolishment of DPI and the elected office of the superintendent, in favor of a State Board of Education that would be appointed by the governor.

The governor's argument is for decentralization of the state education bureaucracy; he has referred to DPI as the "mandate police" (Mayers, 1994, p. 16). The superintendent's counterargument is that any move to make the state superintendent a political pawn of the governor, to dismantle one of the nation's premier state education departments and to reduce local control defies logic and clearly has more to do with power and politics than with our children's educational success. (Schultze, 1994a, p. B4)

The face validity of each argument seems good and in the public interest. However, according to the *Milwaukee Journal*, the real reason for abolishing DPI and creating an appointed State Board of Education is that DPI has been too cozy with the Wisconsin Education Association Council. The council is the state's largest teachers union and a major opponent of choice and charter schools, which the governor favors (Schultze, 1994b). Similarly, an editorial in Madison's *Capital Times* ("Keep Power," 1994) states,

The foes of public education would love to weaken the position of public education's chief advocate. In the name of improving the quality of education, they would undermine what still remains a vital springboard to success for students in every part of this state. (p. 8A)

Politicians will continue to have an influence on education (and sometimes teacher education) in the 21st century because education will continue to be a popular national issue. As public discourse on issues such as school choice, privatization, and support for school meal programs continues, the politicians will be expected to address and make decisions on them.

COURTS

Since the 1960s, there has been increased advocacy for social justice and human rights in the United States, including the rights of students and teachers. Court decisions on students' and teachers' rights, as well as related events leading up to and coming after the decisions, contribute to the curriculum content in teacher education.

Information on students' rights related to the distribution of literature, dress and grooming codes, search and seizure, marriage and parenthood, school records, and due process are a part of the teacher education curriculum. Similarly, the results of race and sex discrimination court cases (e.g., *Brown v. Board of Education*, 1954; *Diana v. State Board of Education*, 1970, 1973; *Larry P. v. Riles*, 1972; *Lau v. Nichols*, 1973) serve as curriculum content for prospective teachers.

Information on teachers' rights related to tenure, strikes, corporal punishment, and tort liability are also a part of the teacher education curriculum. In addition, teacher preparation programs include instruction on academic freedom—teachers' right to make choices about the curriculum they teach.

Whose interests the courts will serve in the 21st century is still a major question. The balance of power on the Supreme Court defies simple description. There is a conservative wing, composed of Chief Justice William H. Rehnquist and Associate Justices Antonin Scalia and Clarence Thomas; a shifting center, composed of Associate Justices Anthony Kennedy, Sandra Day O'Connor, and David Souter; and a liberal wing, consisting of Associate Justices Harry A. Blackmun, Ruth Bader Ginsburg, and John Paul Stevens. This configuration makes it difficult to forecast what decisions the court will render on education and social justice issues.

Court watchers such as Jost (1993) point out that although recent court decisions are to the political right, favoring law enforcement and burdening civil rights litigants, the court also displays a solid streak of judicial restraint (p. 819). With a Supreme Court whose members resist neat pigeonholing and who will probably serve well into the 21st century, educators, especially those concerned with social justice issues, should expect to be influenced by the Supreme Court's decisions, as well as to experience much uncertainty as they await those decisions.

Special Interest Groups

FOUNDATIONS

In the introduction to the spring 1992 issue of *Teachers College Record*, a special issue titled "Philanthropy and Education," editor Ellen Condliffe Lagemann writes,

> Throughout our history and still today, philanthropy has been a major force in the shaping of educational policies and practices. Individual donors and organizations ranging from the American Missionary Association to the American Heart

Association have established colleges and universities, provided funds to construct new buildings, donated libraries and laboratories, and endowed countless professorships, lecture series, research programs, and international exchanges. (p. 361)

The Carnegie Corporation, the DeWitt Wallace–Reader's Digest Foundation, the Ford Foundation, the Kellogg Foundation, and the Lilly Foundation, among others, have a long and active history of participation in the shaping of American education. Gifts in thousands of dollars allow foundations to influence all aspects of education, including teacher education. For example, *A Nation Prepared: Teachers for the 21st Century* (Carnegie Forum on Education and the Economy, 1986), which was generated by the Task Force on Teaching as a Profession and funded by the Carnegie Corporation of New York, argues for major changes in teacher education policies and procedures. Presenting a rationale that school improvement and economic growth are related to reform in teacher education, the report states, "The key to success lies in creating a profession equal to the task—a profession of well-educated teachers prepared to assume new powers and responsibilities to redesign schools for the future" (p. 2). To create a teaching profession "equal to the task," it recommends the establishment of a national certification board for teachers. The purpose of this board is to develop national standards that a teacher has to meet to receive a national teaching certificate. In January 1995, 81 middle and junior high school teachers from 23 states qualified for national certification. In addition, several states announced that they would begin to explore the benefits of this certification procedure (Richardson, 1995).

Lobman (1992) identifies several growing trends of influence that foundations are exerting on education programs, including encouraging and helping universities to integrate the training of professionals from various fields (e.g., education, public health, social work, and public policy) to bring the professions of education, health, and human services closer together, and collaborating and developing partnerships with other donors who are funding similar projects to avoid duplication, streamline funding, share financial risks, use staff expertise and time better, and develop greater political muscle.

That philanthropy will continue to influence teacher education is certain. The critical question is, Will philanthropy support social justice and multicultural education as teacher education heads into the 21st century? It should. In the last century and the first part of this century, philanthropy was in the forefront of efforts to eliminate barriers to education of African American teachers—for example, in its support of historically black colleges and in its support of recruitment and retention of prospective African American teachers. As the 21st century approaches, philanthropic support needs to target teacher education programs that aim to eliminate race, socioeconomic class, and gender inequalities and injustices in educational policy and practices. This is especially true as government funding of education becomes increasingly scarce and as research funding for programs that address diversity becomes extremely difficult to obtain.

BUSINESS COMMUNITY/CORPORATE SECTOR

The education reform movement that started with *A Nation at Risk* in the 1980s demanded more of an education-business partnership. Corporate America charged that high school graduates were entering the workforce unprepared (e.g., Carnegie Forum on Education and the Economy, 1986). Politicians like George Bush and Bill Clinton have responded to these charges with education initiatives that serve to build school-business partnerships. The initiatives have grown from businesses adopting schools and businesspeople becoming mentors in schools to more developed school-to-work transition programs.

Teacher educators are increasingly being required to prepare teachers with a better understanding of education and employment. The Wisconsin Department of Public Instruction has mandated that students who complete an initial professional education program have licensure credits in the area of education for employment. The goals of the courses include helping students to

- Develop understanding of the multiple meanings of work and employment and the role of work in quality of life
- Analyze the changing nature of work and the American workforce
- Design education for employment programs and teaching strategies that are appropriate in relation to the program context

The influence of corporate America on education, including teacher education, has become increasingly stronger since the 1980s. This phenomenon will continue if government funding for education decreases. Because of a shortage of capital, educators will be placed in the position of doing more business with corporate America (e.g., privatizing schools). In fact, the influence of the corporate sector on education has become so strong that now (more than any time in the recent past) the goal of an education seems to be more directly connected to a person's achieving employment than to a person's achieving self-actualization and actively participating in the democratic process.

As the 21st century nears, it is crucial to ask if the U.S. education system is neglecting the development of creative and artistic individuals in favor of persons who can follow rules and are happy punching a time card. Are American schools failing to educate students to deal with the important social and ethical challenges facing society and instead mainly educating them to take their place in a corporate enterprise or a knowledge-based economy? David Rockefeller, Jr. (1992), an acclaimed businessperson and philanthropist, recognizes this point:

> America 2000 may be a start, but its prescriptions do not go deep enough or far enough. Its focus on education's economic imperative is necessary but insufficient with regards to the kinds of ethical, social, and spiritual challenges that confront the nation. (p. 372)

What Americans hear in public discourse is how "our nation is at risk. Our once unchallenged preeminence in commerce, industry, science, and technological innovations is being overtaken by competitors throughout the world" (National Commission on Excellence in Education, 1983, p. 5). What Americans need to hear is that a central purpose of education is to develop self-determination, foster democratic participation, and teach how to challenge the social injustices in the country and throughout the world.

TEACHER UNIONS

Since 1857, when the National Education Association (NEA) was founded, and 1916, when the American Federation of Teachers (AFT) was established, these two organizations have built a long and rich tradition of serving the professional needs of their membership. In addition to looking after the interests of teachers in such areas as salary, fringe benefits, grievance procedures, and overall working conditions, the two associations have had a major effect on the professional development of their members. Both associations disseminate information about professional development through their publications—for example, NEA through the *NEA Research Bulletin* and *Today's Education*, AFT through the *American Educator* and the *American Teacher.*

During the education reform movement of the late 1970s and the 1980s, the two teacher unions became more politically active and more reform conscious. For example, in 1976, NEA supported Jimmy Carter for president, and it has supported democratic presidential and other political candidates in the 1980s and the 1990s. NEA's support of Carter led to the establishment of the Department of Education and closer contact between the union and the White House. Although AFT has historically been noted for its concerns over improving public education, addressing teacher welfare, and establishing a relationship between teachers and organized labor, since the 1980s it has shifted its primary attention to reforms in teaching, such as merit pay and career ladders.

As America moves into the 21st century, both the NEA and the AFT can be expected to continue championing the causes of their members. However, it is equally important that they deal with a reality confronting them: Unionism is undergoing a dramatic change. This change has come about in part because of (a) stronger resistance to unionism from owners and management (e.g., the baseball strike) and (b) employees coming under attack by management (e.g., the air traffic controllers). The 21st century is the time for teacher unions to reassess their sphere of influence, develop new strategies of operation (including forging alliances with school communities), and implement efforts to bring about social justice in educational policy and practices for all students.

EDUCATIONAL INTEREST GROUPS

There are many educational interest groups. For example, most academic disciplines have long-standing associations that can be characterized as interest groups (the National Council of Teachers of

English, the National Council for the Social Studies, the National Council of Teachers of Mathematics, and the International Reading Association, to name a few). Each of these organizations offers services to its members that include regional and national conferences, professional development activities like inservice sessions, and a variety of publications ranging from newsletters and practical classroom suggestions to journals and monographs related to research findings.

Both directly and indirectly, these organizations influence preservice and inservice teacher education programs. For example, the whole-language approach to reading, actively supported by the International Reading Association, has influenced the structure and the content of curriculum in both undergraduate and graduate reading courses. Also, the National Council of Teacher of Mathematics, in its well-publicized document *Professional Standards for Teaching Mathematics* (1991), has proposed standards for the professional development of teachers of mathematics:

> These standards suggest a research agenda with respect to teacher education and learning to teach. There is much that we need to know that cannot be determined from current practice. We need experimentation and careful research, new structures of schools, new intersections between universities and schools, new teacher education programs, school and university professional development programs, teaching and learning with computing technology and other forms of technology and tools, new forms of instruction in university and school mathematics classes, and other aspects of reform. (p. 193)

Unfortunately, these organizations seem more devoted to developing their particular subject matter as a discipline than to seeing the subject matter in relation to the student and his or her life circumstances.

Another example of an educational interest group is the National Coalition of Educational Equity Advocates. This newly formed group comprises several organizations and individuals concerned about quality and equity in education. Among the organizations are the American Association of School Administrators, the American Association of University Women, ASPIRA Association, the National Association for the Advancement of Colored People, the National Education

Association for Bilingual Education, the National Urban League, and the Southeast Asia Resource Action Center. The coalition has been formed because the members believe that the equity issues essential to academic achievement are being ignored in the current pursuit of educational excellence. Particularly addressing teacher education, the National Coalition of Educational Equity Advocates (1994) states,

> By the year 2035, 50 percent of the nation's students will be children of color, many of whom will be of other-than-English language backgrounds, and many of whom will be children of the desperately poor. At the same time, the K–12 teaching force is more white and more female than ever in history. *Not only is the teaching staff less diverse, but teacher preparation programs do not equip prospective teachers with skills they need to effectively teach a diverse student population.* Further, research suggests that alternative routes to certification are producing less qualified teachers, most of whom are teaching in urban areas. Accomplishing systemic education reform for all students will require a significant commitment to professional development. (p. 2, emphasis added)

It is reasonable to assume that educational interest groups will continue their activity as the new millennium nears. Most are organized and have a funding structure that allows them to protect their interests by issuing publications, holding meetings, and coalescing with other groups. It is also reasonable to expect the development of new education and teacher education interest groups. An example would be interest groups that have knowledge and understanding of how to use the information highway and can make it work to their advantage. It is important that these groups take the direction of the National Coalition of Educational Equity Advocates in addressing issues of equity, in addition to developing their subject matter as a discipline.

The Knowledge Industry

FUNDING AGENCIES

Various agencies and organizations specifically allot funds for educational research. At the federal level, this includes the National

Science Foundation and the Department of Education. Other organizations funding research include think tanks and philanthropic organizations. For instance, the Spencer Foundation is funding the evaluation of Milwaukee's private and public school choice program. Agencies funding research and other scholarly endeavors (e.g., lecture series and position papers) will continue to play a significant role in influencing the knowledge base in teacher education in the 21st century.

An important question to be answered is, What "creations of knowledge" will funding agencies actively support? According to Doyle (1990), until recently most of the research in teacher education has followed two themes: quality control and effectiveness. Doyle (1990) states, "Teacher educators have . . . defined as their core problem the search for ways to assure or guarantee the quality of programs and the effectiveness of graduates" (p. 7). He adds that over the past decade, concerns have developed about the knowledge assumptions and the power relations implicit in this line of research, leading to two more research themes: knowledge structures of teaching and teacher empowerment.

Funding for research on these four themes, especially the last two, is important. However, this research agenda does not take into account the teacher and student profile discussed earlier in this chapter, nor does it deal explicitly with issues of social justice and multicultural education (Grant & Sleeter, 1986).

With Congress controlled by Republicans who are advocating cutbacks in most areas of federal spending, it is difficult to be optimistic about funding support for teacher education research and programs, especially for research and programs dealing with social justice issues and multicultural education. Also, foundation funding seems to be relegated to improving standards and developing accountability measures and national boards (e.g., Carnegie Forum on Education and the Economy, 1986). These trends marginalize the guiding principles of social justice and equity. Consequently, the knowledge base regarding the changing student population and successful pedagogical skills is neglected.

RESEARCHERS

Most teacher education programs seem to be guided more by federal and state mandates (e.g., Public Law 94-142 and Wisconsin's

Education for Employment, respectively) and the need to satisfy criteria for accreditation than by the research efforts of education scholars. This is not to say that the efforts of researchers have no influence on teacher education programs. For example, at the University of Wisconsin–Madison, the work of several educational researchers (Kenneth Zeichner, for one) has had both local and national influence on teacher education programs. However, these efforts pale in comparison with the influential forces mentioned earlier. Houston, Haberman, and Sikula (1990) illuminate this point in the *Handbook of Research on Teacher Education*: "There is a tradition in teacher education . . . that each teacher-preparing institution rediscovers its own best way of educating teachers with little or no attention to either other institutions or the research literature" (p. ix).

Federal, state, and local mandates; accreditation agencies; and the traditional way of doing things will continue to marginalize the efforts of researchers to influence teacher education as America heads into the 21st century. If the traditional way of doing things continues, researchers who take social justice issues and multicultural education into account in their research will have an even more difficult time influencing teacher education programs. With this thought in mind, it is clear that those who do traditional research and those who do multicultural research will have to cooperate to have an influence on teacher education programs.

Conclusion

Teachers are fundamental to the educational process. As a result, teacher preparation has a crucial effect on students' learning about and understanding the democratic way of life. The preparation of the teaching force has always been everyone's business, and many want to have a direct influence on it. Mattingly (1975) states in *The Classless Profession*, "In the early nineteenth century, anxious citizens, usually ministers but also a sprinkling of lawyers and doctors, decided that the key to a truly American and democratic public school resided in the teachers of public classrooms" (p. xii). He continues, "These other professionals, The Friends of Education as they were called then, *tried to impart to schoolmen standards modeled upon the new goals and institutions of their own profession*" (p. xii; emphasis added).

In the 21st century, as in the past, agencies will continue to exert their influence on teacher education. Perhaps in a democracy, where so much depends on the education of the citizens, this is as it should be. Nevertheless, the nature of the influence and the reason for the influence must be examined. For those interested in social justice issues, this is paramount because the 21st century is more and more being prophesied as a time of science and technological wonderment, standards and accountability, fiscal constraints, and global economic competition. Concurrently, it is becoming less and less a time of attention to the welfare of the common people, issues of equity and equality, and the United States becoming a truly democratic land for everyone.

In conclusion, I want to return to the ideals of social justice presented by the National Coalition of Educational Equity Advocates ("Social Justice Unionism," 1994): "A desire to help children; hope for the future; service to community; and a conviction that public education is a cornerstone of society's commitment to opportunity, equity, and democratic participation" (p. 12). I urge all agencies that influence teacher education to accept the responsibility to advocate for these ideals. Without a new vision that "revives debate and democracy internally and projects an inspiring social vision and agenda externally, we will fall short of the challenges before us" (p. 13).

References

Ahlquist, R. (1991). Position and imposition: Power relations in a multicultural foundation class. *Journal of Negro Education, 60,* 158–169.

American Association of Colleges for Teacher Education. (1988). *Teacher education pipeline: Schools, colleges, and departments of education enrollments by race and ethnicity.* Washington, DC: Author.

American Association of Colleges for Teacher Education, Research About Teacher Education Project. (1990). *RATE IV—Teaching teachers: Facts and figures.* Washington, DC: American Association of Colleges for Teacher Education.

Brown v. Board of Education, 347 U.S. 483, 493 (1954).

Bureau of the Census. (1990). *1990 census of population and housing: Summary population and housing characteristics of Wisconsin.* Washington, DC: U.S. Department of Commerce, Economic Statistics Administration.

Bush, G. (1988, August 17). If Bush and Dukakis really cared about education. . . . *New York Times,* p. A23.

Bush, G., & Wead, D. (1988). *Man of integrity.* Eugene, OR: Harvest House.

Carnegie Forum on Education and the Economy. (1986). *A nation prepared: Teachers for the 21st century.* New York: Author.

Clark, D. L., & McNergney, R. F. (1990). Governance of teacher education. In W. R. Houston, M. Haberman, & J. Sikula (Eds.), *Handbook of research on teacher education* (pp. 101–118). New York: Macmillan.

Crumpton, R. (1995). State policy and student diversity. In C. A. Grant (Ed.), *Educating for diversity: An anthology of multicultural voices* (pp. 359–370). Boston: Allyn & Bacon.

Diana v. State Board of Education, Civil Action No. C-70 37 R.F.P. (N.D. California, January 7, 1970, and June 18, 1973).

Dilworth, M. E. (1990). *Reading between the lines: Teachers and their racial/ethnic cultures* (Teacher Education Monograph No. 11). Washington, DC: ERIC Clearinghouse on Teacher Education and American Association of Colleges for Teacher Education.

Doyle, W. (1990). Themes in teacher education research. In W. R. Houston, M. Haberman, & J. Sikula (Eds.), *Handbook of research on teacher education* (pp. 3–24). New York: Macmillan.

Gollnick, D. M. (1992). Understanding the dynamics of race, class, and gender. In M. E. Dilworth (Ed.), *Diversity in teacher education: New expectations* (pp. 63–78). San Francisco: Jossey-Bass.

Gomez, M. L. (1990). Teaching a language of opportunity in a language arts methods course: Teaching for David, Albert, and Darlene. In B. R. Tabachnick & K. Zeichner (Eds.), *Issues and practices in inquiry-oriented teacher education* (pp. 91–112). London: Falmer.

Grant, C. A. (1994). Best practices in teacher preparation for urban schools: Lessons from the multicultural teacher education literature. *Action in Teacher Education, 16*(3), 1–18.

Grant, C. A., & Koskela, R. (1986). Education that is multicultural and the relationship between preservice campus learning and field experiences. *Journal of Educational Research, 79,* 197–203.

Grant, C. A., & Secada, W. G. (1990). Preparing teachers for diversity. In W. R. Houston, M. Haberman, & J. Sikula (Eds.), *Handbook of research on teacher education* (pp. 403–422). New York: Macmillan.

Grant, C. A., & Sleeter, C. E. (1986). Race, class, and gender in education research: An argument for integrative analysis. *Review of Educational Research, 56,* 195–211.

Harrington, M. (1984). *The new American poverty.* New York: Holt, Rinehart & Winston.

Houston, W. R., Haberman, M., & Sikula, J. (1990). Preface. In W. R. Houston, M. Haberman, & J. Sikula (Eds.), *Handbook of research on teacher education* (pp. ix–xi). New York: Macmillan.

Jost, K. (1993). Supreme Court preview: Will Justice Ginsburg change the court's balance of power? *CQ Researcher, 3,* 819–839.

Keep power with voters. (1994, December 27). *Capital Times,* p. 8A.

Kirst, M. W. (1974). The growth of federal influence in education. In C. W. Gordon (Ed.), *Uses of sociology of education* (yearbook, pt. 2, pp. 448–477). Chicago: National Society for the Study of Education.

Ladson-Billings, G. (1991, April). *When difference means disaster: Reflections on a teacher education strategy for countering student resistance to diversity.* Paper presented at the annual meeting of the American Educational Research Association, Chicago.

Lagemann, E. C. (1992). Philanthropy, education, and the politics of knowledge. *Teachers College Record, 93,* 361–369.

Larry P. v. Riles, Civil Action No. 6-71 2270, 343 F. Supp. 1036 (N.D. California, 1972).

Lau v. Nichols, 483 F. 2d 791 (9th Cir. 1973), *cert. granted,* 412 U.S. 938 (1973).

Lobman, T. E. (1992). Public education grant-making styles: More money, more vision, more demands. *Teachers College Record, 93,* 382–402.

Marshall, P. (1994). Four misconceptions about multicultural education that impede understanding. *Action in Teacher Education, 16*(3), 19–27.

Mattingly, P. H. (1975). *The classless profession: American schoolmen in the nineteenth century.* New York: New York University Press.

Mayers, J. (1994, December 16). DPI leader fires back at SAVE, governor. *Wisconsin State Journal,* p. 16.

Mills, J. R., & Buckley, C. W. (1992). Accommodating the minority teacher candidate: Non-black students in predominantly black colleges. In M. E. Dilworth (Ed.), *Diversity in teacher education: New expectations* (pp. 134–159). San Francisco: Jossey-Bass.

National Coalition of Educational Equity Advocates. (1994). *Educate America: A call for equity in school reform.* Washington, DC: Author.

National Commission on Excellence in Education. (1983). *A nation at risk: The imperative for educational reform.* Washington, DC: U.S. Government Printing Office.

National Council of Teachers of Mathematics. (1991). *Professional standards for teaching mathematics.* Reston, VA: Author.

O'Day, V., & Smith, M. (1993). Systemic reform and educational opportunity. In S. Fuhrman (Ed.), *Designing coherent educational policy.* San Francisco: Jossey-Bass.

Richardson, L. (1995, January 6). First 81 teachers qualify for national certification. *New York Times,* pp. A1, A9.

Rockefeller, D., Jr. (1992). America 2000 and philanthropy's education agenda. *Teachers College Record, 93,* 370–375.

Romer, R. (1991). Foreword. In National Education Goals Panel, *Executive summary: The National Education Goals report* (p. 1). Washington, DC: National Education Goals Panel.

Schultze, S. (1994a, December 16). Benson sharply criticizes decentralization proposal. *Milwaukee Journal,* p. B4.

Schultze, S. (1994b, December 25). Benson calls for public vote on his office. *Milwaukee Journal,* pp. 1, 3.

Secada, W. G. (1989). Educational equity versus equality of education: An alternative conception. In W. G. Secada (Ed.), *Equity in education* (pp. 68–88). London: Falmer.

Social justice unionism: A working draft—A call to education unionists. (1994). *Rethinking Schools, 9*(1), 12–13.

Spring, J. (1988). *Conflict of interests: The politics of American education.* New York: Longman.

Stone, F. A. (1994). Educational reconstruction and today's teacher education. *Teacher Education Quarterly, 21,* 9–22.

Wisconsin Department of Public Instruction. (1992). *Basic facts about Wisconsin's elementary and secondary schools: 1991–1992.* Milwaukee: Author.

Zimpher, N. L. (1989). The RATE project: A profile of teacher education students. *Journal of Teacher Education, 40*(6), 27–31.

A Response to Chapter 4, "The Influence of Agencies on Teacher Preparation: Social Justice in the New Millennium," by Carl A. Grant

KATHLEEN DENSMORE
San Jose State University

In Chapter 4, Carl A. Grant focuses attention on the ideals of social justice, equity, and democratic participation, seeing public education as the cornerstone of American society's commitment to these ideals. Yet he appropriately highlights the fact that almost in direct challenge to this role for public education, the urban public school student population is increasingly diverse racially and ethnically and from nontraditional families, whereas student teachers continue to be predominantly white and middle class. Grant situates this information in the larger society, where the division between haves and have-nots continues to grow. Given these demographic and economic realities, he argues, when educators and others talk about education reform at any level, they must carefully identify the obstacles to urban youngsters' graduating from high school with a high level and a broad range of knowledge and skills. This identification, in turn, ought to guide analysis of what is needed to ensure the preparation of teachers to understand and work with their students to address these obstacles.

This response to Chapter 4 begins with some underlying assumptions. Next it examines equity issues, including funding, student achievement, and admission to and representation in higher education for both students and faculty of color. Then it addresses the role of teacher education relative to these equity issues. Throughout, the response looks at some of the agencies that influence education, offering suggestions for what should be done.

Underlying Assumptions

The American education system has historically been organized on the premise that only a few students are capable of significant achievements, especially academic achievements. Many believe that only a fraction of the population as a whole is capable of truly benefiting from university education. There is reluctance to recognize the diverse strengths of different people. Yet when one thinks about what is to count as an educated person in the 21st century, one must keep the following two points in mind: (a) The American economy requires more scientists and engineers than ever before, as well as more employees generally who possess a sophisticated knowledge base and strong analytical skills, and (b) although individuals have different proclivities and capacities, everyone in a democracy has a right to learn as much as his or her temperament and talent allow. Greater democracy, freedom, equality, and economic security rest on the widespread development of human capacities. All individuals should be encouraged to develop their intellectual abilities and creativity; education must be organized so that this can happen.

Equity

Funding

Contrary to popular belief, the United States ranks near the bottom among industrial countries on expenditures on K–12 education (Rasell & Mishel, 1990). The Committee for Education Funding claims that there is a need for $25 billion for construction and renovation of facilities alone, excluding higher education (see Karp, 1992). Compounding the lack of overall funding is the widening gap between rich and poor schools (Kozol, 1991). According to a report issued by the Quality Education for Minorities Project (1990), students of color continue to attend segregated and underfunded schools with the least prepared teachers and the most outmoded curricula. Although not all students of color are poor, the number who are is increasing as the overall proportion of children living in poverty increases (Commission on Chapter 1, 1992). Poor families face enormous difficulties in preparing their children for success in school. That is one reason that early childhood programs and health care for babies and mothers facilitate academic achievement (Committee for Economic Development, 1987).

The federal government's overall share of education spending remains small. According to Karp (1992), it peaked at about 9% in the 1970s and dropped to about 6% under Presidents Ronald Reagan and George Bush. Thus over 90% of all funds for education come from state and local sources. Cutbacks in state and federal funding affect not only public schools but higher education. For example, increases in student fees; reduced programs and services for students; and reduced availability of financial aid, grants, and fellowships have diminished higher education opportunities for low-income students—a high percentage of whom are students of color. Furthermore, the refusal of the federal government as well as a federal court to protect race-based scholarships, and the meager funding for bilingual education even though the pedagogical rationale for it has been substantiated (Scarcella, 1990), contribute to decreasing enrollments of students of color at the university level. These figures are part of an overall situation in which an estimated 76% of high-income students complete their bachelor's degrees compared with 4% of their low-income counterparts (Rendón, Hope, & Associates, 1996).

In the present context of budgetary retrenchment, Grant, like many others, concludes that given decreasing funding, schools have little choice but to turn to business for revenues. This is not surprising. The private sector, eager to conquer new markets, is willing to assert its (commercial) influence over public education. Yet is the reduction of public funds for education irreversible? A fait accompli? In terms of the public interest, it is irrational to devote billions of public dollars to such schemes as Star Wars and subsidies for market speculation, rather than to public education and social programs that benefit millions of people.

A separate but related matter is the role of foundations in providing monies for education. Grant appears to assume that foundations function separately from corporations and that they too can be relied on to support education and social justice. It is well established, however, that close ties exist between foundations and the corporate sector of the economy. For example, trustees, largely from the business world, approve the awarding of corporate grants to the nonprofit sector and have a direct form of political control. Corporations also contribute directly to the nonprofit sector—for example, through donations to universities, museums, and health and welfare institutions like the United Way. Concomitant with the financial ties of corporations to the nonprofit sector, thousands of people in business serve on the boards of nonprofit organizations. These boards are private, self-perpetuating, and not publicly accountable unless evidence surfaces of major ethical or legal transgressions (O'Neill, 1989). The most often cited instance of philanthropic organizations promoting social justice through their funding of educational institutions is their support of all-black colleges in the South. That support, however, was based on the fallacious doctrine of separate but equal. This raises questions about the extent to which mainstream philanthropy has actually been in the forefront of eliminating barriers to racial, ethnic, socioeconomic, and gender injustices in educational policy and practices, as argued by Grant. Clearly, though, as Grant also argues, to the extent that foundations provide economic support, they should target education programs that aim to eliminate race, socioeconomic class, and gender inequalities and injustices in educational policy and practices.

In sum, neither the corporate sector nor philanthropic foundations can realistically be a primary source of funding for public education. States must provide a funding base that will allow all local districts to meet education goals (national, state, or local). The traditional reliance on property taxes to fund education makes it difficult for states to equalize school spending even if they are inclined to do so. Difficulties notwithstanding, any plan that seeks large overall increases in funding will also have to address equity issues because expanding education budgets threaten to increase the gulf between rich and poor schools.

Of all the industrially developed nations, the United States, with the most powerful economy in the world, provides the least support to social programs, including K–12 education, while exacting the least support for social programs from its wealthiest corporations and individuals. Historically, public education, as well as public health, Social Security, and myriad other social programs, has been primarily funded from tax revenues. The taxes that most people pay should ensure their access to adequate health, housing, education, safety, and

retirement. Therefore, the withdrawal of funding from public programs such as bilingual education, Head Start, and school lunches,
orchestrated by the furies of private interest since the 1980s and
labeled "a tax revolution" or "getting the government off our backs,"
must be reversed.

Although specific proposals for progressive tax reforms are beyond the scope of this response, a focused and coordinated effort of
government (federal, state, and local), employee unions, and grass-
roots organizing is essential to ensure appropriate policies on bud-
geting and adequate and relevant resources for education at all levels
in all communities. This coordinated effort must also deal with the
root causes of poverty that affect academic achievement. Unfortunately, Grant does not directly address features of the economic context within which low-income students grow up. Education occurs in
the context of a total community; thus meeting social needs is a
condition of raising academic achievement. The key is to provide the
entire socioeconomic environment with the resources to help schools
and teachers carry out their mission.

Government, as a regulator of commerce and labor standards,
should assume a more interventionist role in the economy by exerting
influence over the private and public sectors so that employers have
to pay adequate wages and benefits throughout the nation with
equity for men and women. Work should be created (with requisite
training) that not only pays sufficiently but requires creativity, knowledge, and skill. Furthermore, given the tremendous leap in labor
productivity and net profit produced by scientific and technological
innovations, government, with the support of the majority of working people, must reduce hours of labor so that employers can hire
more people. Knowing that remunerative and challenging jobs are
available in local communities will buttress teachers as they work to
maintain high expectations for all students. Substantial macrolevel
changes, such as changes in the opportunity structures for underrepresented youth, will motivate these youth because they will be
more optimistic about the future and have better incentives for becoming more integrated into society.

Academic Achievement Gaps

Addressing factors such as poverty, health care, and employment
opportunities across diverse communities will address a second equity

issue: academic achievement gaps between low- and high-income students and between white students and most students of color. Once funding agencies recognize the need for change to maximize the potential of the entire population, they can assist teachers and teacher educators in making concrete commitments to prepare more people to participate fully in society. Learning more about how to strive toward widespread mastery of challenging knowledge and skills and placing less emphasis on sophisticated differentiating mechanisms (e.g., specific efforts to track and test) would mitigate against reinforcing educational inequality, maximizing failure, and channeling students into less than constructive paths.

Differential achievement will also be more directly addressed to the extent that teacher educators equip prospective teachers with a wide repertoire of teaching strategies and techniques and with contemporary research on which strategies tend to work best with whom, under what conditions, and why. For example, new teachers must be able to create classroom organizations that allow for meaningful, cooperative small-group learning strategies, individually structured education plans, and peer tutoring—all with multicultural curricula oriented toward problem solving. These strategies have proven to be successful, especially with underrepresented students (Cohen, 1994; Scarcella, 1990). Teachers need initial instruction in new learning strategies. They also need staff development and continuing classroom follow-up to facilitate their implementation of an increasingly sophisticated pedagogy. A later section of this response makes additional suggestions for teacher educators to better serve the unprecedented configuration of race, ethnicity, language, and gender present among students in public school systems today.

Racial and Ethnic Diversity in Higher Education

A third equity issue is admission to and representation in higher education for both students and faculty of color. In addition to being an equity issue, this is a socioeconomic issue: College students in general will be better equipped to contribute to the country's prosperity both economically and socially if they learn from a professoriate that reflects the racial, ethnic, gender, and social class diversity of American society (Collison, 1988). Few faculty of color are available to work with students in higher education, and a declining number of students of color are earning master's and doctoral degrees. Research is sorely needed on why underrepresented teachers have left teaching. These findings can be used both to recruit and to retain people of color in the profession.

The society must make certain that poor and nonwhite youth complete high school, graduate from college, and pursue graduate studies. The quality of high school education must improve for this to happen. Stimulating and relevant multicultural curricula combined with remedial attention and counseling at both the secondary and the university level can help young people complete their education. Attracting more teachers of color (at all levels of the educational system) is one way to improve the educational experiences of students of color, notably African American students and Latinos (Meier, Stewart, & England, 1989). Increasing the number of administrators of color makes the school environment more attractive to minority teachers. Among the steps that might be taken to increase the number of students and faculty of color in schools of education are (a) broadening college admission requirements beyond entrance exams; (b) formulating and implementing institutional goals to diversify university faculty on campuses; (c) examining hiring practices, especially in teacher education programs; (d) examining teacher competency tests for cultural biases; and (e) instituting scholarship and loan-forgiveness provisions for students who teach in certain areas or who teach for a certain period. Specific steps like these, if taken by the appropriate agencies, can contribute to education reform that will develop a multicultural, democratic, and free public education system, one that encourages all persons to develop to their highest capacity.

Teacher Education

Teacher education concerned with social justice should question moves toward greater (standard) selectivity and screening of persons aspiring to become teachers and increased stratification within the field generally. This is parallel to the argument for minimizing educational stratification of students in the public schools. Traditional hierarchies among teachers and among students convey the message that only a few are able to make the most important contributions. At the level of curriculum and instruction, many reform proposals call for making the education of teachers more intellectually challenging.

This is essential if educators intend prospective teachers to provide intellectually challenging classrooms for their future students. Teacher education programs must develop students' analytical skills and conceptual tools to reflect critically on and inquire about different ways of learning, different ways of producing knowledge, their own experiences, and the organization of schooling and society. Reflective inquiry should be treated as a process that may or may not end up with the answers as determined by university professors or school-based educators.

Teacher educators must be prepared to show new teachers how to structure their classes so that students are not merely allowed but required to bring in and share their prior knowledge and experience as it bears on particular subject matter. This develops individual competencies, broadens other students' perceptions of diversity, and helps develop in new teachers an orientation to seeing and under-standing the value in getting to know their students (Delpit, 1995). Similarly, teachers must be taught how and why to consult parents and community leaders and representatives. There is a drastic short-age of communication across cultures and across social categories about who needs to learn what and why. Teacher education programs can create active partnerships with historically black, Latino, and tribally dominated colleges and universities. Joint planning can facili-tate the development and the implementation of more inclusive cur-ricula and provide more diverse faculty to attend to the needs of students. The university in which I teach is taking steps to link teacher preparation programs to urban community concerns. By cooperating with community organizations, prospective teachers have work ex-periences with students (and adults) who are different from them-selves, related to matters that connect them to the lives of diverse youth in ways that are not likely to happen in a school classroom. The intention is to prepare teachers who know how to acquire and use cultural information responsibly and effectively, transforming school failure into success.

Conclusion

For those who think that the obstacles to providing every public school student with a teacher able to assist him or her in becoming a productive, involved, and fulfilled member of society are not primarily located in individual teachers, there is no shortage of recommendations on what needs to be done. In particular, the recommendations for developing and strengthening working relationships between educational institutions and families and communities are promising (e.g., Chavkin, 1993; Fagnano & Werber, 1994; Schneider & Coleman, 1993). Furthermore, research-based recommendations for improving education for underrepresented students are also available (e.g., Hawley & Jackson, 1995; Rendón et al., 1996; Scarcella, 1990). What is missing is sufficient will to divert resources to the development of strategies for reconciling cultural diversity and quality schooling in prekindergarten through graduate institutions.

References

Chavkin, N. F. (Ed.) (1993). *Families and schools in a pluralistic society.* Albany: State University of New York Press.

Cohen, E. G. (1994). *Designing groupwork: Strategies for the heterogeneous classroom.* New York: Teachers College Press.

Collison, M. N. K. (1988, May 25). Neglect of minorities seen jeopardizing future prosperity. *Chronicle of Higher Education,* pp. A1, A20.

Commission on Chapter 1. (1992). *Making schools work for children in poverty.* Washington, DC: American Association for Higher Education.

Committee for Economic Development. (1987). *Children in need: Investment strategies for the educationally disadvantaged* (Statement by the Research and Policy Committee). New York: Author.

Delpit, L. (1995). *Other people's children: Cultural conflict in the classroom.* New York: New Press.

Fagnano, C. L., & Werber, B. Z. (Eds.) (1994). *School, family and community interaction: A view from the firing lines.* San Francisco: Westview.

Hawley, W. D., & Jackson, A. W. (Eds.) (1995). *Toward a common destiny: Improving race and ethnic relations in America.* San Francisco: Jossey-Bass.

Karp, S. (1992, October). Money, schools, and justice. *Z Magazine,* pp. 31–35.

Kozol, J. (1991). *Savage inequalities: Children in America's schools.* New York: Crown.

Meier, K. J., Stewart, J., Jr., & England, R. E. (1989). *Race, class, and education: The politics of second generation discrimination.* Madison: University of Wisconsin Press.

O'Neill, M. (1989). *The third America: The emergence of the nonprofit sector in the United States.* San Francisco: Jossey-Bass.

Quality Education for Minorities Project. (1990). *Education that works: An action plan for the education of minorities.* Cambridge: MIT, Quality Education for Minorities Project.

Rasell, M. E., & Mishel, L. (1990). *Shortchanging education: How U.S. spending on grades K–12 lags behind other industrial nations* (Briefing paper). Washington, DC: Economic Policy Institute.

Rendón, L. I., Hope, R. O., & Associates. (1996). *Educating a new majority: Transforming America's educational system for diversity.* San Francisco: Jossey-Bass.

Scarcella, R. (1990). *The teaching of language minority students in the multicultural classroom.* Englewood Cliffs, NJ: Prentice Hall Regents.

Schneider, B., & Coleman, J. S. (1993). *Parents, their children, and schools.* San Francisco: Westview.

5

The Preparation of Teachers for a Diverse, Free Society

MARTIN J. HABERMAN
University of Wisconsin–Milwaukee

S chools reflect society, but that is not the whole story. Teacher education also reflects society. Rural America was covered with teachers colleges to implement society's desire that farm girls be trained as teachers within 50 miles of their homes. In former times, the commitment of American society to the complete cultural assimilation of immigrants and people of color influenced teacher educators to prepare teachers who would be in close harmony with public schools, teaching the melting-pot vision of America. So today as teacher education is criticized for not being sufficiently multicultural, it is important to remember that teacher education reflects the larger society in much the same way that the public schools do.

To carry this analysis into the present period, current American society entertains several different and conflicting visions. Some constituencies advocate greater multiculturalism, others a return to the melting pot. It cannot be denied, however, that in the past 30 years American society has moved toward greater multiculturalism. This is reflected in countless ways: in the arts and in what is presented as art; in the political system, from actual laws to persons elected to public office and even to jury selection; in the private sector, which emphasizes diversity in products and advertisements; in hiring practices; and most recently, in school curriculum, textbook selection, promotion to principal, and recruitment of teachers. American society has generally shifted from a melting-pot vision to a multicultural one.

This does not mean that America has arrived or that Americans actually live up to their stated values. Clearly, all cultural groups do not have equal life opportunities. Given the high ideals of the Constitution, America will always be a society in process. However, any objective review of government, the media, the education system, and the private sector supports the contention that it is now common and acceptable for Americans to live their lives on three levels: as individuals, as members of some cultural group, and as members of the larger society. In contrast to former times, when the dues for becoming a real American were to reject membership in any other cultural group, the current, common American value is that Americans may be participants in another cultural group as well as in the general American society. Indeed, being a proud member of another cultural group is not only allowed but regarded as a badge of merit. Again, the larger society is not in complete agreement on this issue, and many constituencies still openly argue against hyphenated Americans. This disagreement is reflected in teacher education, with some faculty openly or passively resisting preparation of future teachers to deal with diversity.

The problem faced by teacher education, however, is more than trying to give society what it says it wants. Teacher education is not a tabula rasa, but an already existing enterprise with overly full enrollments, faculties trained in particular doctoral specializations, and programs ensconced in universities with historical patterns of doing things. Rather than fill a multicultural void, making university-based teacher education more multicultural would require a total reconstruction. Although this is possible, some teacher educators are finding it more effective to create new, alternative certification programs that are multicultural to start. Again, the point is that teacher education reflects the larger society, with all its confusion and mixed signals as well as its clear directives. On this last point, for example, the fact that 41 states plus the District of Columbia offer alternative certification reflects a genuine need to find teachers who can be effective in multicultural, poverty-area schools. At the same time, these states have thick tomes of written requirements for teacher education programs. In effect, almost all states encourage major urban school districts to take the lead in preparing their own teachers, whereas the states hold universities to very detailed, complex standards in traditional teacher education programs.

There are five obstacles to university-based teacher education becoming truly multicultural:

1. Future teachers are not just ill prepared to deal with diverse populations; they are ill prepared to deal with any population of children and youth in cultural terms.

2. People do not choose to be teachers because they want to deal with children and youth in cultural terms. This problem is an important precondition of the first one.

3. The knowledge base in teacher education uses personality constructs, not cultural constructs, to explain human behavior.

4. Teacher educators who guide practice (student teaching, field work, etc.) rely on explanations other than cultural ones to understand and predict children's behavior.

5. The approach in traditional preparation programs is to educate the neophyte that *normal behavior* and *normal development* in children and youth are synonymous with "healthy and desirable behavior and development."

I have written less about the last problem than I have about the others, so I discuss it in this chapter. Those supporting traditional teacher education programs generally regard urban living, poverty, cultural diversity, and the like as conditions that cause individual children to develop special needs. The psychological paradigm for children growing up in urban poverty and violence is that they suffer the range of ailments and emotional impediments to normal development typical of children who grow up in a war zone (Garbarino, Dudrow, Kostelny, & Pardo, 1992). This type of conceptual stance relegates distinctive cultural backgrounds and societal influences to being other forms of exceptionality, conceptually akin to other handicapping conditions. Similarly, the term *minority* has become merely another euphemism for an adverse condition that intrudes on an individual's development and learning. This explains why many Euro-American teachers and teacher educators continue to use the term minority even when most of the children and youth in a given school district are a numerical majority. This approach does not teach pre- and inservice teachers to define *normal* as "typical." If they knew the meaning of normal, they would realize that children who grow up in violent neighborhoods or in poverty are making perfectly normal responses to undesirable social conditions. Instead, teacher educators typically teach neophytes to make the concept of normal synonymous with the concept of healthy and desirable. Therefore, if children grow up in adverse conditions, they are not developing normally or making normal responses or even being normal; they are learning bad behaviors, and bad behaviors cannot possibly be normal. When one lays naive multiculturalism onto this limited way of perceiving growth and development, the result is frequently insensitivity and nascent racism. Minority status cannot be perceived as a normal condition if the perceiver regards it as a less than desirable status and a handicapping condition. In this way, even when there is the numerical reality of a new majority, the perceiver holds on to the label of minority to signal that there are serious handicapping conditions with a majority of individual children in a particular school, city, or total society.

These confusions in meaning have led to different approaches to teacher education. Supporters of traditional forms of teacher education prepare future teachers to deal with all forms of individual "abnormality" (i.e., undesirable things that should not have happened and that impede "normal" development) on an individual basis. No matter how many children suffer from poverty, are caught in violence, or are persons of color, even if they total 100% of a particular constituency, they are perceived and taught as children with special needs because the knowledge base in traditional teacher education is conceived and offered on that paradigm.

This is not merely an abstract issue of word definition. Such usage reflects the conceptual understanding of a large number of inservice teachers in the major urban school districts. Many practicing teachers seriously and honestly believe that most or all of their students should not be in their classrooms because the children are not achieving at "normal" grade levels; are "abnormal" in their interests, attention, and behavior; are not emotionally suited to school; and need special classes or teachers trained to work with exceptional individuals. In some urban areas and in some schools within those districts, many teachers judge over 90% of their students to be people whom they should not have to teach because the students are not "normal" (Payne, 1984).

Before I proceed to an analysis of multiculturalism in American schools, I want to place America in an international context. Among the approximately 240 nations in the world, there is almost complete agreement on what constitutes the basis for nationhood. From Bosnia to Rwanda and from Turkistan to Cyprus, it is assumed that every ethnic group has an inherent right to its own country. The several exceptions to this general assumption are countries that are not free societies, countries like Iraq and Nigeria in which one group has effectively subjugated another.

Among the world's free nations, though, exceedingly few are dedicated to the concept of multiculturalism, that is, to the notion that various cultures can and should live together on an equal basis in the same society. These few are all former members of the British Empire. Even among them, there is tension: The French Canadians support a robust secessionist movement, as do the Protestant Irish. In Great Britain itself, the Welsh and the Scots have persisting secessionist movements. The United States, Australia, and South Africa alone support political and public policy dedicated to the equal treatment of many ethnic groups within a united general society.

This international context is frequently overlooked in discussions of multiculturalism. In terms of what the world regards as "normal," nations are built for and by specific ethnic groups. The dreams of Americans and some few other nationalities are clearly an "abnormal" expectation: that ethnic groups can be maintained and even enhanced at the same time that they live peacefully and equitably and contribute to a common larger society. In America's adolescence of only 200 years, it is still to be determined if these multicultural expectations can be realized.

The Need to Specify the Purpose of Multiculturalism

Future educators may well look back on current efforts to make school curricula more accurately reflect cultural diversity and term this period the Great Multicultural Curriculum Wars. Experts and advocates define multiculturalism in various ways, but agree that the concept calls for a restructuring of schools. At the same time, publishers, school boards, administrators, and teachers in school districts across America see themselves as making school programs more multicultural without making significant changes in present forms of schooling. Are the advocates of restructuring and the promoters of making current forms of schooling more efficient talking about the same multiculturalism?

These divergent views reflect the fact that proponents of greater multiculturalism usually begin with the assumptions that multiculturalism is good and that more of it would be better. This is not to say that they never define multiculturalism. Quite the contrary: They define it in a great variety of ways. What is less typical of their arguments are clear statements of (a) the problems that greater multiculturalism will resolve; (b) the procedures for implementing the particular form of multiculturalism being advocated; and (c) the specific objectives that will be achieved—that is, what will success look like? Unless these questions are addressed and the answers are coherently connected, there will continue to be incomplete stabs and superficial efforts at multicultural reforms.

In some cases, multiculturalism is defined as a process, that is, as ways in which teachers and students interact as they teach, learn, and live together in schools. In other cases, multiculturalism seems to be a product, that is, a curriculum to be learned, with new forms of knowledge to be achieved and evaluated. A third approach is to define multiculturalism in terms of presage criteria, that is, information that one can obtain about a school before setting foot in it: the ethnic backgrounds of the teachers, students, and administrators; the curriculum materials in use; the number of languages used in the school program; the nature of parent involvement in decision making; and the criteria used for determining students' achievement.

These approaches are not always mutually exclusive. Advocates frequently view greater multiculturalism in more than one way. They seldom consciously recognize that they are using two or more ways simultaneously because they rarely connect the problems they are addressing to the objectives they are advocating. Following are the major ways in which reformers seem to use multiculturalism in their various, frequently conflicting advocacies.

Multiculturalism as a coexistence of cultures. Should Western civilization continue to be the basis of most of the school curriculum, or should school curriculum also reflect a major emphasis on the historical, intellectual, and cultural development of Asian, African, South American, and Middle Eastern peoples?

Multiculturalism as personal values, human differences, and life choices. Should school curriculum continue to assume the existence of a common set of societal mores that should be taught in school, or should school curriculum help students decide how to make life choices from a variety of lifestyles?

Multiculturalism as a nation of diverse cultural groups. Should school curriculum be directed at achieving one America to which all groups must accommodate and in which all individuals must learn to participate, or should school curriculum enhance and honor cultural diversity in an already multicultural society?

Multiculturalism as social justice and equity. Should school curriculum reflect society as it is, or should school curriculum teach students to participate in efforts aimed at equalizing opportunity and treatment for all individuals and groups?

Multiculturalism as a process of making teaching and learning more relevant. Is multicultural curriculum essentially various forms of new content to be learned, or is multiculturalism essentially a process of connecting the existing curriculum with students' lives to make their learning more meaningful and relevant?

Multiculturalism as total school climate. Is multicultural curriculum any particular component(s) of the school program, or is it everything that occurs in school under the aegis of the school?

Multiculturalism as worldwide environmental cooperation. Should school curriculum continue to emphasize the "right" of Western societies to exploit the world's natural resources to satisfy their highly consumptive lifestyle, or should school curriculum teach a use of natural resources that reflects the concerns of scientists, naturalists, and other societies?

Multiculturalism as learning to compete in a worldwide economy. Should school curriculum prepare students for jobs and careers in today's American economy, or should school curriculum prepare students to compete successfully in the worldwide economy of tomorrow? To what extent can the school-to-work thrust also become a multicultural curriculum?

It is possible to combine the responses to these eight issues in ways that create a meaningful whole. The best way to implement all visions or any particular one is to select and train neophytes who are more disposed to a multicultural ideology at the outset.

Teachers' Perceptions of Multiculturalism

Because of societal pressures, particularly in large urban school systems, there is a widespread effort to use school curriculum and materials as a means of forcing teachers to teach in new, more multicultural ways. The assumption is that if new texts, videotapes, supplementary reading materials, and other forms of instructional materials are introduced, then teachers will in effect be trained to function differently. The strategy is not without merit. It is certainly a more direct approach than trying to change preservice program requirements. It is also more effective because the overwhelming number of preservice teachers never take jobs in major urban school districts, and half of those who do, quit or fail in 3 years or less.

However, making changes in public school curriculum as the vehicle for multicultural inservice teacher education has a downside. It is like reading a catalog of spare parts for machines that have never been built, written by persons who have used very few (or none) of the parts but have collected the descriptions from others or simply made them up. After examining current texts, handbooks, and source books on how to make schooling more multicultural, one has a clear impression of the difficulty of trying to derive a comprehensive understanding. These materials deal in cursory ways with—or omit altogether—complex issues about the nature of teachers and teaching, learners and learning, and schools and the community. The various proponents of multiculturalism must be clear about their positions and assumptions so that teachers who use the material they advocate can have a context for understanding where they are coming from, what they hope to accomplish, and why. Without greater amplification and clarity, much of the how-to-do-it material on multicultural teaching reads like recipes for jejune activities. Much is written and discussed about multicultural education, but what is actually done in classrooms is bits and pieces of odds and ends conducted in fits and starts. The influence of this disjointed approach on teachers' development is not much different from the influence on children and youth.

Following are some of the critical issues that advocates might at least address. To continue to ignore these issues and simply hold workshops on specific new multicultural content and ways of teaching it will ensure that the present state of confusion continues.

1. Can the particular multicultural program being advocated be implemented within the existing school curriculum, or must the curriculum be expanded?

2. Is the program to become part of the elementary school program, become part of the social studies program, or be integrated at all grade levels into all subjects?

3. Can the program be implemented by teachers using any form of instruction, or are some forms of instruction more appropriate than others?

4. Can teachers implement the program within their existing role, or will their responsibilities have to be reconstructed?

5. Can teachers implement the program as individuals, or must they work in teams or as a total school faculty and staff?

6. Is the multicultural content needed by teachers knowledge that they can be expected to know right now or to learn in due time, or will they be expected to teach it without really knowing it themselves?

7. What is the nature of American society being advocated? What is the vision of diversity being taught? Does it include groups based on gender, age, and physical condition as well as on language, race, ethnicity, religion, and culture? Does the content to be learned also emphasize goals related to self-concept, awareness, and the advocacy of equitable treatment for others?

8. Does the program emphasize cultural diversity as an international, national, statewide, districtwide, or school building issue?

9. Will the learnings gained in the program be assessed by traditional means, or will new forms of evaluation be needed?

10. Are practicing teachers merely ignorant of the program being advocated, or do they hold values that actively prevent them from implementing it? Do proponents of new and particular approaches to multiculturalism have a plan for changing widely held, deep-seated teachers'

values? Do they assume that teachers will simply lay
aside lifelong belief systems?

On this last point, none of the curriculum materials with which I
am familiar even recognizes that what teachers currently believe is of
any importance or that the effect of any new curriculum will have to
be strained through teachers' perceptions. The problem is that although only a fraction of 1% of school budgets are devoted to staff
development, even an intensive inservice program is unlikely to
change the way in which experienced white or black or brown teachers look at gender or race issues (Sleeter, 1992).

Inservice teachers tend to be fixed on denying the existence or
usefulness of subgroups in American society. In a study of 227 experienced teachers, a colleague and I asked them to identify what they
perceived to be the goal of multicultural education (Haberman & Post,
1995). Regardless of experience, sex, subject, grade level, or amount
of education, the respondents overwhelmingly chose the first two
levels described in Table 5.1, either denying the need to teach about
or be sensitive to cultural subgroups (Level 1) or identifying tolerance
as the most appropriate goal for teachers and schools (Level 2).

Fewer than 5% of the respondents perceived that Levels 3, 4, and
5 were either necessary or desirable. Therefore, the goal of inservice
education for teachers should be to move them in the direction of
Levels 3, 4, and 5. Furthermore, inservice teachers need to see that all
children and youth require three types of development: learning
related to their individuality, learning related to their cultural groups,
and learning related to the larger society (Haberman & Post, 1990).

Either through selection of teachers initially or through retraining
subsequently, teacher educators must deal with practicing classroom
teachers as part of the solution. In spite of the difficulties presented
thus far, there are better ways to address the problem of making
school curriculum more multicultural. Although there are still no
model school systems, there are numerous model schools in which
carefully selected faculty have implemented their multicultural perceptions and programs.

Unless advocates of particular multicultural programs address
these issues forthrightly, faculty development will continue to be a
source of confusion and an obstacle. Although proponents cannot
solve the problem by simply stating their views or preferences, they

TABLE 5.1 Levels of Goals for Multiculturalism Perceived
　　　　　by Teachers

Level	Goal	Explanation of Goal
1	Denial of subgroups	Children and youth would learn that all people are individuals—distinct personalities—regardless of their backgrounds.
2	Tolerance	Children and youth would learn that all people have to learn to live together in this world regardless of their differences. Cooperation and tolerance are vital.
3	Heterogeneity	Children and youth would learn that every person comes from some ethnic group and that all groups are equally fine.
4	Advocacy	Children and youth would learn that the United States is made up of many racial, ethnic, and religious groups and that each must be protected and enhanced.
5	Change	Children and youth would learn that all Americans have a responsibility to change the discrimination and the prejudice in American society against certain groups.

SOURCE: From "Multicultural Education: Teaching in the Real World" by M. Haberman and L. Post. In A. C. Ornstein (Ed.), *Teaching: Theory Into Practice*. Copyright © 1995 by Allyn & Bacon. Reprinted/adapted by permission.

have a responsibility to admit that there is a need for continuous teacher development and to state how they would meet this need.

The Reactive Effect of Diversity in Urban Schools

At the same time that experts and reformers focus on implementing their particular visions of multiculturalism, the schools are not in a static condition; they are being transformed. This transformation is almost entirely a reactive phenomenon, not a proactive effort to educate new (or old) majorities to the more diverse society of the 21st century. The current situation must be a curious one for experts in and advocates of multiculturalism. At the same time that they feel frustrated and stonewalled by schools, the schools are actually changing in important ways in an effort to manage and control student populations that are becoming more culturally diverse and falling into greater poverty all the time. Admittedly, more metal detectors, more building-safety aides, more student suspensions, more alternative schools for "troublemakers," increases in the number of special education students, more minimum standards tests for promotion and graduation, more adjudicated delinquents, and more GED study for dropouts are not the advocacies of multicultural reformers. Schools make these types of changes to stay the same, but because the changes transform schools into more repressive, authoritarian places, they need to be recognized as critically important trends. Commonly grafted onto these management and control policies are cosmetic efforts at greater multiculturalism: textbooks with people of color, observance of Martin Luther King Day, a Cinco de Mayo or "Juneteenth" celebration, and pictures in hallways of more representative heroes and heroines. What school authorities fail to recognize is that reactive policies aimed at greater control mitigate their efforts to create a positive climate; teach critical thinking and not rote learning; demonstrate mutual respect among teachers, students, and parents; and inspire students to see value in learning.

Other school changes, although reactive, have the potential for being positive: child development centers in high schools for students' children, realistic and useful sex and health education, and viable career education that unites school and the world of work. The jury is still out on whether schools can even respond in these ways, let alone proactively implement them, because to do so requires changing traditional mores and school practices.

At present, half of the nation's children are concentrated in nine states. By the year 2000, there will be a majority of minorities in 39 major districts and in 12 states (Hodgkinson, 1992). If present trends continue, the idealistic goal of having all children (including those currently labeled majority) receive a more multicultural form of schooling will not be realized. Indeed, children and youth already in multicultural and poverty-area schools will not receive any version of multiculturalism. What seems likely is that reactive changes, motivated by fear and the need to control, will continue to make schools serving students in poverty and from multicultural backgrounds more repressive.

Multiculturalism as Craft Knowledge and Practice

Classroom teachers in American schools are faced with daily decisions that may reflect group differences in race, language, religion, sex, age, ethnicity, income, education, employment, family structure, or combinations of these. Even place of residence (e.g., rural or urban), political affiliation, or the presence of handicapping conditions can be a basis for group differences. Unlike the definitions of other societies, the American definition of cultural group is variable and complex. Most of the world uses structural definitions; that is, a cultural group has its own language and religion. American society uses functional definitions; that is, a person's membership in a particular group can explain and predict his or her behavior. As a result, diversity in America may refer to gang membership, income level, or sexual orientation. These criteria may be as powerful as race, language, or religion in explaining behavior.

Only by understanding the expanded, functional definition that American society uses to define cultural groups can one even recognize the examples that follow as issues of multicultural schooling. It is my contention that to prepare teachers for the real world who have any hope whatever of being effective in truly multicultural schools, teacher educators must arrange for them to have practice and on-the-job coaching regarding situations such as these.

Example 1

It is mid-October in Ms. Butler's first grade. Class is going well. The children are very involved, enthusiastic, and cooperative. Ms. Butler shows her pleasure with them by planning at least one special activity each day that she knows they will enjoy. The activities have proven to be true learning experiences. They involve art, music, poetry, dance, cooking, parties, field trips, or construction of some kind.

The activity that the class enjoys most is celebrating birthdays. The children learn to plan and carry out a party. They also cooperate, socialize, and practice respecting one another. The activity has come to mean a lot to the class and to the children whose birthdays are being celebrated.

Ms. Butler is now gathering materials for Halloween. She plans to read stories, use creative writing activities, do artwork and construction, and perhaps even put on a class play. Several of these activities, like the birthday parties, will be among the special ones that seem to mean so much to the children and that the teacher uses to reward the class for its good work.

One of the quieter girls brings in a note from her mother. The note states that the family members are Jehovah's Witnesses and do not celebrate birthdays. The note also conveys the mother's objection to her daughter's participating in any Halloween activities. The letter concludes with the statement that celebrating birthdays and Halloween is not part of the public school curriculum.

Example 2

Mr. Williams teaches math in the eighth grade. He has established a relationship of trust with his several classes. Almost all the youngsters demonstrate that they want him to be their teacher by the respect that they show him. For his part, Mr. Williams is pleased to be there and enjoys the students.

Mr. Williams has great empathy for the students. He has an almost uncanny ability to see the world as 13- and 14-year-olds living in urban poverty do. He grew up in the neighborhood and is a graduate of the neighborhood high school. His classes involve friendly bantering and an undertone of pleasant chatter. As students work on math problems in groups or at the blackboard, or as they answer the teacher's questions, there is clearly a good feeling in the room.

Mr. Williams's style is one of coaching. He moves around while he encourages or praises particular students' efforts. The chatting and the sharing and the laughing are a constant background and seldom get out of hand. Occasionally, Mr. Williams will tell the class or a particular student to keep the volume down. Clearly, there is very good rapport between the teacher and the students. Clearly also, Mr. Williams has a great sense of humor and a quip for every occasion.

Two of the girls in one of his classes are pregnant. One of the girls reports that her boyfriend was recently shot and killed. The other girl has told Mr. Williams that the father of her child is a 14-year-old in another middle school.

The other students in the class all know about the condition of the expectant girls and frequently comment on their situations. One of the girls is expecting twins; the other is expecting a girl. Occasionally, students ask Mr. Williams to set aside the day's math lesson to have a baby-naming contest, or they request an activity specifically focused on the girls' condition.

Mr. Williams is uncomfortable discussing the girls' situation with them or with the class, and he stays with the math lessons. As each week passes, he feels more and more helpless and inadequate at responding to the girls and to the class, whereas the youngsters seem more and more eager to initiate discussions or ask questions about the girls' condition.

Example 3

Ms. Brown is doing a good job in the third grade. For the past 3 years, she has been concentrating on becoming a better science teacher. In addition to completing more university course work in science, she has attended special summer programs on the particular need of children in poverty to do better in science, have more hands-on activities, and develop as independent thinkers. Also, Ms. Brown has attended workshops on the special need to encourage young girls in science. She feels strongly about this work because her family encouraged her to become a teacher rather than an environmental scientist so that she could get a job and earn enough to help put her younger brother through medical school.

Inspired by her substantial inservice education in the teaching of science, Ms. Brown has developed several methods of teaching that emphasize the children asking questions and engaging in critical thinking. Some of the activities continue for as much as half an hour at a time and involve the class in explaining discrepant events. The events appear to be counter to common sense and frequently motivate the children to deal with materials, equipment, or elements that are behaving in ways that the children would not predict. When she is using these methods, Ms. Brown reminds the children that they must constantly question her, ask why and how, and never assume that what she says is true simply because she is the teacher.

The third-grade class is learning a lot. Some of the children's experiments and demonstrations are coming from the eighth-grade science curriculum.

Ms. Brown is especially pleased with the progress of the girls. There does not seem to be any difference in achievement or interest between the boys and the girls. Ms. Brown is also an enthusiastic coach and frequently repeats the admonition that the children must question everything, always seek evidence, and take nothing on authority.

After school one day, the father of one of the quieter girls in the class comes to the door and asks to speak with Ms. Brown. He has recently arrived from Mexico. He carefully explains to Ms. Brown that he has always taught his children respect for adults. Respect means that they keep quiet, listen, and do what their parents and older people tell them to do. The father tells Ms. Brown that his daughter will finish elementary school, but not go to middle school; she is needed at home to help take care of the younger children. He has taken off work to visit Ms. Brown because his little girl has come home from school crying, saying that she is supposed to "not believe" the teacher. The father makes it clear that he is not seeking an explanation or more information. He has come to deliver a clear message to Ms. Brown: First, his little girl will become a woman like her mother, not well educated and certainly not a scientist. Second, his little girl will be taught to listen to and not to doubt her elders or authority.

Example 4

Mr. Johnson has become a secondary school social studies teacher because he wants to make youngsters successful participants in American society. He made it out of the ghetto, and he wants to help others succeed in the larger society.

Mr. Johnson is in his first year of teaching. He is trying hard but feels that he has a long way to go before he will be comfortable with his students or they with him. He has been attempting to personalize the material so that the students can identify with the historical characters in the curriculum. Thus far, he has been able to involve a few students in his classes. Most are apathetic; some put their heads down and do not participate at all. Very few turn in any homework. Several of the students in his homeroom just show up for lunch and attend no classes.

Mr. Johnson is trying hard to understand and relate to his students. When students are suspended or expelled, he makes a point of meeting with them. He tries to find out what is going on, and he solicits students' perceptions of what is happening to them. The typical conference involves Mr. Johnson trying to get more information and understand his students better. He frequently asks, "Why did you do that?" Whether the youngster has been involved in a fight or whatever the situation, the typical response is silence. Mr. Johnson frequently feels very frustrated, and although he thinks that most of the students respect him, he has not been able to learn more about why they engage in fighting and other behaviors that they know will get them suspended.

A few of the youngsters have educated Mr. Johnson about the various gangs in the neighborhood—their symbols, their colors, their rituals, and the blocks that they control. Mr. Johnson believes that learning this information has helped establish rapport, but he does not think that the information has helped him better understand their school behavior, or what he can do to help them want to do better in school.

Last week, a 17-year-old returned to Mr. Johnson's classroom, to which he was assigned by the courts after murdering another youth. Mr. Johnson asked the young man in a private meeting after school why he had killed the other youngster. The young man replied, "'Cause he needed killin', that's why." The young man made this comment in a flat, unemotional manner that made Mr. Johnson shudder.

* * *

To what authority do these teachers refer in order to say or not to say something, to do or not to do something? More precisely, what is the objective of these teachers' responses? Are they selected or prepared to say to themselves, "I know what's right and wrong, and I do it"? That would be the kind of sociocentric position typical of teachers in homogeneous schools that are in total harmony with their communities, representative of small-town America circa 1920. Do these teachers take the position of a relativist: "Everyone must determine what's right and wrong for himself or herself"? Is the teacher's role simply one of a clarifier, asking each student or parent, "How do you feel about what you believe?" Is the teacher a bureaucratic functionary who announces, "In this school the rule is that we all . . . "?

My own view is that there are goals of public education in the general society that must transcend the preferences of particular cultural groups or individuals. Taking the four examples in order, I think that Ms. Butler should continue to celebrate birthdays, Mr. Williams should advise the school nurse and parents to make sure that prenatal care is provided, Ms. Brown should continue to instruct females so that they achieve in science, and Mr. Johnson should promulgate the value that killing is wrong. To certify people as teachers who are reluctant or incapable of acting in these situations is not to prepare teachers for the reality of diverse schools. The four examples of conflict presented here are few in number and relatively minor in intensity compared with the hundreds of such episodes that practicing teachers face in multicultural classrooms in the course of their careers. At the heart of multicultural education is the teacher's recognition that children and youth can and should be taught to function on three levels: as individuals, as members of one or more cultural groups, and as members of the general society. To do this, the teacher must be selected on criteria that include ideology and be prepared through on-the-job coaching to deal with the inevitable conflicts that will arise among the diverse individuals and groups in American society. Otherwise, teacher educators perpetuate the myth that American diversity has only a folk-fair side, in which different cultural groups learn one another's dances, foods, and dress, and not a conflict-resolution side in which various groups learn to live together.

On-the-Job Practice as Teacher Education

Multicultural programs will have to deal with the types of issues that I have raised regarding the real conditions of teachers' practice in schools. If multicultural advocates are serious about what their advocacies might actually mean in the lives of children and youth, they must do more than hire on with publishers interested in selling neat new collections of activities and lessons that are graded by level or divided by subject. Similarly, using teacher committees or nonprofit organizations to compile handbooks of activities for classrooms without addressing the types of issues that I have raised will maintain multicultural curricula at a superficial level similar to new ways of making paper-bag turkeys or better ways of making volcanoes.

There is no way to pursue new curricula—particularly curricula as emotionally charged as multicultural ones—without simultaneously addressing the issue of on-the-job teacher education and the conditions under which teachers work. The opportunities in this challenge are well worth the effort. Teachers can be models of learners as they work to develop greater awareness themselves. Students and their families can become resources and not simply inadequate objects of input. There can be little question that future schools will change in response to the greater diversity of the new majority. Without planning, the changes may very well create school climates of greater control and restriction. With planning, classroom teachers may be proactively involved in making *multicultural* a meaningful word in the effect that schools have on children and youth and not another euphemism for schools with more safety aides.

In 1969, Smith concluded that there had to be a major overhaul of teacher education before teachers would be adequately prepared to work with children of any social origin:

> Racial, class, and ethnic bias can be found in every aspect of current teacher preparation programs. The selection processes militate against the poor and the minorities. The program content reflects current prejudices; the methods of instruction coincide with learning styles of the dominant group. Subtle inequalities are reinforced in the institutions of higher learning. Unless there is scrupulous self-appraisal, unless every aspect of teacher training is carefully reviewed, the changes initiated in teacher preparation as a result of the current crises will be, like so many changes which have gone before, "merely differences which make no difference." (pp. 2–3)

Twenty-four years later, a remarkably thorough summary of the teacher education literature seeking evidence of how teachers are being prepared for cultural diversity demonstrates that little has changed. Even searching for reports that were not research pieces or published documents generated an exceedingly small literature. Zeichner (1993) concludes that

> there is a lot of evidence that the situation hasn't changed much in the 24 years since Smith delivered [his] condemnation of teacher education. . . . If teacher education programs were successful in educating teachers for diversity, we might not have today such a massive reluctance by beginning teachers to work in urban schools and in other schools serving poor and ethnic- and linguistic-minority students. Just educating teachers who are willing to teach in these schools,

however, only begins to address the problem of preparing teachers who will successfully educate the students who attend these schools. Educating teachers for diversity must include attention to the quality of instruction that will be offered by these teachers. More of the same kind of teaching, which has largely failed to provide a minimally adequate education to poor and ethnic- and linguistic-minority students, does not improve the situation. (pp. 4–6)

In a review of the teacher education literature from 1960 through 1990, Weiner (1991) concludes that not only is the urban knowledge base missing, but faculty refuse to acknowledge that they "lack this understanding—and need to acquire it" (p. 168).

A review of the literature for preparing teachers for children in poverty from diverse cultural groups leads to the conclusion that a lot less is going on than meets the eye. Universities remain committed to basing their programs on the age of the learner, the content to be taught, and the handicapping conditions of children and youth. Operationally, poverty, urban character, and cultural diversity are typically defined as special conditions. Teachers are prepared to teach children and youth characterized by these conditions in the same way that they are prepared to teach persons with handicapping conditions: by taking an additional course. Such traditional teacher education continues to assume a universal knowledge base (all normal children develop in the same ways and pass through the same developmental stages) rather than a contextual one. The focus is on the individual as the unit of analysis rather than on any cultural group that socializes the individual. The concepts of educational psychology continue to dominate teacher preparation, limiting it to one knowledge base rather than multiple bases.

What is contextual teacher education? It focuses on particular ethnic groups in particular schools, with particular needs, problems, and aspirations. In this form of teacher education, the knowledge bases for teachers do not emanate from one limited scholarly discipline or from universal questions (e.g., How do all children learn?). Rather, this form begins with specific, practical questions (e.g., How can violence be reduced in this school in St. Louis?) and brings interdisciplinary approaches to bear on the search for solutions.

In the future, the preparation of urban teachers may become the responsibility of more than one profession and include interprofessional and interdisciplinary approaches. To meet the needs of children and youth in the real world, future teachers will have to be prepared to access the services of the full range of human service professionals: nurses, physicians, dentists, social workers, and more. At present, the literature demonstrates more initiatives—and more comprehensive ones—by educators of medical, health, and human service professionals who seek to work with schools and teachers than it does initiatives by teacher educators who seek to work with health and human service institutions and professionals (Casto & Julia, 1994). If future teachers of children and youth in urban poverty will need to be interdisciplinary practitioners, will traditional programs of teacher education be able to respond to all of America's children in any serious, major way, or will they continue to add a course or a requirement to maintain existing programs? Because both poverty and cultural diversity will probably continue to increase, the pressures on traditional forms of teacher education are also likely to increase. Concurrently, the number of teachers prepared on the job in multicultural school situations will continue to increase. Effective multicultural teacher education involves selecting those who are predisposed to multiculturalism at the outset and coaching them on a situation-specific basis as they function in the role of teacher.

References

Casto, R. M., & Julia, M. (1994). *Interprofessional care and collaborative practice.* Pacific Grove, CA: Brooks/Cole.

Garbarino, J., Dudrow, N., Kostelny, K., & Pardo, C. (1992). *Children in danger.* San Francisco: Jossey-Bass.

Haberman, M., & Post, L. (1990). Cooperating teachers' perceptions of the goals of multicultural education. *ACTION in Teacher Education, 12,* 161–169.

Haberman, M., & Post, L. (1995). Multicultural education: Teaching in the real world. In A. C. Ornstein (Ed.), *Teaching: Theory into practice* (pp. 337–353). Boston: Allyn & Bacon.

Hodgkinson, H. L. (1992). *A demographic look at tomorrow.* Washington, DC: Institute for Educational Leadership, Center for Demographic Policy.

Payne, C. M. (1984). *Getting what we ask for: The ambiguity of success and failure in urban education.* Westport, CT: Greenwood.

Sleeter, C. (1992, Spring). Resisting racial awareness: How teachers understand the social order from their racial, gender and social class locations. *Educational Foundations,* pp. 172–189.

Smith, B. O. (1969). *Teachers for the real world.* Washington, DC: American Association of Colleges for Teacher Education.

Weiner, L. L. (1991). *Perspectives on preparing teachers of at-risk students in urban schools, 1960–1990.* Unpublished doctoral dissertation, Harvard University.

Zeichner, K. (1993). *Educating teachers for cultural diversity.* East Lansing, MI: National Center for Research on Teacher Learning.

A Response to Chapter 5, "The Preparation of Teachers for a Diverse, Free Society," by Martin J. Haberman

BARBARA G. BURCH
California State University, Fresno

In Chapter 5, Martin J. Haberman presents a number of truisms, compelling arguments, and provocative ideas that cause reflection on current practices and beliefs as well as reconsideration of some basic assumptions that guide decision making and actions in preparing teachers for today's schools. Haberman's basic commitment lies in ensuring the preparation of teachers who can teach all children, recognizing that both schools and American society have moved toward greater multiculturalism. He begins with the notion that schools reflect society; therefore, teacher education must prepare teachers who are in close harmony with public schools. He concludes with the observation that effective teacher education involves "selecting those who are predisposed to multiculturalism at the outset and coaching them on a situation-specific basis as they function in the role of teacher" (p. 130). Between these ideas, Haberman recounts the many ways in which educators have attempted to respond to the growing diversity and multiculturalism of American society, the passive resistance to this reality among some teacher educators, and the tendency to cling to historical patterns of doing things.

Definitions

Regarding Haberman's position on how educators are addressing multicultural education in schools and in teacher preparation programs, educators seem to have spent so much time defining multicultural education and focusing on the materials available for use in classrooms that they have lost some of the meaning that must be reflected in living a commitment to multicultural education. Preparing teachers for a diverse, free society means preparing teachers who can teach all children, irrespective of differences in their learning capacity, lifestyles, access to resources, neighborhoods, social conditions, gender, religion, ethnicity, race, and economic status.

Perhaps educators' use of the terms *diversity* and *multiculturalism* has become rhetorical and routine, to the point that it obscures their full meanings of the words. Haberman freely interchanges them. There is a tendency to associate multiculturalism principally with matters of race and ethnicity, thereby limiting the likelihood of capturing the full spirit and intent of this critically important concept. This tendency is reflected in Public Agenda's research for *First Things First*, which found that "nine in ten Americans (95%) support the idea of schools teaching 'respect for others regardless of their racial or ethnic background' " (as cited in Johnson, 1995, p. 14).

Haberman cites various characterizations of multiculturalism, calling them conflicting advocacies. Although one might make a compelling case for any or all of the characterizations, I am concerned that educators not overlook or set aside the single factor in a child's life that most affects his or her success as a learner: poverty. The Children's Defense Fund's 1994 yearbook states, "Family income is a far more powerful correlate of a child's IQ at age five than maternal education, ethnicity and growing up in a single-parent family" (p. 3). This same publication notes the finding of a U.S. Department of Education report, published during the Reagan administration, that every year a child spends in poverty adds two percentage points to the chances that he or she will fall behind in school.

Haberman raises a number of penetrating questions about the ways in which educators are attempting to implement multicultural education in schools and in teacher education programs. It is puzzling that he does not comment on the role of the teacher education faculty in relation to what they believe. Teacher educators must accept responsibility for what they are modeling. To what extent are teacher education faculty conveying appropriate attitudes and behaviors relative to their commitment to multiculturalism and diversity?

The Unique Needs of Urban Schools

Haberman directs much of his attention to the nature and the challenges of diversity and multiculturalism in urban schools. With more than 80% of Americans living in metropolitan areas and sending their children to urban schools, there is certainly legitimacy in being concerned about the needs of those schools. Haberman takes the position that the knowledge and the skills needed to teach effectively in urban schools are so unique and special that it is not possible to train teachers for these schools properly in generic teacher education programs. He contends that it is possible to train teachers appropriately for urban schools only when the entirety of their pedagogical preparation takes place in the urban school setting. At the same time, he suggests that teachers in America's diverse society must be able to teach all children, irrespective of individual differences, socioeconomic conditions, ethnicity, or situational context. If all teachers are in fact trained to be able to teach all children, then these well-trained teachers will also be prepared to teach children and youth in urban schools. There is no question that teachers in urban schools face many and enormous challenges, but teachers in almost every kind of setting find themselves facing increasingly complex situations and multiple obstacles to doing their jobs well. Dysfunctional families, lack of parental involvement, declining communities, issues of safety and disorder, conflicting values, and myriad social and economic problems affect teachers to some degree in almost every community.

I agree with Haberman's notion that to be truly effective in all kinds of settings, teachers must have practice and on-the-job coaching fitted to the uniqueness of the settings in which they are teaching. However, I do not believe that it is reasonable to expect basic initial teacher preparation as it is now defined and operationalized to do all of this. Some of this training is a natural part of the yet-to-be-clearly-conceptualized continuum of professional development for teachers. This continuum must be defined in part by the nature of the actual practice setting in which a teacher teaches and must include continuing professional development and support systems to equip teachers to meet the unique needs of the workplace.

One of Haberman's most compelling and provocative points is that schools are typically responding to the challenges of changing populations by imposing more controls. Although many of the controls are designed to make schools safe and prevent violence, they "transform schools into more repressive, authoritarian places" (p. 121).

Teacher Values and Decision Making

The chapter includes four minicases in which teachers are presented with situations that call for decision making in the face of some type of conflict involving cultural differences and values. The cases raise the question of what source of authority teachers should use to make decisions in value-conflict situations. Haberman's answer is that some goals of public education must transcend the preferences of particular cultural groups or individuals. This is a critically important proposition, and it sends a powerful message to teacher educators to define what those goals are and how they translate into teacher education programs. At the 1996 annual meeting of ATE, David Berliner spoke to this point in describing teaching as a "moral craft." Teachers must develop an articulative dimension that enables them to make informed judgments based on a set of beliefs about what constitutes good education, Berliner contended. The overarching disposition, the ideology that all teachers must possess, he went on, must be compatible with doing the best of all that educators know about children, teaching, learning, and schooling in a democratic society. Ideology, he emphasized, determines who one is and enables one to take value positions about what is good and what ought to be.

The Delivery Systems

I could not agree more with Haberman's argument that universities err by basing their preparation programs on age of learner, content to be taught, and handicapping conditions of learners, and by having students take an additional course to meet exceptional or special preparation needs. He contends that teacher education should be more contextually oriented, "focus[ing] on particular ethnic groups in particular schools, with particular needs, problems, and aspirations" (p. 129). Teacher educators would do well to look at their own models of teacher preparation and their assumptions. They are guilty of moving teacher candidates into and through teacher preparation programs in lockstep fashion. They tend to prescribe a predesignated number of courses or credits regardless of differences in backgrounds, experiences, and prior learning among teacher candidates. Completion based on time and units is not a sound basis for ensuring well-prepared teachers.

Haberman is insightful in recognizing that "to meet the needs of children and youth in the real world, future teachers will have to be prepared to access the services of the full range of human service professionals: nurses, physicians, dentists, social workers, and more" (p. 130). Preparation of urban teachers, in particular, may become the responsibility of more than one profession. Dean Corrigan expands on this premise in Chapter 6 and elsewhere. I would not limit interprofessional collaboration and cooperation to those who will be teaching in urban schools, because in every community setting, irrespective of type, teachers must be able to support the individual needs of children and youth in their classrooms. They cannot do this working in isolation from other community service providers.

Haberman's emphasis on the unique contextual elements in which a child comes to school and learns must not be lost. Educators are all painfully aware of the pace and the scope of demographic change in America's communities and schools. Teachers working with children only within the schoolroom cannot successfully accommodate the change. Families, communities, and neighborhoods shape and influence the lives of children; they also influence the way in which a teacher must teach to be effective with the children of those families and communities.

Meeting children's physical needs is paramount in addressing their educational needs; neither a hungry child nor a physically ill child can concentrate on learning. The extent to which social and emotional needs of children are met in their daily lives will dictate their academic performance. Although the extent to which schools should meet these needs has long been debated, it is neither good educational practice nor ethical behavior for educators to pretend that they can create a nurturing and supportive learning environment for children whose social and emotional needs are unaddressed. It is difficult to accept schools' ambivalence on whether they can or should attempt to redress deficiencies in the homes and the communities of schoolchildren. The following piece makes the point well:

WHY ARE CHILDREN NOT A PRIORITY?

If one in three victims of physical abuse were corporation presidents . . . , it'd be considered a national crisis.

If 60 percent of aged people weren't getting shots that could save their lives, it'd be a scandal.

If 3 million police officers were so poorly paid that their families were living in poverty, we'd do something about it.

And if the U.S. mortality rate for Olympic athletes was higher than [the rates of] the 19 industrial nations, we'd suspect something was dreadfully wrong.

Yet we have an astonishing capacity as a nation to absorb and shrug off all of these enormities when they happen to infants and small children. (R. Reno, as quoted in Busse & Jehl, 1994, pp. 18–19)

Restructuring

Haberman raises a particularly compelling question: "Are the advocates of restructuring and the promoters of making current forms of schooling more efficient talking about the same multiculturalism?" (p. 114). Banks and Banks's (1993) definition of multicultural education suggests an affirmative answer: "Multicultural education is an idea, an educational reform movement and process designed to change the structure of educational institutions to give all students an equal chance to achieve academically in school." The authors use the term *multicultural education* to mean "a total school reform effort designed to increase educational equity for a range of cultural, ethnic, and economic groups" (p. 1).

The arguments and the position that Haberman presents have been growing in importance and concern. In 1971, at the national conference of the Association for Supervision and Curriculum Development, Jerome Bruner questioned whether there should be a fundamental

restructuring of the entire educational system, well beyond the curriculum revision stage for which he was so well known. He commented on the appalling effects of poverty on the lives of children.
American education in 1970, Bruner argued, "had passed into a state
of crisis. It had failed to respond to changing social needs, lagging
behind rather than leading." He noted that his

> work on early education and social class . . . had convinced
> [him] that the educational system was, in effect, a way of
> maintaining a class system—a group at the bottom. It crip-
> pled the capacity of children in the lowest socioeconomic
> quarter of the population to participate at full power in the
> society, and it did so early and effectively. (Bruner, 1971,
> p. 26).

If a Woods Hole–type conference were held in 1971, Bruner remarked, it would not take place in a rural, coastal setting.

> More likely, [it] would gather in the heart of a great city. The
> task would center around the dispossession of the children of
> the poor and the alienation of the middle class child. . . . The
> issues would have to do with how one gives back initiative
> and a sense of potency, how one activates to tempt one to
> want to learn again . . . , and the curriculum would later be
> addressed not as a subject but as an approach to learning and
> using knowledge. (p. 26)

Bruner was also concerned about how to sustain learning and
make it compelling. He referred to an extraordinarily moving book
called *Letter to a Teacher: School Boys of Barbiana* (Rossi & Cole, 1970)
about a Tuscan hill town in Italy where

> the children . . . had failed so many times in so many ways in
> school that they had given up generation after generation—
> consigned to unskilled labor. A priest came to the parish. He
> started a school in which nobody was to fail, a school in
> which it was expected that everybody had to pass. It was
> everybody's responsibility to see that everybody in the class
> mastered the lesson before anybody could go on to the next
> lesson. (as quoted in Bruner, 1971, pp. 27–28)

Bruner extolled this example of the powerful force created for effective learning by a community in which members shared a sense of compassion and responsibility for one another. The strategies used were cross-age tutoring, peer groups, and learning communities.

Bruner went on to note an educational problem of the first order:

> We shall kill ourselves as a society and as human beings unless we direct our efforts to redressing the deep, deep wounds that we inflict on the poor, the outcast, those who somehow do not fit within our caste system. For the very young, the extent of being out, in not having a chance as an adult . . . very quickly reflects itself in loss of hope in the child. When a group is robbed of its legitimate aspiration, its members will aspire desperately and by means that outrage the broader society, though the means are efforts to sustain or regain dignity. (pp. 27–28)

Twenty-five years ago Bruner was saying that America must find ways of reformulating schools as institutions.

Imperatives for the Future

The most challenging children and youth to teach are those whose needs are greatest. Table 5.2 dramatically portrays what is driving the demand for changes in schools.

Haberman firmly makes the case that teachers must teach all children and teach them well. Teacher educators have a great moral obligation to fulfill, and they cannot fulfill it without addressing and modeling multiculturalism.

In a 1987 monograph, Haberman writes,

> The future of a democratic society is only as promising as the vision of its "ordinary" people. . . . As a democratic society, we will in the future be tested on how well we learn to resolve our problems, and this will, in large measure, derive from the quality of our educational system. What the wisest parents want for their children, all Americans must want for their children. To make a democratic system work, we must conceive of education as a common good, not as a personal one.

TABLE 5.2 Moments in America for Children

Every 9 seconds	a child drops out of school.
Every 10 seconds	a child is reported abused or neglected.
Every 14 seconds	a child is arrested.
Every 25 seconds	a baby is born to an unmarried mother.
Every 32 seconds	a baby is born into poverty.
Every 34 seconds	a baby is born to a mother who did not graduate from high school.
Every 1 minute	a baby is born to a teen mother.
Every 2 minutes	a baby is born at low birthweight.
Every 3 minutes	a baby is born to a mother who received late or no prenatal care.
Every 4 minutes	a child is arrested for an alcohol-related offense.
Every 4 minutes	a child is arrested for a violent crime.
Every 4 minutes	a child is arrested for a drug offense.
Every 10 minutes	a baby is born at very low birthweight.
Every 15 minutes	a baby dies.
Every 2 hours	a child is killed by firearms.
Every 4 hours	a child commits suicide.
Every 7 hours	a child dies from abuse or neglect.

SOURCE: Reprinted with permission from *The State of America's Children Yearbook 1996*. Washington, DC: Children's Defense Fund, 1996.

> To fail to recognize that principle of education as a common good—that every child's education enhances the nation and that every undereducated person is a potential drain and threat to the nation—is to back into a future that will become increasingly dangerous. (p. 1)

Haberman's chapter in this book offers a strong case for the issues that teacher educators must address and the direction that they must pursue as the new millennium approaches.

References

Banks, J. A., & Banks, C.A.M. (Eds.). (1993). *Multicultural education issues and perspectives* (2nd ed.). Boston: Allyn & Bacon.

Berliner, D. (1996, February 27). *Research and social justice.* Address to the 76th annual meeting of the Association of Teacher Educators, St. Louis.

Bruner, J. (1971). [Address]. In R. R. Leeper (Ed.), *Dare to care/dare to act: Racism and education* [Addresses and statements at the 26th annual conference of the Association for Supervision and Curriculum Development, St. Louis] (pp. 25–28). Washington, DC: Association for Supervision and Curriculum Development.

Busse, C., & Jehl, J. (1994). New beginning for children and families. *Thrust for Educational Leadership, 24*(3), 18–19.

Children's Defense Fund. (1994). *The state of America's children: Leave no child behind* (1994 yearbook). Washington, DC: Author.

Children's Defense Fund. (1996). *The state of America's children yearbook 1996.* Washington, DC: Author.

Haberman, M. (1987). *Recruiting and selecting teachers for urban schools.* New York: ERIC Clearinghouse on Urban Education, Institute for Urban and Minority Education; Reston, VA: Association of Teacher Educators.

Johnson, J. (1995). *Assignment incomplete: The unfinished business of education reform.* New York: Public Agenda.

Rossi, N., & Cole, T. (Trans.) (1970). *Letter to a teacher: School boys of Barbiana.* New York: Random House.

6

Teacher Education and Interprofessional Collaboration: Creation of Family-Centered, Community-Based Integrated Service Systems

DEAN CORRIGAN
Texas A&M University

In decisions made every day, Americans place children at the very bottom of the agenda with grave consequences for the future of the nation. It is intolerable that millions of children are physically and emotionally disadvantaged in ways that restrict their capacity to learn, especially when we are aware of the terrible price that will be paid for such neglect, not just educationally, but in tragic human terms as well.

ERNEST BOYER, *Ready to Learn*, 1991

The most vivid truth in the human services is that no single profession can adequately respond to the complex problems facing children and families. It will take interprofessional collaboration, public awareness, financial support, and a renewed commitment to the notion that "it takes a whole village to raise a child."

Moreover, integrated service systems cannot by themselves solve the problems of poverty and poor quality of life; that will take jobs and a new sense of urgency. Business and industry must be full partners with human services. Indeed, everyone has a part to play in creating healthy, humane communities.

In this chapter, community is envisioned in the way that Tonnies (1887/1957) defined it years ago: community of kinship, place, and mind. Community of kinship emerges from the kinds of relationships among people that create a unity of being, similar to that found in families and other closely knit collections of people. Community of place emerges from the sharing of a common habitat or locale for sustained periods. Community of mind emerges from the bonding of people around common goals, shared values, and shared conceptions of being and doing. Together, the three kinds of community represent webs of meaning that link diverse groups of people by creating among them a sense of belonging and a common identity as human beings who are capable of affection and caring for others as well as themselves (Sergiovanni, 1994). America's future depends on the ability of its citizens to create healthy, humane communities and on the commitment of its leaders to act on the values embodied in such communities.

Tomorrow's schoolteachers, counselors, principals, and other educators need to learn how to collaborate with partners in other human service professions such as health care, social work, and criminal justice, who serve the same clients. In addition to preparation in their particular specializations, these professionals must (a) possess a common core of knowledge that is derived from the problems faced by their clients; (b) have access to interprofessional education programs that prepare them to work together across agencies in family-centered, community-based delivery systems; (c) understand the policies of integrated services at the national, state, and local levels; and (d) learn the political strategies necessary to implement and influence these policies. At the heart of this effort must be a commitment to advocacy for America's most vulnerable children and families.

Centrality of Purpose

The first priority of all the partners involved in designing teacher education and interprofessional collaboration should be agreement on purposes. The severe shortcoming of past reform efforts was that they focused on means, with little consideration for ends. Purposes were not clear enough, nor consequences powerful enough, to sustain them (Corrigan, 1992a).

The important question at the outset of any discussion on ways to improve education is, What results are to be achieved? In this debate, discussants must understand the origins of American education and its uniqueness compared with education in other countries. America's schools are based on the principle of no rejects, as stipulated in Public Law 94-142, the Education for All Handicapped Children Act (Corrigan, 1978). America's schools are not screening stations for society's other institutions. By law, professional educators must design and implement free, appropriate education programs for all the children of all the people, including children of minorities, children who are economically disadvantaged, and children with special learning needs. In a democracy, what is or is not done for those on the edges, those most in need, determines the effectiveness of the whole system. What the best and wisest parents want for their children, the community must want for all its children (Dewey, 1900).

The important questions about education are, (a) Who should be educated? (b) What curriculum should be taught? (c) What teaching methods should be employed? (d) What textbooks, supplementary materials, and media should be used? and (e) How and on what criteria should students, schools, and teachers be evaluated? These questions must be answered in terms of the purposes to be achieved.

Furthermore, the characteristics and the competencies of the teachers needed, and the kind of teacher education required to prepare these teachers, must be rooted in the ends to which teaching and teacher education are directed. The important questions about teacher education are, (a) What should teachers know and be able to do? (b) Who should be selected for professional preparation? (c) What knowledge and skills should teacher candidates be taught? (d) What values, attitudes, and convictions should they possess? (e) How should the program be organized? (f) What pedagogy should be used? (g) What preparation should teachers have in order to work with other professionals who serve the same children and families? and (h) How should teacher education and interprofessional education programs be designed, implemented, and evaluated? The answers to these questions, too, must be relevant to the purposes of American education.

In an institution charged with the education of a free people, it makes little sense for teachers to think that they are being responsible to their clients solely by teaching children to read, write, and compute, if they are also producing what C. Wright Mills has called "happy robots" (Corrigan, 1992b). In a democracy, critical thinking skills are as basic as literacy itself. Furthermore, teaching students to read, write, and do math and science with technical proficiency only, but neglecting to convey the purposes for which these skills are to be used, is to produce a potential menace to society. Reading can be a lethal weapon in the hands of a person who uses it to build a better bomb to blow up the house of a neighbor who has a different skin color. As Ducharme (1988) points out, education is for making a life as well as for making a living.

Therefore, evaluation of the outcomes of America's schools, and of teacher education, must go beyond test results. Using test scores as the sole indicator of excellence ignores many equally important qualities unmeasured by tests but important to learn in school—for example, making good judgments about people and situations, having the courage and the ability to know when to persist in risk-taking situations, making choices and seeing them through to completion, and demonstrating a sense of loyalty and a concern for the human rights of others as well as one's own rights. Students need to learn such skills along with the three Rs if they are going to obtain and keep a job, be a good parent, be a successful community member, and live a satisfying life.

The most rigorous, most ecologically valid, most educationally significant form of educational evaluation, says Eisner (1990), will secure its data outside classrooms and schools, not inside them. What people think about, what they talk about, how analytic and critical they can be, what they pursue, what kinds of values they express, what they do: These are the significant results of education.

Too often, teacher educators have acted as if education is a purposeless activity with no relationship to the great problems of the time. Too often, they have maintained the illusion of neutrality. They have been so enamored of the *means* of education (credit hours, degrees, structures of programs) and the technology (television, computers, testing) that they have neglected the *ends* of teacher education. There is no such thing as value-free teacher education. There is only the choice to be conscious and clear about values, or to conceal and confuse them.

Threats to America's Children

The starting point in defining the purposes of integrated services, teacher education, and interprofessional development should be the actual needs, problems, and conditions of America's children and their families. As documented in *The State of America's Children* (Children's Defense Fund, 1994), conditions are so bad that they can no longer be ignored. More children are living in extreme poverty today than in any year since 1975, when such data were first collected. The increase in poverty has been particularly dramatic for America's youngest children. In 1992, 25% of all children under 6 years of age were poor, as were 27% of all children under age 3. Children comprise the nation's poorest and fastest-growing poverty group (National Commission on Children, 1993). African American and Hispanic children are 2 to 3 times more likely to live in poverty than white children. Ten percent of poor children are from the inner city (National Commission on Children, 1993). Poverty is not restricted to minorities, however; among whites it rose from 9.7% in 1973 to 15.6% in 1992, the highest rate of increase for any racial group (National Center for Health Statistics, 1993).

Current conditions in which children live signal the need for changes in America's social institutions and in professional practices:

- Violence permeates the environments of families at all socioeconomic levels. Twenty-five percent of child deaths are due to injury. Homicide is the fourth leading cause of death among children 1–9 years of age, the third leading cause among adolescents 10–14 years of age, the second leading cause among youth 15–19 years of age (Maternal and Child Health Bureau, 1993).

- Prejudice, racism, and polarization divide Americans. In far too many places, individual differences are ridiculed rather than viewed as a source of richness. The racial isolation described in the Kerner Commission report (Kerner, 1968; Seigel, 1969) over 25 years ago persists in America. Riots still occur (e.g., in Los Angeles), and the consequences are no longer limited to cities.

- Family structures and roles are changing. Over half of all new marriages are ending in divorce, leaving 15.3 million children living with one parent, the mother in over 90% of the cases. Also, 23% of new babies are born to single mothers (National Commission on Children, 1991).

- Child care services are not available to help parents meet the enormous responsibilities of rearing a child while employed full-time, or to meet the needs of single-parent families. In 1991, 58.4% of mothers with children of preschool age were working, nearly double the level in 1970. Over the same period, working mothers of school-age children increased from 43.0% to 74.4% (Maternal and Child Health Bureau, 1993).

- Homelessness is reaching epidemic proportions. Single-parent families are the fastest-growing segment of the homeless population, now representing 34% compared with 27% in 1985. Moreover, one of every five homeless children is of school age. Every night, 65,000–100,000 children are homeless. Currently, there is a shortage of affordable housing. Seven million low-income renters are competing for 4 million housing units (Bassuk, 1991).

- Mental disorders occur in the lives of 20% of children under 18 years of age (National Institute of Mental Health, 1993). In 1991, about 2.7 million children were reported to state authorities as abused or neglected, an increase of 6% over 1990 and 40% over 1985 (National Commission on Children, 1993). Substance abuse is on the rise, creating serious disruptions in the lives of children and families, as well as threats to their health and safety. Teenage suicides have increased at an unprecedented rate. In 1991, as many as 1 in 12 high school students attempted suicide (Maternal and Child Health Bureau, 1993).

- Health facilities and schools are serving children with whom they have never had to deal. AIDS has become a serious threat to the nation's children. Twenty-five percent of American babies are born to women who receive inadequate prenatal care, and the consequences are being felt in the number of low-birthweight babies who later exhibit low school performance (National Commission on Children, 1993). The average cost of health care per child is about half of that for adults and a seventh of that for the elderly. In 1991, one of six children had no health coverage at all (National Center for Health Statistics, 1993).

- Value systems are being transformed as children see materialistic rewards coming from dealing drugs and engaging in other illicit activities rather than from working at the kinds of jobs that can be obtained as a result of schooling. The increasing number of young people out of school and out of work with no skills to make a living is a ticking time bomb (Levin & Bachman, 1972; Lewit, 1992). Eighty-two percent of America's prisoners are high school dropouts, and more and more adolescents are being tried in adult courts (Texas Education Agency, 1993).

- Schools see more and more children who are doomed to fail before they ever start. One of three 6-year-olds is not ready for formal education (Boyer, 1991). Once in school, untold numbers cannot learn adequately because they come to school hungry, suffer neglect or abuse at home, or have birth defects and illness. The children from poor families usually find themselves at the bottom of the heap (Kozol, 1991).

Interrelationships

What is most important to recognize about these conditions is their implications for children and families at risk, for community agencies, and for the professions sanctioned by society to serve them. These implications can be visualized by placing children and families at the center of community services and examining the interrelationships of entities, information flows, and activities (see Figure 6.1).

Actions taken by one entity in the system influence the environment in which the other entities exist and consequently the behavior and the products of those entities. Orland (1990), for example, has documented the relationships between the number of years that children spend in poverty and their academic success. Poor children are more likely than their nonpoor counterparts to be low academic achievers, to repeat grades, and to drop out of school (National Center for Children in Poverty, 1990). Dropping out of school influences future employment, level of income, and health (U.S. Depart-

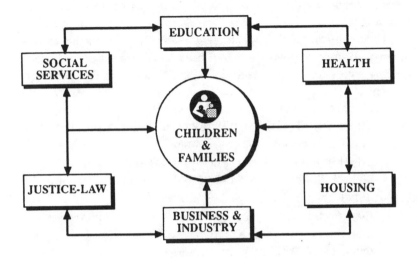

Figure 6.1. Interrelationships of Entities, Information Flows, and Activities

ment of Health and Human Services, 1992). Dropouts are 3½ times more likely than high school graduates to be arrested and 6 times more likely to become single parents (National Commission on Children, 1991).

Children of unmarried teenage mothers are 4 times more likely than children in other families to be poor, and they are likely to remain poor for an extended period (National Commission on Children, 1991). Poverty, lack of education, and teenage pregnancy relate to form a self-perpetuating cycle. Thirty-one percent of 8th- and 10th-grade female dropouts in 1990 left school because they were pregnant; 28% reported that they would likely return to school if child care were available there (National Education Goals Panel, 1992).

Degree of poverty, access to equal education, availability of family support, opportunity for health care, and incidence of violence interact in every community. They affect employment (Lewit, 1992); incarceration and crime (Levin & Bachman, 1972; Texas Education Agency, 1993); immunization rates, mortality rates, suicide rates, and levels of drug abuse and child abuse (Hamburg, 1992; National

Center for Children in Poverty, 1990); enrollment in postsecondary education (National Education Goals Panel, 1992); and the ability of the workforce to compete in the global economy (U.S. Department of Labor, 1991).

These interrelationships have far-reaching economic consequences. Bruner's (1993) studies of the cost of neglect provide convincing evidence of the need for a more cost-effective strategy, prevention:

- The birth of each low-birthweight baby costs about $21,100; a normal birth costs $2,800.
- The children at highest risk account for only 1%–4% of the population, but they claim 20%–40% of the health care dollar.
- Every "class" of school dropouts earns $237 billion less than an equivalent class of high school graduates; governments lose $70 billion in tax revenues.
- Children of teenage parents cost society $16.6 billion each year.
- Prison alone costs $20,000 per person per year; additionally, there are construction costs ($160,000 per cell), legal costs, and costs of probation officers.

The paybacks from a prevention strategy are clear (Bruner, 1993):

- Preschool saves $3–$6 for each dollar spent (Berrueta-Clement, Schweinhart, Barnett, Epstein, & Weikart, 1984).
- Prenatal care saves $3.38 for each dollar spent.
- Early immunizations save $10 per person in subsequent medical costs.
- Nutrition for needy women and their children saves $3 for each dollar invested.

Consideration of the foregoing information indicates that it is in everyone's interest to work together to improve the delivery of services through collaborative, family-centered, community-based integrated service systems. The future conditions of all Americans are inextricably interlocked.

Implications for Schools

When one steps into a schoolhouse today, it does not take long to realize that the persistent life situations of many students and their families (drugs, suicide, AIDS, teenage pregnancy, crime, lack of jobs, poverty, etc.) call for multiple-agency, multiple-profession responses. To accomplish their primary job of intellectual development (creating humane centers of intellectual inquiry, creating communities of learning), educators must work with their professional partners in the rest of the human service delivery system.

Educators in schools have at least three main functions:

1. To teach relevant knowledge. The primary function of the American school is to develop the intellect so that all students can make intelligent decisions regarding the complex problems that children and families face today. In today's political climate, this function will not be accomplished without controversy. The more that knowledge deals with values and the solution of real community problems, the more controversial it is likely to be. Professional teachers must be prepared to defend intellectual inquiry, critical thinking, and the free exchange of ideas in America's schools (Corrigan, 1992b).

2. To connect children and their families with other agencies that deal with the health and human service needs of the community. Because schools are the community institution that most children attend nearly every day, and because schools are directly connected to families, school leaders have a major responsibility for helping to mobilize community resources.

3. To collaborate with local, state, and national policymakers in developing policies that support integrated service programs and interprofessional education.

The fact that schools have an advocacy role for children and are the institution that all children attend does not necessarily mean that education, health, and human service professionals should provide all their services on the school site. The extent to which the school becomes the site for access to services will depend on the community. In many communities, however, the school is already a community center, serving people of all ages throughout the day and the evening with a wide variety of family-centered programs (Dryfoos, 1994; Lawson, 1994).

Interacting Components of One System

Central to the concept of integrated services and interprofessional education as a means for reforming education, health, and human service delivery is the recognition that schools, colleges of education, and community agencies should be interrelated and interacting components of one system. The American school and American teacher education must be a part of the community, and vice versa. Lawson (1994), in reporting lessons learned from his journey throughout the United States studying schools, universities, and communities involved in interprofessional collaboration, points out that family-centered, community-based schools are engaged in more than structural change. They are changing purpose and substance by actually developing family-friendly support environments.

Working in partnership with other agencies, tomorrow's schools will become hubs in a network for facilitating access to various components of human services. Through collaboration with other agencies, schools will foster interprofessional teams (persons from education, health, social work, business and industry, etc.). Some schools will be called *interprofessional development schools*. Beginnings already exist in schools where there are social workers, psychologists, child care workers, nurses, other health professionals, tutors, mentors from business and industry, adult literacy specialists, and more.

Now that professional development schools are under way, it is an appropriate time to add an interprofessional dimension to their design. In fact, interprofessional development schools may be the best setting in which to start interprofessional training and research because that is where the interface of professions is taking place and where it will take place in the future. Interprofessional development schools have great potential as preservice and inservice professional development centers and as vehicles for enhancing collaboration.

In addition to interprofessional education at the bachelor's and master's level, there must be preparation programs at the doctoral and postdoctoral levels for selected leaders in each of the participating professions. This cadre of professionals, already licensed in their specializations and highly respected by their colleagues, will receive special training in interprofessional collaboration, policy development, and design and implementation of preservice and inservice interprofessional programs. Whether they are teachers, school principals, physicians, social workers, psychologists, child care workers, health care providers, urban planners, family counselors, or some other type of specialist, these leaders will gain the knowledge, the skills, and the values to view problems and issues from a broad perspective. They will know how to build bridges of understanding across the participating professions.

New Developments in Interprofessional Education

There has not been widespread development and implementation of programs linking education and human services since the Bicentennial Commission of the AACTE (Howsam, Corrigan, Denemark, & Nash, 1976) proposed it in the mid-1970s. Recent events, however, suggest that the time for this idea has come again (Corrigan, 1993). The Board of Directors of AACTE has made collaboration with other professions serving children and youth one of its top three priorities. Through a grant to AACTE, the DeWitt Wallace–Reader's Digest Fund has provided Jackson State University and the Universities of Louisville, New Mexico, and Washington with funds to incorporate health and human services into their training programs for educators (Corin, 1994). Also, the DeWitt Wallace–Reader's Digest Fund has given Fordham University a grant to establish the National Center for Social Work and Education Collaboration, and nine institutions have received grants through this center to introduce interprofessional education into social work preparation (Fordham University, n.d.): Boston College; California State University, Long Beach; Clark Atlanta, Eastern Washington, Howard, Washington, and Wayne State Universities; and the Universities of Houston and Utah. Furthermore, the Danforth Foundation's Leadership Development

Program has made community-based interprofessional leadership training a major priority. Additionally, the American Educational Research Association, the Office of Educational Research and Improvement of the U.S. Department of Education, and the National Center on Education in the Inner Cities, in conjunction with AACTE and ATE, recently sponsored an invitational interprofessional conference, "School-Linked Comprehensive Services for Children and Families" (Office of Educational Research and Improvement, 1995).

In its third report dealing with reform, *Tomorrow's Schools of Education*, the Holmes Group (1995) recognizes that education reform depends heavily on restructuring professional schools, orchestrating new working relationships with other colleges and departments of the university as well as with public schools, and fostering the commitment and the will of school and university administrators and faculty and other human service professionals to effect massive change in educational policy and practice.

In 1993, ATE created the National Commission on Leadership in Interprofessional Education, which includes policymakers, trainers, and practitioners from 10 professions involved in creating family-centered, community-based integrated service systems. In addition to other activities, the ATE commission has become a vehicle for national dissemination and a partner in three interprofessional development grants awarded by the Maternal and Child Health Bureau of the U.S. Department of Health and Human Services in 1994, to Western Oregon State College, the University of Vermont, and the Hawaii Medical Association. All three grants involve education, health, and social work, even though each program is sponsored by a different profession. The purpose of the funds is to support collaboration among the three projects, and with the participating professions, through the ATE commission.

The goal of the Western Oregon project, which is based in the College of Education, is to assist selected colleges and universities in developing educational offerings that will cross-train students in various disciplines so that on graduation they can effect integrated services at the local level. The project will accomplish its goal by identifying family-centered, community-based projects across the nation that have been successful in integrating services and by studying the knowledge, the skills, and the values needed by service providers in those settings. Then, with the assistance of the ATE commission, the project will develop criteria to select a number of colleges and universities to join the three Maternal and Child Health Bureau grantees in developing curricula and training programs for integrated services that are based on the best practices found in the aforementioned communities. Commission members who themselves are engaged in implementing integrated services or interprofessional education programs will provide some of the technical assistance (Fredericks, 1995).

The goal of the Vermont project, which is based in the Department of Social Work, is to improve service delivery to children with special health needs and their families by (a) compiling, evaluating, and disseminating exemplary models of community-based services and (b) designing and implementing interprofessional education. The major collaborative groups of the project are families, students, and faculty. The program development process will move from family and professional collaboration to interprofessional education to family and interprofessional education and practice. Expected outcomes include changes in college curriculum, changes in community practice approaches, and changes in the ways in which children and families receive services. The Vermont project has compiled and disseminated a literature analysis and is collaborating with the Oregon project on expanding it (Bishop, 1995).

Hawaii's project, which is sponsored by a medical association, will be implemented in the context of the existing Healthy and Ready to Learn Center (HRTL), a one-stop health, education, and family support center serving culturally diverse families on the coast of Oahu. The program includes the Medical Home, whose purpose is to promote collaborative relationships among health, education, and social service providers serving young children and their families by developing a model for preservice and inservice professional training to provide family-centered, community-based, coordinated care. Project staff will train regional HRTL staff to implement and field-test identified elements of collaborative practice. Linkages will be created between the HRTL and university training programs to offer interprofessional training opportunities to pediatric and obstetrics-gynecology residents and doctoral candidates in education and social services (Sia & Taba, 1995).

The efforts of the ATE commission will be enhanced by its work with the three Maternal and Child Health Bureau grantees. From their unique settings, they bring a diversity of thought and study and a commitment to sharing lessons learned that will help the commission achieve its purpose (Corrigan, 1994).

Characteristics of Interprofessional Education Programs

A review of over 50 case studies of interprofessional education programs compiled by the ATE commission indicates that institutions often begin building their programs with a seminar held in conjunction with field experiences in a variety of human service settings serving children and families (schools, health agencies, social service offices, criminal justice organizations, etc.). Instructors usually include adjunct faculty who work as practitioner mentors in field sites and professors from affiliated departments in the university, participating as interdisciplinary teams.

The next step in building interprofessional education programs is team-taught interdisciplinary courses designed to provide a common body of knowledge and skills relevant to the creation of family-centered, community-based integrated services. Courses are taught in several departments, but are cross-listed, with the credit hours distributed to the home department of the instructors. Team teaching, dual appointments, and centers and institutes are other strategies used to facilitate cross-department programs.

Appendix 6.1 identifies a few interprofessional development programs getting under way. It also highlights some of their characteristics.

Lessons Learned in Program Development

At the conference "School-Linked Comprehensive Services for Children and Families," the Task Force on Interprofessional Education (1995), with representatives from 17 universities, summarized the lessons that its members had learned from their experience in developing programs:

1. Learning occurs in multiple contexts.
2. Real experience is the best teaching method; simulation is okay; the didactic approach is the worst. Espoused theory must be translated into theory in use.

3. Professional behavior must be driven by personal vision to enable children and families to deal with problems.

4. No one model of or approach to teaching collaborative behavior is desirable.

5. The learning process determines what will be learned.

6. Experiential learning with clients develops bonding and advocacy.

7. Collaborative practice involves simultaneous renewal.

8. In trying to change the status quo, interprofessional education will confront many barriers.

9. Interprofessional collaboration must begin with individuals, requiring vision and respect for and understanding of colleagues.

10. Overall vision must begin with family, from prenatal form on up.

11. Service structure must be adaptive, fluctuating between centralization and decentralization for task completion.

12. Attitude and orientation are as important as skills and knowledge in promoting relationships rather than individual isolation.

13. Respect for social, ethnic, and professional differences is required of professionals who are working together.

14. Universities could be part of the answer, not part of the problem.

15. Interprofessional education must be grounded in history, culture, and local relationships.

16. Leadership requires letting go and giving over; it involves creating conditions so that others can succeed.

17. Mutual respect for all participants is essential.

18. Involvement of all players in initial planning promotes development of ownership.

19. Interprofessional education must be understood as a developmental process; therefore, programs must ensure continued support and linkage to similar-minded colleagues.

20. It takes more than education agencies to develop interprofessional collaborators.

21. Interprofessional collaboration is done best when it is coequally governed.

22. Interprofessional collaboration is time consuming, difficult, complex, expensive, necessary, fun, and challenging.

23. As a field, interprofessional collaboration is already highly competitive and in danger of becoming the victim of turf battles among the professions involved.

24. Interprofessional collaborators need to be watchful of their language in communicating both among themselves and outside the professions.

25. Interprofessional collaborators need to avoid project mentality.

26. There are many experts who can work with interprofessional collaborators to develop outcome measures and evaluation schema; accountability is essential to credibility.

27. Interprofessional education does not depend on school-linked services; it is broader. Achieving intended outcomes requires more than school-linked services.

Reflections and Guiding Questions

Until recently, the response of policymakers to each crisis in education, health, and human services was to develop a categorical program. The primary strategy for change was to set up model programs or projects. Most of these models continued only as long as government or private funding lasted, or until their particular advocates died or moved on to other priorities (Corrigan, 1992a).

As education, health, and human service concerns have expanded and grown in complexity, it has become more and more evident that many agencies serve the same clients (Hodgkinson, 1992) and that professional responsibility for specific services is often uncoordinated and dysfunctional. An increasing number of state policymakers and legislators now recognize that new organizational relationships at the family and community level must be developed among schools, universities, health agencies, and other human service organizations; a systemic, collaborative approach is imperative. Fifteen states have already passed legislation fostering collaboration across state agencies and local communities (*State Education Leader*, 1994).

Calls to put the pieces together have come from policy analysts and practitioners as well as politicians. *Within Our Reach* (Schorr & Schorr, 1988), *Together We Can* (Office of Educational Research and Improvement, 1993), and *Principles to Link By* (American Academy of Pediatrics, 1994) represent just a few of the recent publications that demonstrate wide-ranging interest in integrated services and interprofessional education.

However, although reports are filling bookshelves and integrated service systems are increasing rapidly, university interprofessional preparation programs and research efforts to support them are just in the early stages of development. As on other occasions, the universities are playing catch-up. Most of the university professors engaged in the interprofessional development programs described in this chapter are pioneers on their campuses. They are often more closely linked to their community partners than to the traditional decision makers in their institution. Largely dependent on foundation grants or other sources of outside financing, they are extremely concerned about university financial support over the long haul for the difficult task of changing professional preparation in education, health, and human services.

The changed circumstances described in this chapter have special implications for those who work in the professional schools and colleges that serve as the training and research arms of their professions. In addition to discovering new knowledge and integrating knowledge from the various disciplines, professional schools and colleges have a responsibility to inform practice. Professors who educate practitioners for integrated services must confront reality: If they do not model collaborative behavior, future providers are unlikely to understand the importance of such coordination or be prepared to function in the unified systems that are emerging.

The education profession, in conjunction with the other human service professions, must identify the particular knowledge, skills, and values needed by educators to be effective collaborators with other human service providers, and vice versa. They must ensure that such knowledge, skills, and values become part of the curriculum in each field of specialization and are appropriately infused into interprofessional programs. In addition, the participating professions must develop creative ways to make appropriate knowledge and related skills a part of continuing education efforts.

Mandating new laws and policies is not enough to change practitioners. They must have the opportunity to learn the new knowledge and skills necessary to make the needed changes. Professional development, which is so often left out of legislation and budgets, is the key to reform. Change in professional practice and change in the training and research arms of each participating profession must take place simultaneously. Reform in one part of the system without reform in the other will not work.

Following is a beginning set of questions to guide discussion of integrated services and interprofessional collaboration:

1. What is meant by family-centered, community-based, integrated service systems?

2. What are the implications of using existing conditions in the lives of America's children and families as the starting point for deriving the purposes and the content of collaborative programs, and then evaluating the outcomes?

3. What do children and families need from service providers? How should the expectations of children and families influence the development of integrated service systems and interprofessional education programs?

4. What are the barriers to interprofessional collaboration? What strategies can reduce these barriers? What has facilitated interprofessional collaboration?

5. What is the role of each professional partner (educator, health care provider, social worker, criminal justice officer, etc.)? How can the professional partners help one another better understand their particular roles in an integrated service system?

6. What do schools and community agencies expect of universities, and what do universities expect of schools and community agencies? Can interprofessional collaborators use preparation programs as vehicles for service as well as for learning? How do interprofessional collaborators ensure that programs are sensitive to diverse settings and populations?

7. What should be the content of preservice and continuing interprofessional education programs to prepare current

and future educators, health care providers, social workers, and criminal justice personnel to create integrated
service systems? What kinds of curricula, instructional
approaches, and field experiences should be used? When
and where should they take place?

8. What should be the design of programs at the doctoral
   and postdoctoral levels to prepare a cadre of leaders in each
   of the professions who can move with confidence across
   human service settings and link various parts of the system? What must these leaders know and be able to do as
   interprofessional practitioners, university and community trainers, policymakers, and authors of legislation?

9. What policies and legislation are being developed at the
   local, state, and national levels to enhance and support
   the concept of collaborative delivery of services? How
   does categorical funding create unnecessary barriers to
   effective implementation? What policies are needed to
   allow flexible access to financial support, yet maintain
   accountability for program results? What additional
   policies need to be developed, and at what level?

10. What research and evaluation designs are appropriate
    for the studies that are needed? How do interprofes-
    sional collaborators design research that considers the
    whole system rather than isolated components? What
    are the purposes and the characteristics of participatory
    research? How do interprofessional collaborators bring
    service providers and children and families into the de-
    velopment of programs and the design of evaluation
    from the beginning? What is the most effective way to
    disseminate the best of research and practice so that inter-
    professional collaborators can learn from one another?

11. How can research address the measurement of outcomes
    that reflect the goals of multiple agencies, and how can it
    consider the multiple variables associated with interpro-
    fessional collaboration? How do interprofessional col-
    laborators describe relational qualities such as respect
    and caring and make them count in evaluation? What
    strategies are needed to communicate research findings
    to broad nonprofessional audiences?

12. How can the attitudes and the actions of decision makers be changed to give serious attention to all the foregoing questions?

The Challenge

In view of the conditions of children and families documented in this chapter, the overriding question that university personnel must ask themselves is, Are we obsolete? If they are not to become obsolete, they must connect professional preparation programs to the solution of society's problems. They must transform the preparation of human service professionals.

The human service professions have important work to do, together. They and society have to get beyond the "I'll take care of mine; you take care of yours" syndrome. They have a common stake that they must accept and profess to others. Interprofessional collaboration is not an option today; it is a necessity and an obligation of professional leadership.

In the face of mounting public criticism, almost every university in America seems to be engaged in a reexamination of its missions, but to date, very few have given the future of America's children a high priority in their deliberations. This situation is difficult to reconcile in a country in which one of every four children lives in poverty and 65,000–100,000 are homeless on any given night in the week. Higher education—indeed, society in general—needs a new generation of visionary university leaders who, in the tradition of the land grant idea of public service, can restore a sense of social purpose to the American university. The nation needs leaders who are personally involved in the mission of community building.

If the human service professions were to coalesce, they would constitute the largest workforce in the country. The potential of such a coalition to touch all spheres and levels of influence would be unequaled. Especially if coalition members kept their values straight and kept their focus clearly on the common goal of creating healthy, humane communities for America's children and families, they would represent power with a purpose.

APPENDIX 6.1

Characteristics of Selected
Interprofessional Education Programs

California State University, Fresno, Center for Collaboration for Children and Families

The development of an interprofessional academic program at California State University, Fresno is the direct result of having the Center for Collaboration for Children and Families on campus (Smith, 1993). The Multiple Subjects Credential Program at the university prepares early childhood education students to teach in elementary schools, with an emphasis on their developing and working in interprofessional, interdisciplinary collaboratives.

Professional preparation is integrated into three semesters of course work, fieldwork, and student teaching. Two interprofessional courses are required. A content course called Cultural Foundations Seminar exposes students to the terminology, the principles, and the public policy associated with interprofessional collaboration involving education, health, and social services. Students also design and analyze different collaborative models. In a fieldwork course titled Psychological Foundations Fieldwork, students observe children and families in real settings, develop a case study, and design an interprofessional service plan based on their observations and understanding of interprofessional collaboration. The classes are intended to help students develop their own philosophy of early childhood education and interprofessional collaboration.

California State University, Fullerton, School of Human Development and Community Service

The School of Human Development and Community Service at California State University, Fullerton offers two graduate-level integrated service courses (Topol, 1994). One is primarily content based; the other is field based. The course work demonstrates an integrative approach to curriculum development. The content-based course, Theory and Methods of Services Integration, is a theory course with some fieldwork required. The content includes the state of current service delivery systems, the changing environment of children and families, the nature of collaboration at the policy level, community-based service development and implementation, and outcomes-based funding and evaluation. One objective of the course is to provide students with the knowledge and the tools to understand the philosophy, the history, and the current state of collaborative service delivery.

In the second course, Practicum in Services Integration, students work in interdisciplinary teams in a setting in which integrated services are provided to families and children. They report on their experiences and findings. Through observation and participation in the field and involvement in seminars, students learn to identify the needs assessment and program evaluation processes most appropriate for design and implementation of collaborative services. In addition, students become able to evaluate current service delivery systems and design integrated ones. The practicum builds on the theory course and introduces additional theory from analysis of field experiences, readings, and group discussion.

Members of several service-providing departments participate in the program. Teams from elementary and bilingual education, nursing, child development, human services, educational administration, and criminal justice contribute to the program and to the Center for Collaboration for Children. Because many of the students and faculty in the program are also professionals in the community, the academic education offered reaches both students and practitioners.

Miami University, Institute for Educational Renewal

The program at Miami University in Ohio (Lawson & Briar, 1994) focuses on academically oriented public service. Content is directly related to the needs of children and families to be served in community-based, culturally competent, consumer-driven, integrated service systems.

Schools and social systems are partners. Service providers representing several agencies have been located at the same site. Services offered vary according to site. They involve school-community consortia, family support and housing services, economic development, and neighborhood revitalization. In a full-semester clinical experience, education students work with social workers, health care professionals, and academically oriented public service teachers learning to provide comprehensive family-centered services.

The Institute for Educational Renewal plans to extend curriculum linkages and field experiences to all the disciplines and community-based agencies needed to provide the interdisciplinary knowledge base for integrated service delivery. Undergraduate courses will be offered as part of general education, open to all students in the university; other interdisciplinary courses will be offered in the inter-professional graduate program. The departments involved include Family Studies and Social Work; Physical Education, Health and Sport Studies; and Educational Leadership.

Figure 6.2 presents a conceptual curriculum model designed by Lawson and Briar (1994) that they call the Interprofessional Village. Two excellent publications recently produced with support from the Danforth Foundation offer amplification of this curriculum and other components in the development of interprofessional education and integrated services: *Serving Children, Youth and Families Through Inter-professional Collaboration and Service Integration: A Framework for Action* (Briar & Lawson, 1994) and *Expanding Partnerships: Involving Colleges and Universities in Interprofessional Collaboration and Service Integration* (Lawson & Briar, 1994). These publications are an essential resource for any institution interested in developing interprofessional programs.

Seattle University, Community Service Learning Partnership

The Master in Teaching (MIT) program at Seattle University (Anderson & Guest, 1993) is a four-quarter, 60-credit-hour teaching licensure program that admits two cohorts of 50 students each year. It involves integrated, team-taught courses, extensive and varied pre-student-teaching field experiences, and a post-student-teaching course in which students reflect on their experiences and new knowl-edge. Interprofessional education and collaboration are the foci of the content courses as well as the field experiences.

At the center of the MIT program is the community internship, which is a two-term program requirement. It extends the student's experience beyond the university classroom into the community. Prospective teachers study and experience the role of the educator as

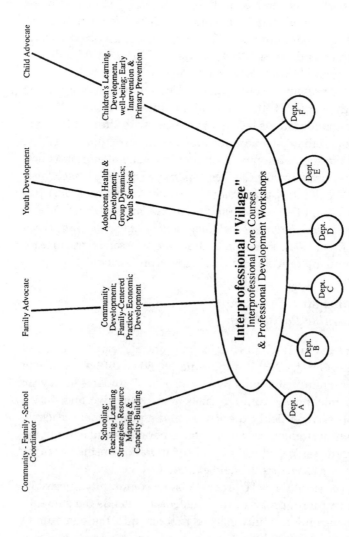

Figure 6.2. Interprofessional Village Model of Interprofessional Education and Integrated Services

SOURCE: From *Expanding Partnerships: Involving Colleges and Universities in Interprofessional Collaboration and Service Integration* by H. Lawson and K. H. Briar, Oxford, OH: Miami University, Institute for Educational Renewal; St. Louis, MO: Danforth Foundation. Copyright © 1994 by the Institute for Educational Renewal. Reprinted with permission.

a partner in developing collaborative efforts. MIT students learn to work with social workers, counselors, public administrators, nurses, physical and occupational therapists, psychologists, clergy, law enforcement personnel, lawyers, and physicians.

Several general outcomes are expected from participation in the community internship: that the students will (a) develop the knowledge, the skills, and the attitudes necessary for interprofessional collaboration to meet the needs of youth and families; (b) be able to identify a variety of human service agencies that can assist teachers in addressing students' needs; (c) demonstrate a personal commitment to social responsibility; and (d) develop the attitudes and the interpersonal skills needed to work effectively with culturally diverse groups of students. Pursuit of these four goals helps prospective teachers see children and families at the center of an interprofessional network of service providers.

Members of the MIT program expect the participating community agencies to (a) work with the intern to design an experience that allows direct contact with agency clients and professionals; (b) provide orientation and training needed to help ensure a successful internship; (c) engage in analysis and reflection activities with the intern; and (d) complete an evaluation of the intern's accomplishments.

University of New Mexico, Interdisciplinary Collaboration Program

The Interdisciplinary Collaboration Program at the University of New Mexico (Kane, 1993) was conceived over a number of years by a group in the College of Education. A reorganization of the College of Education that disbanded all departments, a request for proposals from AACTE, and a growing interest throughout the college in interprofessional education created the environment from which the program formed.

Students and practitioners from several professions participate in the program: (a) preservice elementary and middle school education students; (b) preservice community health education students; (c) preservice family studies students; (d) practicing teachers and professional staff in elementary and middle schools; and (e) professionals working in community health, social service, and criminal justice agencies. Possible future participants include medical, counseling, and educational administration students.

The program emphasizes collaboration between individuals, not organizations. The fundamental operating premise is that persons must get to know one another and develop relationships based on mutual respect and trust. Other premises are that (a) schools and agencies want specific and concrete results for children in a short period; (b) program staff want to create a mechanism that will produce information on how to foster collaboration; and (c) an increased level of participation from school and community agency personnel is desirable.

Interprofessional training in the program is context oriented; that is, it emerges from the needs of students and professionals as they work through the problems of children, youth, and families. Training for interdisciplinary collaboration occurs in several forums. Cross-professional information is integrated into foundation courses for future teacher educators, community health educators, and family studies professionals. Field placements are critical cross-training components. Bimonthly seminars are conducted for students and community practitioners at a local community center, where participants establish working relationships with one another and approach issues associated with providing support and services to children and families. Monthly debriefing meetings for students and faculty address successes, lessons learned, and the problems students are experiencing in their field placements. Students' evaluation of experiences and identification of needs provide feedback to the faculty, from which they build future learning experiences.

References

American Academy of Pediatrics. (1994). *Principles to link by: Integrating education, health and human services for children, youth and families* [Final report of a conference involving more than 50 organizations concerned with children, youth, and families]. Washington, DC: Author.

Anderson, J., & Guest, K. (1993, February). *Meeting the needs of children and youth: Seattle University's community service program for preservice teachers.* Paper presented at the meeting of the American Association of Colleges for Teacher Education, San Diego.

Bassuk, E. (1991). Homeless families. *Scientific American, 265*(12), 66–72.

Berrueta-Clement, J. R., Schweinhart, L. J., Barnett, W. S., Epstein, A., & Weikart, D. (1984). *Changed lives: The effects of the Perry preschool program on youths through age 19.* Ypsilanti, MI: High Scope.

Bishop, K. (1995). *Partnerships for change* [Grant description]. Burlington: University of Vermont, College of Education and Social Services.

Boyer, E. (1991). *Ready to learn: A mandate for the nation.* Princeton, NJ: Carnegie Foundation for the Advancement of Teaching.

Briar, K. H., & Lawson, H. (1994). *Serving children, youth and families through interprofessional collaboration and service integration: A framework for action.* Oxford, OH: Miami University, Institute for Educational Renewal; St. Louis, MO: Danforth Foundation.

Bruner, C. (1993). *Examining the costs of failure.* Unpublished manuscript, Center for the Study of Social Policy, Washington, DC.

Children's Defense Fund. (1994). *The state of America's children: Leave no child behind* (1994 yearbook). Washington, DC: Author.

Corin, N. (1994). AACTE/DeWitt Wallace–Reader's Digest Project fosters interagency collaboration. *AACTE Briefs, 15*(9), 2–3.

Corrigan, D. (1978). The political and moral contexts that produced P.L. 94-142. *Journal of Teacher Education, 29*(6), 10–14.

Corrigan, D. (1992a). Reflections on thirty years of building collaborative efforts. *Teaching Education, 4*(2), 1–10.

Corrigan, D. (1992b, Winter). Reinventing the American school. *Kappa Delta Pi Record, 28*(2), 35–42.

Corrigan, D. (1993, September-October). An idea whose time has come—again. *ATE Newsletter, 27*(1), 6–7.

Corrigan, D. (1994). Future directions of partnerships in education: Schools, universities, and human service systems. In M. J. O'Hair & S. J. Odell (Eds.), *Partnerships in education: Teacher education yearbook II* (pp. 281–292). Fort Worth, TX: Harcourt Brace.

Dewey, J. (1900). *The school and society.* Chicago: University of Chicago Press.

Dryfoos, J. G. (1994). *Full service schools: A revolution in health and social services for children, youth, and families.* San Francisco: Jossey-Bass.

Ducharme, E. (1988). The purpose of American education today: Concerns and assertions. In D. Corrigan (Ed.), *The purposes of education today: Conceptions of schooling* (pp. 9–20). Washington, DC: National Association of State Universities and Land-Grant Colleges.

Eisner, E. (1990). What's the purpose of school? *ASCD Update, 32*(10), 4.

Fordham University, National Center for Social Work and Education Collaboration. (n.d.). *Supporting children and families in the public schools* [Brochure]. New York: Author.

Fredericks, H. D. (1995). *Higher education curricula for integrated service programs* [Grant description]. Monmouth: Western Oregon State College, Teaching Research Division.

Hamburg, D. A. (1992). *Children of urban poverty: Approaches to a critical American problem.* New York: Carnegie Mellon University Press.

Hodgkinson, H. L. (1992). *A demographic look at tomorrow.* Washington, DC: Institute for Educational Leadership. (ERIC Document Reproduction Service No. ED 359 087)

Holmes Group. (1995). *Tomorrow's schools of education.* East Lansing, MI: Author.

Howsam, R. B., Corrigan, D. C., Denemark, G. W., & Nash, R. J. (1976). *Educating a profession.* Washington, DC: American Association of Colleges for Teacher Education.

Kane, W. (1993). [Response sheet: Program information on integrated services and interprofessional education]. Unpublished raw data, University of New Mexico, Albuquerque.

Kerner, J. (1968). *Two societies* (Report of the National Advisory Commission on Civil Disorders). Washington, DC: U.S. Government Printing Office.

Kozol, J. (1991). *Savage inequalities: Children in America's schools.* New York: Harper.

Lawson, H. (1994). Toward healthy learners, schools, and communities. *Journal of Teacher Education, 45*(1), 62–70.

Lawson, H., & Briar, K. H. (1994). *Expanding partnerships: Involving colleges and universities in interprofessional collaboration and service integration.* Oxford, OH: Miami University, Institute for Educational Renewal; St. Louis, MO: Danforth Foundation.

Levin, H. M., & Bachman, J. G. (1972). *The effects of dropping out: The costs to the nation of inadequate education* (Report prepared for the Select Committee on Equal Educational Opportunity of the U.S. Senate). Washington, DC: Congress of the United States. (ERIC Document Reproduction Service No. ED 072 171)

Lewit, E. M. (1992). Dropout rates for high school students. In R. E. Behrman (Ed.), *The future of children: School-linked services* (pp. 127–130). Los Altos, CA: Center for the Future of Children.

Maternal and Child Health Bureau. (1993). *Child health USA '92.* Washington, DC: Maternal and Child Health Information Resource Center.

National Center for Children in Poverty. (1990). *Five million children: A statistical profile of our poorest young citizens.* New York: Author.

National Center for Health Statistics. (1993). *Children's health.* Unpublished report, National Center for Health Statistics, Office of Public Affairs, Washington, DC.

National Commission on Children. (1991). *Beyond rhetoric: A new American agenda for children and families.* Washington, DC: Author.

National Commission on Children. (1993). *Just the facts: A summary of recent information on America's children and their families.* Washington, DC: Author.

National Education Goals Panel. (1992). *The National Education Goals report: Building a nation of leaders.* Washington, DC: U.S. Government Printing Office.

National Institute of Mental Health. (1993). *Children's mental health.* Unpublished report, National Institute of Mental Health, Epidemiology and Psychopathology Research Branch, Washington, DC.

Office of Educational Research and Improvement. (1993). *Together we can: A guide for crafting a profamily system of education and human services.* Washington, DC: U.S. Government Printing Office.

Office of Educational Research and Improvement. (1995). *School-linked comprehensive services for children and families: What we know and need to know.* Washington, DC: U.S. Government Printing Office.

Orland, M. E. (1990). Demographics of disadvantage: Intensity of childhood poverty and its relationship to educational achievement. In J. I. Goodlad & P. Keating (Eds.), *Access to knowledge: An agenda for our nation's schools* (pp. 43–58). New York: College Entrance Examination Board.

Schorr, L. B., & Schorr, D. (1988). *Within our reach: Breaking the cycle of disadvantage.* New York: Doubleday.

Seigel, I. H. (1969). *The Kerner Commission report and economic policy.* Kalamazoo, MI: W. E. Upjohn Institute for Employment Research.

Sergiovanni, T. J. (1994). Organizations or communities? Changing the metaphor changes the theory. *Educational Administration Quarterly, 30,* 214–226.

Sia, C., & Taba, S. (1995). *Health and education collaboration project* [Grant description]. Honolulu: Hawaii Medical Association.

Smith, D. O. (1993). [Response sheet: Program information on integrated services and interprofessional education]. Unpublished raw data, Center for Collaboration for Children and Families, Fresno, CA.

State Education Leader. (1994). [Newsletter of the Education Commission of the States; special issue on interagency collaboration] *13*(1), 1–16.

Task Force on Interprofessional Education. (1995). [Notes from session at conference, "School-Linked Comprehensive Services for Children and Families"]. Unpublished report.

Texas Education Agency. (1993). *Family and community support: Coordinated education, health and human services.* Austin: Author.

Tonnies, F. (1957). *Community and society* [Gemeinschaft und gesellschaft] (C. P. Loomis, Ed.). New York: Harper & Row. (Original work published 1887)

Topol, K. (1994). [Response sheet: Program information on integrated services and interprofessional education]. Unpublished raw data, Center for Collaboration for Children, Fullerton, CA.

U.S. Department of Health and Human Services. (1992). *Healthy children 2000: National health promotion and disease prevention objectives related to mothers, infants, children, adolescents, and youth.* Boston: Jones and Bartlett.

U.S. Department of Labor. (1991). *What work requires of school: A SCANS report for America 2000.* Washington, DC: Author.

A Response to Chapter 6, "Teacher Education and Interprofessional Collaboration: Creation of Family-Centered, Community-Based Integrated Service Systems," by Dean Corrigan

ROY A. EDELFELT
University of North Carolina at Chapel Hill
North Carolina State University

In Chapter 6, Dean Corrigan makes a convincing and impressive case for interprofessional education. I concur intellectually with his premises. However, persuading the professions to integrate their services is another proposition. At times, Corrigan seems to be so deep into his subject that the ordinary reader might not fathom his contentions. For example, as he admits, integrated service systems alone cannot solve the problems of children and families in poverty. Jobs, a new sense of urgency, and a wide range of partners are a beginning step toward solving that problem, but there are other barriers. Of a different order, yet just as serious, are such obstacles as achieving cooperation among professions, decreasing turf protection, developing a greater concern for the common welfare, and reducing selfishness among professionals.

Certainly, all will benefit if Corrigan's vision becomes a reality. As he suggests, America's future is at stake. In the current political climate, though, the community of place and kinship that he advocates is elusive. The society is large, complex, and impersonal. Community of mind may be more possible. If people are aware of and care about the conditions that Corrigan reports, they can think about and act to resolve the crisis. There can be bonding around common goals, as there is bonding around the Bill of Rights and the Constitution. My recommendation is to strive for community of mind, to revive the notion of caring about all the nation's citizens and to rekindle Americans' commitment to doing so.

Collaboration and Centrality of Purpose

Corrigan's observation that teachers, principals, counselors, and other educators should learn how to collaborate with partners in other human service professions is on the mark. Learning how to collaborate is no easy matter, however. Acquiring common knowledge, preparing to work together across agencies, understanding the policies of integrated services, and learning the political strategies to implement and influence those policies—those tasks constitute a tremendously ambitious agenda. It is multidimensional. In contrast, the professional preparation of educators is seldom multidimensional. Not only is teacher education subject centered, it is profession centered. Teacher educators slip too easily back into their own professional concerns and programs. Corrigan does this as he outlines the important questions of teacher education instead of sticking with the context of interprofessional education. Then, as he addresses the problems that must be faced and the results that must be achieved, he addresses the confluence of human activity necessary for integrated services and interprofessional education.

In writing about education, Corrigan does not describe how it might extend into the total growth of the individual, nor how it would contend with environmental influences outside the school. When he suggests that human services should address "persistent life situations," however, he offers an inkling of a new concept of human service. In addition, professionals must gain empathy for people who are different, people who were born into difficult circumstances, who live in substandard environments, who have been raised with values that digress from middle-class norms, and whose life experiences have been influenced by unique, often tragic twists of chance.

Goals for Teachers

The list of competencies and characteristics that Corrigan expects teacher education programs to produce in new teachers is complete but overwhelming. It goes beyond overwhelming when he augments the already extensive goals to be achieved in an undergraduate program with preparation for working with other professionals in serving children and families. Maybe he should have suggested a fifth-year internship to accommodate both teaching and interprofessional goals.

The most important of his goals for teachers—and the one that is most often neglected—is that of helping teachers develop positive, humane values, attitudes, and convictions. How teachers would behave as a result of those dispositions and persuasions is only implied. This would have been a good time to endorse again the importance of the teacher of teachers modeling an integrated interprofessional approach.

Corrigan's belief that test scores should never be used as the sole indicator of the achievement of school students or prospective teachers is essential to the philosophy that he advocates. Particularly admirable is his calling for assessments of prospective teachers' competence in "making good judgments about people and situations, having the courage and the ability to know when to persist in risk-taking situations, making choices and seeing them through to completion, and demonstrating a sense of loyalty and a concern for the human rights of others as well as [their] own rights" (p. 145).

Threats to America's Children

The evidence that Corrigan presents on the needs, the problems, and the conditions of American children and families makes a solid case for action. The emphasis is appropriately on persons who are poor and disadvantaged. Concentrating only on that segment of society may be too limiting, however. Many middle- and upper-class children and families live vapid lives and need support and assistance. It might be better to think of all people as requiring integrated services. Abuse, a lack of caring, and a need for human services are present across society, even though need may be well hidden or unadmitted among the more privileged classes.

As Corrigan points out, the relationship of one hardship to another tends to complicate growth and development and quality of life. The domino effect may stop only when there is some human service intervention. Strongly suggested in what Corrigan advocates is interdependence. Professionals as well as laypersons have much to learn about living in interdependent communities. There is too much stress today on independence.

Implications for Schools

On the subject of implications for schools, Corrigan's identification of three main functions of education is helpful but not sufficiently complete. Functions 2, connecting children and families with other health and human service agencies, and 3, collaborating with policymakers at local, state, and national levels to support integrated services, are not generally operational in schools today, but should be. Function 1, teaching relevant knowledge, misses the social and civic responsibility of school. As Corrigan states and implies elsewhere in the chapter, there is more to schooling than developing the intellect.

A real problem in creating a center for interprofessional human services is the matter of location. Corrigan notes that the school is the one place that all children attend. He then concedes that all human services need not be provided on the school site. He does not go far enough, though. The institution of school as Americans have known it may be obsolete. Some communities may need a community development center, a place where all the human services are available. Professional or interprofessional development schools could be such places, provided that they expand their services beyond education. If all or most human services contribute to growth and learning, development, and the enhancement of life, then creating a service center makes sense. It may also eliminate waste, overlap, and redundancy. It could be more effective and efficient, as Corrigan suggests—a one-stop service.

Preparation for Leadership

The minor attention that Corrigan gives to the preparation of leaders for interprofessional human service centers is to be expected. Too little is known as yet about how and what to do with leader preparation. Most of the trailblazers have learned by doing. Documenting their learnings, developing case studies of how and why the pioneers have become what they are, would be instructive. Care should be taken not to reduce such knowledge quickly to prescriptive courses of study. Learning by doing should remain a central part of leadership development.

In addition to what Corrigan suggests for leadership training, there should be study of professional cultures, professional hierarchies, and the real and the assumed complexity and intricacy of various professions.

Reporting on Projects Under Way

Corrigan's brief reporting on projects under way brings a reality to the theory and the philosophy presented in the chapter. Interprofessional education and integrated services are not just talk. There are live projects out there that demonstrate interprofessional human service activities. It will be important to learn how these programs fare: whether they continue after grant funds terminate, whether ownership develops in the institutions where pilots are operating, whether funding becomes a regular part of public or private support. Also important to learn will be whether changes take place in community human service practices, whether professional preparation programs are effective, and most important, whether programs improve the lives of children and families.

Sharing news on interprofessional education programs is very helpful, and selecting some that are under the leadership of professionals other than educators testifies to the many human service agencies that are engaging in interprofessional projects. Summarizing the lessons learned in the short history of interprofessional education begins to establish criteria for evaluating programs and provides guiding principles for new programs.

Conclusion

Breaking the mold and changing the culture in professional programs in universities will be difficult. Cross-department collaboration is often difficult. Bridging chasms separating professional schools is even more challenging. Adding to that becoming more service oriented, doing more than dispensing knowledge, and altering research to address persistent life situations means changing priorities and practices and establishing different policies and reward systems. If preparation programs also become vehicles for service, there must be radical revisions in higher education.

There is among university faculty the knowledge to implement such programs. Whether there is the wisdom and the commitment to take the risks necessary remains to be seen. Corrigan is right in declaring, "Interprofessional collaboration is not an option today; it is a necessity and an obligation of professional leadership" (p. 162).

If such programs address the problems of children and families, if they inform practice, model behavior, and integrate knowledge and service, that will be a great achievement. The dream is worth pursuing.

7

Partnerships for Quality Teaching

RICHARD W. RILEY
U.S. Department of Education

The executive and legislative branches of the federal government are in the middle of a battle over congressional plans to make drastic cuts in K–12 and higher education. President Bill Clinton is fighting to protect Pell Grants, Direct Lending for college students, Head Start, Goals 2000, Title I, Safe and Drug-Free Schools, educational technology, and other key programs.

President Clinton is also fighting proposals to cut Eisenhower Professional Development Grants. Cuts would deny teachers the training that they need to help students reach higher academic standards. Eisenhower Grants help school districts improve professional development through high-quality programs in core academic subjects. They also support schools in forming collaborations with colleges and universities.

Recently, the U.S. Senate took a step in the right direction. It voted to restore more than $1.7 billion in cuts to education and to bring the fiscal 1996 appropriation level very close to the 1995 level. Goals 2000, Title I, Safe and Drug-Free Schools, educational technology, and School-to-Work—all of these and other programs were restored to higher levels, but still not quite the levels we would like. Summer jobs and Head Start were also restored to nearly full health.

That is the good news. The not-so-good news is that the House of Representatives has not budged from the appropriations bill that it passed last year, which calls for unprecedented cuts of nearly $3 billion in education. This includes the elimination of Goals 2000.

What is so tragic about these cuts is that they are not necessary to balance the national budget. The president has proposed a plan that would protect America's investments in education and training over the next 7 years and still balance the budget. ATE and AACTE are working together and with the Department of Education on many of these issues.

The president and I cannot sit idly by and watch these attempts to undermine efforts to improve the quality of teaching and learning in America's classrooms. We have the greatest admiration for the nation's teachers and teacher educators. We watched with alarm and sadness as previous administrations often made teachers the scapegoats for the schools' problems. We decided to move in a new direction, developing partnerships with teachers and colleges to make education better. Together, we have achieved great breakthroughs. The reauthorization of the Elementary and Secondary Education Act gives teachers real flexibility to innovate. The reauthorization of the Office of Educational Research and Improvement makes its research and information resources much more accessible. The Gun-Free Schools Act will give teachers and children the chance to teach and learn, not dodge bullets. The Family Involvement Partnership for Learning will encourage parents to take more responsibility for their children's education and to reconnect with teachers.

One of our proudest moments came when the president signed the Goals 2000 act. Goals 2000 encourages states and communities to raise standards, and it promotes collaborative efforts between schools and higher education to advance teacher training. Already, many districts and schools are using their Goals 2000 money for professional development.

Goals 2000 also makes teacher education one of the eight National Education Goals. The goal declares, "The nation's teaching force will have access to programs for the continued improvement of its professional skills and the opportunity to acquire the knowledge and skills needed to instruct and prepare all American students for the next century." The National Education Goal for teacher education sends the message, loud and clear, that teacher preparation and continuing professional development must play an essential role in education reform. When I visit schools across the nation, particularly schools that have turned themselves around, I am constantly reminded of the importance of quality teaching. I say to a principal or an administrator,

"What is the most important reason for your success?" The answer very frequently is, "Good teachers and good staff development."

With this in mind, I established the Department of Education's professional development team to examine the best available research and exemplary practices and to develop principles that could guide teachers and policymakers. Hundreds of educators and organizations helped the Department of Education develop these guidelines.

The result is "Principles of High-Quality Professional Development" (U.S. Department of Education, n.d.). The principles focus on such important issues as resources, research, time, planning, evaluation, standards, and use of technology. These principles are grounded in the philosophy that teacher development does not end with graduation from college but is a careerlong process. A high-quality teacher education program attracts talented and diverse candidates, prepares them well, provides them with strong support during induction, and helps them as teachers update their knowledge and skills throughout their careers. In other words, it accomplishes what educators are trying to achieve for the nation's children: learning for a lifetime.

I recognize that the career-long continuum to which I refer is different from what exists in most schools today. Schools lack support systems for beginning teachers; the profession throws them into the pool and watches them try to stay afloat. The profession should be supportive from the beginning, and even earlier. It must make a serious commitment to recruiting teachers as early as possible, long before college. Moreover, it should think of professional development for experienced teachers as more than a one-shot workshop or an inconsequential graduate course. Professional development programs must demonstrate that they truly make a difference in teacher performance and student achievement.

I also urge you to strengthen collaborations and encourage the sharing of expertise. When teachers leave the nation's schools of education, their professors should not just wish them a happy life and never see them again. Professors should welcome teachers back after they have been out in the real world, for they will have good ideas for improving teacher education. Furthermore, professors should go into the elementary and secondary schools and share their experience and ideas. The doors should be open on both ends.

I mentioned technology earlier. The world is changing dramatically. I used to tell folks that I lived in Greenville, South Carolina. Now I tell them that I live at "secretary@ed.gov." We need to make sure that teachers become comfortable and creative users of information technology. This too will take more than a 1-day methods course for preservice teachers.

That is why I have sought the partnership of teachers, business leaders, and others, looking for the best ways to make computers available in schools. This process will soon be completed, and President Clinton will announce our Technology Initiative early next year. The administration's goal is to provide all teachers with the training that they need.

On the subject of partnerships, I emphasize the importance of reaching out to others, particularly parents. Teacher education programs ought to prepare teachers to work closely with families. Currently, only half of all states require parent involvement training for teacher certification, and most programs concentrate on early childhood and elementary school training. I would like to see that extended to all grades because the importance of family-school connections cannot be overemphasized. Educators must focus on this issue like a laser beam.

In the information age, no task is more important, no responsibility greater, than teaching. I was reminded of this recently when I traveled with the president to Northern Ireland. Children in Northern Ireland go to either Catholic or Protestant schools. There is no integration. In the public schools in America, the melting pot is boiling over. Children of all races, faiths, languages, and nationalities are thrown together. Students with disabilities and special learning needs are an increasing challenge for teachers in classrooms that are already overcrowded. Many students come from poor, troubled families, and often they are no strangers to violence. Moreover, the problems are everywhere—in the suburbs and rural areas as well as in the cities. American educators educate the world, and they must deal with a world of challenges.

Teacher education programs must help cushion the shock. They must have a healthy dose of "real-world relevancy."

Teachers should not have to do the job alone, of course. Parents, businesspeople, social workers, health care professionals, safety officials, and others should be involved.

A new generation of young people is out there, and millions more—record numbers, in fact—are coming along. Some call it a tidal wave of teenagers. That is why the job that teacher educators are doing is so important to America. They should recognize the challenge, work to meet it, and feel good about their great contributions.

I close by quoting Pat Conroy, author of *The Prince of Tides*, a fellow South Carolinian, and a friend of mine. Pat has written a new novel called *Beach Music*. In it, the character Jack McCall thinks of his friend Ledare, who is teaching Jack's young daughter Leah. Seeing Leah grow under Ledare's tutelage, Jack observes, "One can do anything, anything at all, if provided with a passionate and gifted teacher." I believe that America can do anything if provided with gifted, well-prepared teachers.

Reference

U.S. Department of Education. (n.d.). *Building bridges: The mission and principles of professional development* [Brochure]. Washington, DC: Author.

8

Building a Strong Foundation: The Importance of Knowledge and High Standards in Improving Teacher Education

SHARON PORTER ROBINSON
Office of Educational Research and Improvement
U.S. Department of Education

We in the Office of Educational Research and Improvement (OERI) are pleased to have had a chance to support the National Congress on Teacher Education because the congress represents a good beginning toward collaboration and the creation of new partnerships in this extremely important field of teacher development and support. It has been reassuring to hear comments such as "We need to do this again" and "We need to replicate this back home" from so many participants.

I must offer a challenge, though. Meetings like the National Congress on Teacher Education should always build on what has been learned previously. If the groups represented at the congress come together again, they should be asking the next generation of questions, based on evaluating their diverse experiences in bringing about changes and refining the challenges shared in the course of the first congress. We in OERI eagerly await the congress's action recommendations. As Secretary of Education Richard Riley and various other representatives of the U.S. Department of Education have indicated, we are determined to bring a new kind of coherence and power to all the programmatic activities within the Department of Education that support the development of teachers and other educators. This power will come from something that sounds very simple but can be very difficult. We are trying to apply what is known to what is done across the Department of Education. Whether in the Office of Elementary and Secondary Education, Vocational and Adult Education, or Special Education, or in OERI, we are trying to ensure that all of our efforts to encourage excellence and diversity in the educator workforce are based consistently on the best that is known. We will require time and resources for inquiry, reflection, and action that will result in continuous improvement. That is a high standard, an important one that I ask teacher educators and other stakeholders to consider as essential.

In that vein, it is well worth noting that ATE and AACTE, through their elected and staff leaders, set a high standard for collaboration in organizing the National Congress on Teacher Education. Leonard Kaplan brought the idea to OERI and was a determined advocate and a strong catalyst for getting various groups together and beginning this conversation. There has been a true spirit of cooperation between ATE and AACTE that we in OERI hope will be continued for the betterment of the entire teacher education community, including the many other stakeholders represented at the congress. I also want to acknowledge publicly the very committed and competent support for the congress from the Department of Education, especially from my special adviser for professional development, Joseph Vaughan, and Secretary Riley's senior adviser on teaching, Terry Dozier, and from various program offices across the agency.

We believe that the Department of Education comes to this partnership with some legitimate credentials. The department is, in fact, involved heavily in the process of change. We are struggling to understand how to cull the most valid and valuable knowledge from what is out there and to build on it to help practitioners and policymakers create strategies that will support all learners across this country. Our mission is a long-term commitment that can be met only if we are good at creating an organization that will be guided by rigorous inquiry, responsiveness to our customers, and continuous improvement. Our goal is to create a department that has the capacity and the culture to become stronger, leave a legacy of support for change and improvement, and leave a widely shared vision of high expectations for and devotion to every learner in America. I think that the Department of Education has found many ways to institutionalize this message. Many of our staff understand what change entails, and we come as colleagues to work with other stakeholders in improving the preparation and career-long development of teachers.

The nation is coming to understand that if we in the profession are going to bring about the kind of meaningful reform that we are discussing, it has to begin with qualified teachers who have the capacity to bring new knowledge and new technology to meet the needs of an increasingly diverse student population. That should be our shared vision, and we must find ways to define, expand, and enrich it and—most important—to make it a reality.

But teachers cannot do the job alone. There has been much discussion about creating learning organizations in schools and higher education institutions and in their various communities. Many of the interests inside and outside education institutions that must be represented in a true community of learners were represented at the congress, but we in the profession must strive to be even more inclusive and more open to good ideas from whatever sources are available.

There have been discussions of what a profession is, what role knowledge plays in a profession, and what research does to support a profession. There has been an examination of the cycle of continuous knowledge development and use that must be the foundation of a profession. Expanding, nurturing, and sharing that knowledge in appropriate and relevant ways gives vibrancy and credibility to practice.

That is perhaps the most challenging aspect of teacher education today. Two essential questions are, How do teacher educators ensure for themselves access to and understanding of knowledge about competent practice? and, How do they share that knowledge with those who require it to make professional decisions that address the talents and the needs of all students? These questions should drive the definition of what needs to change and the strategies for reform in teacher development, whether the focus is on recruitment, preparation, licensing, and induction of beginning teachers or the continuing development, support, and recognition of experienced teachers. How is the profession using knowledge about competent teaching practice?

Quality control in teaching is another confounding factor. Virtually all the states are wrestling with how to improve the licensing of new teachers through efforts like the Interstate New Teacher Assessment and Support Consortium. Across the nation, the profession is wondering how to recognize accomplished teachers newly certified through the arduous process designed by the National Board for

Professional Teaching Standards (NBPTS). Heated and passionate debates about accreditation have been raging, as they have about alternative routes to teacher certification. All of this really comes back to the basic question, Do standards really matter, and if so, whose standards must they be?

I hinted earlier at my answer to that question. Standards should matter, and they should belong to those who are members of the teaching profession, whether they are teaching in schools, higher education institutions, or other settings. Standards should be based on what the profession agrees is the best available knowledge about competent practice. Standards represent the only benchmarks that the profession can use to decide what are legitimate criteria in licensing, certification, and accreditation, indeed in teacher development writ large. If there are no standards, anything at all will yield a product that someone will be willing to call competent, or worse, will yield teachers that no one will be willing to call competent. Unless teachers and teacher educators exercise professional responsibility to guard the integrity of professional practice, there will be no assurances of the quality of persons entering the professional community. A profession cannot survive, indeed does not exist, without standards that society holds as rigorous and valid. It is as simple as that.

How do teacher educators contribute to standards that matter? They have to agree on what they know while leaving freedom for legitimate differences about what that knowledge means for improving practice. The investments of OERI and its predecessors have produced many findings that are relevant to defining standards. Educators sometimes get together and make meaning out of those findings, and the profession gains new content, new strategies, and new ways of instructing and supporting learning. Sometimes when a new approach is derived from those findings, like cooperative learning, within a short time everyone is doing it. That is, everybody is doing something and calling it what the new approach is, even if in some cases that something bears little more than superficial resemblance to the actual research-based approach. People are able to do that because the profession does not have standards. A research colleague who was doing an evaluation of a new teacher development program in California a few years ago lamented to me that she was having a difficult time finding a control group. Even though the new initiative had just begun, everybody had something they called the innovation. Teacher educators clearly do not yet have a common definition, in most cases not even a common language, about what is known. There is not a strong consensus on the knowledge base that supports teaching. Perhaps the only way that the profession can achieve that consensus is to hold another congress, get some good facilitators, close the doors, have a good debate, and then announce to the world what has been decided. Although I suspect that is not the best way to get the job done, the profession does have to identify the knowledge that it embraces. That is what defines all of us teacher educators.

From this knowledge, we in the profession can bridge to the standards of practice that we need for licensing, certification, accreditation, and teacher development in general. If the profession is willing and able to agree on that knowledge and what it means for practice, we will have addressed the issues of excellence, diversity, and unity simultaneously.

An analogy from another profession may help illustrate the point. Educators constantly hear medical analogies of varying degrees of appropriateness, but I think that what I am going to describe contains many valuable lessons for teacher educators. In medical education, there is an approach called problem-based learning. One module using this approach focuses on a patient who presents himself to his family physician with a 2-month history of increasing shortness of breath. He is admitted for further workup. The medical students go through the module by first meeting and interviewing the actual patient and then at every subsequent step being presented with several options that they might explore. Their analysis as a team is evaluated by their guide, their teacher, and the team comes up with a diagnosis and a prescription. If some medical students cannot be present at the interviews because of sheer numbers or because they are on another campus, they can participate through use of interactive technology.

One reason that medicine can present its cases in this way is that it has agreed on definitions and standards about all the diagnostic and prescriptive procedures that practitioners might consider. It has standards of practice that the profession agrees are acceptable. Problem-based learning allows flexibility in what courses of action to take, given the particular case, and it encourages collegial approaches in deciding what needs to be done. In this case, it puts the emphasis on teacher as guide rather than as purveyor of knowledge. The students have the primary responsibility for understanding the patient, exploring options, and deciding jointly on a course of action. In other words, they learn by doing under the guidance of a teacher who is there to make sure that no harm is done to the patient. Moreover, this medical school is willing to say when something is not up to standards. Student learning can be productive because the definitions of content and skill requisites are clear.

Teacher educators, whether based in higher education institutions, schools, regional service centers, or other settings, have to find the same courage. They have to define models of practice that will ensure that all prospective and practicing teachers have opportunities to learn to respond to all students in competent ways and with creative, caring, and wise professional judgments. They have to agree on standards that will define quality in everything that they do. Then, they have to have the courage to evaluate rigorously and authentically and make judgments about what is up to standards and what is not. Otherwise, as the size and the diversity of the student population increases over the coming years, a workforce will be there, and its members will be called teachers, but many may not be qualified in the ways that the profession, the students, and the nation's future demand.

Furthermore, if teacher education programs cannot ensure their customers that their graduates are of high quality, the temptation to produce teachers through quick and superficial alternative means will be heightened, especially in areas of shortages. It is reasonable to assume that, as is now the case, these alternative-route programs will be of mixed quality. Undoubtedly, some entrepreneurs will recognize opportunities for profit and seize the moment. I am not against free enterprise, and I am certainly not against profit. I do care deeply about quality, and I ask teacher educators and the diverse stakeholders represented at the congress to join me in a revolution to create both a demand for and a supply of high-quality teacher education and teaching practices. Every student in every classroom in America is entitled to a teacher of excellence who can respond to his or her talents and needs.

9

Agenda for Tomorrow

ROY A. EDELFELT
University of North Carolina at Chapel Hill
North Carolina State University

This chapter summarizes the action plans prepared by members of 20 small groups at the National Congress on Teacher Education. It also reflects the evaluations submitted at the close of the congress.

Discussion was the feature of the congress. Participants met four times from Sunday noon to Tuesday noon—a total of 4 hours and 30 minutes—to discuss and debate issues on four themes, each a motif for a half-day session: (a) linking teacher development to conditions of teaching in schools and colleges and student achievement; (b) recruitment, selection, preparation, and support needed to staff schools in the 21st century; (c) changes needed in policy and practice, research, and partnerships to create and maintain high-quality teacher preparation and professional development; and (d) recommendations for action plans to effect the changes needed in policy and practice, research, and partnerships.

Chapters 2, 3, 4, 5, and 6, by Mary E. Diez, Nancy L. Zimpher, Carl A. Grant, Martin J. Haberman, and Dean Corrigan, respectively, were prepared especially for the congress and sent to participants in advance of the meeting. Together with the keynote speech by Mary Hatwood Futrell (Chapter 1) and the address by Richard W. Riley (Chapter 7), they constituted the major inputs to participants before and during the congress. There was also, of course, the experience and the expertise that participants brought to the meeting. Sharon

Porter Robinson's presentation (Chapter 8) was delivered at the closing session and therefore did not provide input into action plans.

Almost all the action plans reflect the concept of teacher education as a continuum, beginning with recruitment and extending through selection, initial preparation, clinical experiences, internships, licensure, induction, inservice education, teaching experience, professional certification, and career-long professional development. The concept of a continuum may have become prominent partly because of the way in which the congress was orchestrated; that is, the themes may have implied a continuum. On the other hand, the time may have come when the stakeholders clearly see teacher education as a continuum because of the interrelatedness of its phases. In the past, efforts and activities in teacher education have seldom been addressed as a continuum. As teaching becomes a full-fledged profession, they must be. In the words of one participant, "Learning to teach is lifelong."

A second and almost unanimous proposal from the small groups is that teacher education be knowledge based and that all assessments of it explore and ascertain the database on which it operates.

A third theme running through action plans is more emphasis on research: identifying, conducting, disseminating, using, and validating it, in all phases of teacher education.

The action plans deal with eight categories of proposals:

1. *Process and activities:* extensive further discussion by a wide variety of stakeholders, replications of the congress at the state level, organization of local summit meetings and forums, another national congress, and a National Congress on Teacher Education as a separate but related entity

2. *Participants:* involvement of representatives from a much-expanded realm of stakeholders—the public, businesses, legislatures, and other human service professions, as well as education and professional associations—in future deliberations on reforms

3. *Phases of teacher education:* equal attention to all phases of teacher education (necessary to achieve improvement)— recruitment, selection, preparation, clinical experiences,

induction, licensure, inservice practice and education, certification, and career-long professional development

4. *The substance of preparation:* continuation of the search to
identify and maintain (a) a knowledge base in professional studies and clinical experiences and (b) a solid general education; and further investigation of the nature and
the scope of teacher adequacy in the disciplines

5. *Governance:* collaboration and partnerships with schools,
professional organizations, unions, learned societies,
health and human service groups, citizens, legislators, and
other individuals and groups that deal with children and
professional preparation; national accreditation through
the National Council for Accreditation of Teacher Education
(NCATE); and self-governance, possibly with a National
Congress on Teacher Education as a separate but related
entity (analogous to the set-up in professional sports)

6. *Resources and time:* reasonable budgets, administrative
support, adequate staffing, and a restructuring of the
teacher's schedule

7. *Public relations and policy development:* publicity for the
ideas generated by the National Congress on Teacher Education and establishment of policies and mechanisms to
undergird the social and administrative systems of the
institutions responsible for education and human services

8. *Autonomy and interdependence:* recognition of state sover-
eignty in education—for example, encouragement to each
state to hold its own congress, thereby increasing input
from stakeholders on the substance and the direction of
teacher education at the level at which decisions are made

The remainder of this chapter summarizes and analyzes recommended actions in specific areas, sometimes at the local, state, or
national level only, other times at two or three of these levels. In many
ways, teacher education functions within state boundaries. In other
ways, it is a national enterprise. Teacher educators themselves oper-
ate in a national market, and the speed and the breadth of communication and the ease of travel erase state boundaries in many matters.

Summary and Analysis of Action Plans

Recruitment

Suggestions on recruiting people to teaching abound in the action plans. There is a call to rethink what the teacher of the future should be in terms of changing needs in education. There are suggestions to recruit a more diverse population (particularly minorities and high-demand candidates), target academically gifted students, attract teachers through partnerships with secondary schools and community colleges, connect with historically black colleges, and provide a career ladder for paraprofessionals. There is a challenge to find and develop tools and techniques for selecting sensitive persons, assessing candidates' attitudes toward students and their potential for teaching, and addressing ideology and the ability to nurture learning in children (portrayed by one group as teachers for children).

The action plans give minor attention to the dilemma of supply and demand. Information on the adequacy of the supply of teachers and the needs of employers for teachers has been a perennial problem. The many ways in which the 50 states collect and report supply-and-demand data and the absence of reliable means of forecasting complicate the problem. National and state data and mechanisms to predict, plus ways to provide remedies for shortages and oversupply, are badly needed. A partial solution might be scholarships to attract teachers, particularly to rural and urban areas.

State and Local Concerns

The plans express a need to review current practices in teacher education at the state level, examine state laws and regulations, and assess their efficacy and currency. (The legal control of teacher education is, of course, at the state level.) For example, the plans recommend assessments to confirm that prospective teachers are exposed to best practices. Highlighting and disseminating best practices is a recurrent suggestion in the plans. Interest in inspecting teacher education at the state level introduces the notion of boundaries, such as how much state requirements constrain teacher education, whether state approval is provincial, how much colleges and universities collaborate with public schools, and whether teacher education is responsive to urban and rural needs.

Local concerns in the action plans include whether adequate linkages exist with disciplines in the arts and sciences, whether exemplary practice is modeled, how much valued content is taught, and whether students are being exposed to teachers with exceptional skills. There is strong support for school-college partnerships and for collaboration among schools within the university and with other human service groups that deal with children. The purpose of these alliances would be to address the broad array of social, health, and psychological problems that children and families face.

Clinical Experiences

The action plans identify early field experiences, extensive clinical experiences in a variety of settings, and extended internships as necessary components of preservice education. Particularly prominent in the plans are exposures to schoolwork and study in addition to a focus on teaching skills—on topics such as multicultural education, health and social services, use of technology, integrated curriculum, and assessment of student learning. A number of action plans call for significant interaction with other human service preprofessionals, training in cohorts, and stronger support for nontraditional students. Training in cohorts represents a way to eliminate fragmentation, which leaves the prospective teacher responsible for synthesizing courses and other experiences, and to promote synthesis and continuity through longitudinal relationships with peers.

There is a clear and loud insistence on data-based teacher education, expressed in various ways. Teacher educators must help prospective teachers develop a thirst for inquiry from the time that they first enter teacher education. Action research skills must be emphasized along with the traditional quantitative and qualitative research skills so that teachers can be producers of and contributors to the knowledge base of professional practice.

The action plans call for states to adopt common standards for teacher licensure (with appropriate local adaptations) such as those enunciated in *Model Standards for Beginning Teacher Licensing and Development,* by the Interstate New Teacher Assessment and Support Consortium (INTASC; 1992). There is encouragement for a common set of program standards for state approval and national accreditation by NCATE. There is also support for the standards of the National Board for Professional Teaching Standards (NBPTS) and advocacy of their use for professional development and performance appraisal in local school districts.

Several plans would establish and find resources for a national task force or consortium to bring together the many groups working on standards—NCATE, INTASC, NBPTS, the National Association of State Directors of Teacher Education and Certification (NASDTEC), the ATE Quality Standards Commission, and so on. The goal: to establish common or core standards and develop processes for applying those standards. The consortium could reduce overlap and expense, some of which might be allocated to applying standards. The consortium might also serve to ensure that preparation (and licensure), induction, certification, accreditation, and continuing professional development are addressed more evenly. With common standards, the proposal for encouraging national reciprocity in teacher licensure would be simplified. With ease in moving across state lines, reciprocity across the nation could be connected to national retirement and pension systems for teachers. Most higher education personnel already have that option through the Teachers Insurance and Annuity Association.

Induction

Induction into the *job* of teaching receives major attention in the action plans. This may be no surprise because few states have established policies, adequate funding, or trained mentors for the induction of beginning teachers. Induction into the *profession* of teaching, however, garners little attention.

Proposals for induction into the job of teaching include assessing the causes, the nature, the successes, and the failures of existing induction programs; determining the effects of good mentoring; studying the effectiveness of the ways in which mentors are assigned; and examining the quality of the initial assignments and the orientations given to beginning teachers.

For beginners and for experienced teachers, action plans call for user-friendly situations to ensure that teachers have time for reflection, professional development, writing, planning, team building, revitalization, validation of models of instructional delivery, action research, and connection with colleagues and school units. Conditions of work in schools influence greatly what even outstanding beginning (or experienced) teachers are able to do. Until teachers' assignments and schedules become more practitioner friendly, even the best teacher education program may be for naught.

Proposals for quality support and supervision of beginning teachers include surveys of existing induction programs, their level of funding, and the results achieved. There is also encouragement to establish state policies on induction that contain adequate funding. A related proposal is to establish state-level standards and rewards for selection and preparation of school-based educators who supervise preservice and beginning teachers.

Practicing Teachers

Proposals for practicing teachers include promotion of positive teacher initiatives to ensure quality K–12 educational experiences and creation of partnerships with other human service professionals to ensure delivery of adequate services in local communities. One plan suggests pairing volunteer education and arts and science faculty to offer peer coaching to teachers. Another plan advocates an interdisciplinary, inter- and intraprofessional sense of community that would change the culture of teaching and teacher education. Whether the interest in changing the culture of schooling is meant to suggest the creation of interprofessional development centers (erstwhile schools), as Corrigan's chapter suggests, is not clear.

One plan calls for educators to identify a vision—for example: "We're here so that children can learn. All children learn, all teachers learn, in a healthy community." What is done in school should be evaluated against such a vision. Everything that does not contribute to the vision should be jettisoned.

Many plans call for professional development schools and interprofessional collaboratives to improve teacher education and to promote partnerships between higher education and public schools. Several proposals suggest incorporating preservice clinical experiences into induction and continuing professional development while addressing preparation, licensure, induction, certification, and continuing education equally. Often, in suggesting the examination of professional development schools and other best practices, the plans recommend collection and dissemination of successful models. There is wide agreement on, and frequent mention of, discovering and disseminating best practices, and on doing this through a clearing-house—an ERIC center or a comparable agency. Such an effort should encompass every conceivable aspect of teacher education.

There is a proposal to broaden the concept of teacher education and school improvement by conducting a meta-analysis of each area of the teacher education continuum to discover what works.

The Reputation of Teacher Education

Creating a better public persona for teachers and improving the reputation of teacher education are the subjects of some action plans. Teaching and teacher education have never enjoyed high public standing in the United States, partially because of their histories. Only recently have states required elementary school teachers to hold college degrees; until the 1940s most elementary school teachers were prepared in normal schools or teachers colleges. High school graduation was for just a small portion of youth until the early 1900s. It is no surprise, then, that teacher education, one of the newest professional schools in the university (introduced in the 1940s and the 1950s), rates low in prestige. Unfortunately, even the major achievements of the teaching profession and teacher education are seldom well publicized. Table 9.1 sets forth some of them. Additional achievements are that over the 124 years represented in Table 9.1 on pp. 198–199, from 1869 to 1993, the percentage of 5- to 17-year-olds enrolled in school increased from 57.0 to 91.7 and the percentage of 17-year-olds graduating from high school grew from 2.0 to 72.6 (National Center for Education Statistics, 1995).

One proposal for improving the reputation of teaching is to initiate a national campaign representing teaching as the noblest of professions or as learning for a lifetime. The profession's status might be enhanced by showcasing successes better and more frequently, with an emphasis on how education improves the quality of life; involving parents and citizens more in decision making; and raising public awareness of what is happening in education. Another suggestion is to build bridges to the public to demonstrate teachers' accountability and responsibility for the education of all children. Furthermore, there are suggestions to conduct public relations campaigns to promote the status of teachers, establish political alliances to improve the image of the profession, and mount a national action plan to increase the influence of teachers—all to enhance the prestige of the profession. Still another proposal is for teacher educators to work with the public to promote improvement, the notion being that mutual support would improve education's credibility. Last, and perhaps most important, is the idea of promoting public education as essential for participating in and advancing a democratic society (the theme of ATE's 1997 annual conference).

In another vein, one action plan recommends establishing an interdisciplinary, interagency cohort of professionals, possibly in several locations, to provide advice on and to model in practice the kind of reform ("retrofit") of preservice and inservice teacher education that would serve the needs of children and families in the current milieu.

Policy

In the policy arena, one plan proposes calling on President Bill Clinton to convene a National Congress on Teaching and Learning with a larger number and a greater variety of stakeholders to influence national policy regarding teaching and teacher education. The projected result would be a report (readable and sound-bite worthy) to rival the challenge issued in *A Nation at Risk* (but with a positive spin). It might highlight Goals 2000, particularly Goal 7. The plan calls for immediate action on this effort. (Concern is expressed that energies will go into a book rather than into a policy agenda—that is, that the emphasis will be on rhetoric rather than on action.)

Another proposal is to convene a second National Congress on Teacher Education in September 1996 to highlight the importance of education in the United States as a means of fostering a democratic society. It should include all the constituents of the first congress but seek broader representation from business, the learned societies, the human services, preservice teachers, and parents and children. Each person would participate as a representative of a constituency rather than as an individual. In addition, the second congress should select a National Ambassador for Education to speak for it on crucial issues. The most important first step is to create a positive image for teacher education. To that end, the second national congress should devote time to defining what a teacher is, in language that the public can and will understand. A major event might be organized to give focus to these efforts—such as Hands Across the Classroom, a major march on

TABLE 9.1 Growth of the United States, Education, and Teacher
Education, 1869–1993

| | | | Public School Enrollment | |
| | | | --- | --- |
Year	No. of States	U.S. Population	Elementary School	Secondary School
1869–1870	37	39,818,000	6,792,000	80,000
1879–1880	38	50,156,000	9,757,000	110,000
1889–1890	44	62,948,000	12,520,000	203,000
1899–1900	45	75,995,000	14,984,000	519,000
1909–1910	46	90,492,000	16,899,000	915,000
1919–1920	48	104,512,000	19,378,000	2,200,000
1929–1930	48	121,770,000	21,279,000	4,399,000
1939–1940	48	130,880,000	18,833,000	6,601,000
1949–1950	48	148,665,000	19,387,000	5,725,000
1959–1960	50	179,323,000	27,602,000	8,485,000
1969–1970	50	201,385,000	32,597,000	13,022,000
1979–1980	50	224,567,000	27,931,000	13,714,000
1989–1990	50	246,819,000	29,152,000	11,390,000
1992–1993	50	255,028,000	31,081,000	11,735,000

SOURCE: From National Center for Education Statistics (1995); Andrews,
Andrews, and Pape (1996); Clark and Guba (1977); Frazier et al. (1935); and
Stinnett (1974).

Washington, or Lights On for Education. The 1996–1997 school year
should be organized to spotlight schools, with a focus on best practices across the country.

No. of Public School Teachers	No. of Institutions Preparing Teachers			No. of States Requiring Bachelor's Degree for Certification	
	Normal Schools	Teachers Colleges	Total Institutions	Elementary School Teachers	Secondary School Teachers
201,000	69	0	78	0	0
287,000	No data	0	No data	0	0
364,000	204	0	234	0	0
423,000	289	2	No data	0	2
523,000	247	12	379	0	3
657,000	326	46	No data	0	10[a]
843,000	212	134	839	2[a]	23
875,000	103	186	No data	11	40
914,000	5	138	1,005	21	42[b]
1,387,000	0	55[c]	1,150[c]	39	51
2,131,000	0	16	1,246	47	52
2,300,000	0	10 (est.)	1,365 (est.)	52[b]	52
2,860,000	0	0		52	52
3,017,000	0	0	1,332[d]	52	52

a. The District of Columbia is included in this figure and the following figures in this column.
b. Puerto Rico is included in this figure and the following figures in this column.
c. This is a 1961 figure.
d. This is a 1995–1996 figure.

A final suggestion for influencing policy is that the U.S. Department of Education's Office of Educational Research and Improvement be provided with a succinct list of projects to fund and support. This could be a topic for state congresses.

Participants, Resources, and Timetables

Details of Action Plans

The action plans designate the partners for each action recommended, the resources needed, the parties responsible for action, and a target date for accomplishment of a recommended action. This chapter excludes such detail. People in many situations in the country will need to determine for themselves the resources that they need, assign responsibility in their particular circumstances, and set their own timetable. The important task in this chapter is to collect the ideas that the small groups generated.

There are, however, some things to learn from the details. For example, the variety of partners recommended is more broadly based than is customary. In most projects in American teacher education, too few stakeholders have been involved in devising plans and carrying out actions. As a consequence, teacher education has failed to reap the benefit of broad input and has hardly ever taken advantage of the opportunity to generate wide ownership for an improvement. When noneducators have participated, the social distance between them and educators has often been great. Even in projects involving teachers and administrators, their roles have usually been subordinate. For example, student teaching, a cooperative endeavor between schools and colleges, has frequently been a one-sided arrangement in which colleges use schools for clinical experiences and schools reap few benefits and rewards. These are among the reasons that change has been slow. The collaboration and the partnerships proposed in action plans should help remedy such situations.

Many of the proposals have been part of the rhetoric in teacher education for years, but action has lingered far behind talk. The plans under discussion in this chapter should fare better because they call for wide involvement, which should produce understanding of and appreciation for change that has the full concurrence of stakeholders.

Partners

Partners in most proposals are individuals, professional associations, learned societies, government or quasi-government agencies, business and industry organizations, and groups that represent different segments of the society. The individuals, and the persons who speak for the groups—experts, power and authority figures, decision makers, elected and appointed officials, and others—appear to be the people and the elements of the society who need to tackle and solve the problems that the action plans address. The ordinary people, the parents and the citizens of communities, should also participate. The scope and the complexity of the proposals that have been made require, even demand, the involvement of many societal factions. Teacher education and the education of children have a broad effect on the society. In the long term, little is as important as the quality of education that citizens receive in their early years. There is a direct relationship between productive living and quality of life, and a good education.

Educators have often assumed that they know what is best for the learner and for the preparation of those who teach the learner. Today, the world is changing too fast for anyone to assume that he or she knows what is best for every child and every teacher. In addition, unless the learner is engaged in the learning process, little will be remembered and have meaning. As a consequence, education must be a cooperative process, one that is continually evaluated to ensure its relevance for the particular learner, the context, and the content being taught. The action plans from the congress demonstrate a commitment to that concept in specifying the partners that participants would engage to achieve their action plans.

The most significant characteristic of the partners included in the action plans is the breadth of types of people and organizations. Perhaps because there were many different types of stakeholders present at the congress, the plans envision a much broader aggregate of partners. That should continue to be so. Colleges of education should be less self-serving and take leadership by opening up participation in preparing teachers.

Very little is said about protecting turf or sharing power and authority. Sharing control and expense will continue to be an issue. Many plans suggest identifying successful models. Descriptions of effective governance in teacher education and in collaborative projects with other human service personnel and organizations would help. Collection and dissemination of such data are high on the list of recommendations.

Resources

Foremost among the resources prescribed are informed, talented people and financial support. Broken down further, that prescription includes time, staff, leaders, publications, technology, and equipment. Access to journals, ERIC clearinghouses, studies of undergraduate programs, professional development schools, and professional development is essential. In the technology category are computers, modems, electronic systems, the World Wide Web, and home pages. With regard to people, specifications also include the need for persons from many sectors with commitment, energy, resolve, spirit, connections, and human relations skills.

Responsibility

The various action plans assign accountability for their diverse proposals to different individuals and organizations, depending on the nature, the emphasis, and the complexity of the proposal. The relationship between resources and responsibilities often presents a Catch-22–type dilemma. Without at least some resources, proceeding with many of the action plans will be difficult; without achievement, finding resources to further action plans will be difficult. Fortunately, people will carry forward a number of action plans by volunteering to do so, by taking on overloads, and by folding proposals into existing endeavors. All three approaches have been evident in actions since the congress.

One of the responsibilities that ATE and AACTE must accept is documentation of the achievements at local, state, and national levels in pursuing the action plans developed at the congress. Demonstrating that the congress has been more than talk will be essential. Many participants suggest that the goal of a second congress should be to assess progress on action plans of the first congress. Assistant Secretary of Education Robinson makes that challenge in Chapter 8.

Granted, many of the proposals will take more than a year to achieve; participants admit that. Plans can, however, be assessed in terms of the degree of progress achieved. Participants expect progress, having set various target dates—1996, 1997, 1998, and as far ahead as 2001. There can be a different set of questions raised at the next congress. Careful documentation will prompt those questions. A report card on the action plans of the congress would be appropriate—and a way to assess if all the satisfying talk became something more than rhetoric.

References

Andrews, T. E., Andrews, L., & Pape, C. (Eds.). (1996). *The NASDTEC manual 1996–1997: Manual on certification and preparation of educational personnel in the United States and Canada.* Dubuque, IA: Kendall/Hunt.

Clark, D. L., & Guba, E. G. (1977). *A study of teacher education institutions as innovators, knowledge producers, and change agents.* Bloomington: Indiana University Press.

Frazier, B. W., Betts, G. L., Greenleaf, W. J., Waples, D., Dearborn, N. H., Carney, M., & Alexander, T. (1935). *National survey of the education of teachers: Vol. 6. Special survey studies.* Washington, DC: U.S. Government Printing Office.

Interstate New Teacher Assessment and Support Consortium. (1992). *Model standards for beginning teacher licensing and development: A resource for state dialogue.* Washington, DC: Author.

National Center for Education Statistics. (1995). *Digest of education statistics 1995.* Washington, DC: U.S. Government Printing Office.

Stinnett, T. M. (Ed.). (1974). *A manual on standards affecting school personnel in the United States.* Washington, DC: National Education Association.

10

A Plan for Action

LEONARD KAPLAN
Wayne State University

We will be criticized if we do something.
We will be criticized if we do nothing.
Since criticism is inevitable,
Let us do something.

ANONYMOUS

A plan for action issuing from the National Congress on Teacher Education should correspond to the initial set of purposes established for the meeting. The purposes were to

- Highlight and clarify the issues, contributions, and successful practices in teacher education throughout the nation and within local and state contexts and agendas
- Bring together representatives from major constituencies so that each may hear and become more aware of the objectives/recommendations of all organizations
- Further define and publicize the difficulties and problems confronting efforts to improve the teacher education process
- Better understand the knowledge base inherent in the teaching/learning process
- Develop a clear statement about the role of teacher development and higher education in relation to children's learning

- Provide recommendations to practitioners, policymakers, legislators, researchers, and other key education constituents (ATE & AACTE, 1995, p. 6)

The National Congress on Teacher Education was a success. Evaluations from participants ran the range from "good meeting" to "spectacular event." Thus the planners are proud of this first effort. They are mindful, however, that satisfying talk is not enough to solve problems or make improvements. If in a year or two, teacher educators are discussing the same issues, then the congress will not have fulfilled its mission. For years, teacher educators have attended meetings that offered promise but delivered less. Hearts and minds were in the proper place, but resolve for action was short. During the planning for the congress, committee members never left a planning session without a discussion of where our deliberations would go after the congress.

Chapter 9 presents and synthesizes the outcomes of the congress. I make some effort in this chapter not to plow fields already cultivated. However, a plan of action is required. Many of the action items that follow are suggested or implied in the earlier chapter, but they require more emphasis.

Action Item 1. The momentum and the energy that the congress generated must not be lost. One clear outcome is a strong recommendation that state and regional units of ATE and AACTE sponsor their own congresses, using the input and the process developed for the national congress. Many of the materials needed for such meetings are contained in this book. The format for process is available from the national ATE office in Reston, Virginia. Obviously, each state or regional unit will build its own agenda around local concerns and will make some adjustments. However, the major themes of teacher educators, as identified at the congress, are appropriate throughout the United States.

ATE may want to consider another congress a few years hence, or in the year 2000, as a celebration of entering the next century. The latter would certainly keep such a meeting in the "event" category.

Action Item 2. ATE and AACTE should enter into a broad collaboration that includes representation from many other agencies and groups (stakeholders) interested in the initial and continued preparation of teachers—business, industry, health, government, social services, parents, communities, teachers, administrators, and other professional associations. This expanded collaborative (large but manageable) will help formulate positions that reflect consensus on such topics as the following:

1. Quality standards for teachers, teacher educators, and institutions that produce teachers
2. The role of equity (gender, racial, ethnic, age, geographic, and economic) in the preparation of teachers
3. Licensure and certification
4. Ways in which interprofessional collaboration can enhance the quality of the nation's teaching force
5. Ways in which improved teaching results in better and more student learning

Action Item 3. Each state or region should develop a political action plan. This is particularly relevant in an election year. The plan should not endorse any political party or candidate. Rather, it should establish a set of principles, practices, and ideas that offer further insight into the decisions that move the profession. Local, state, and national policymakers may appreciate input regarding effective practice before rather than after they make decisions, and educators can decide to back candidates who support the positions represented in the principles.

Action Item 4. The profession must identify best practices. As it does, more data will become available to support the new consensus. Individuals, institutions, states, and regions are encouraged to produce more action research to support best practice theory. ATE and AACTE have a responsibility to document best practices and other achievements recommended by the congress.

Action Item 5. When ATE and AACTE work together, they represent the major voices in teacher education. They now have in place a joint committee to discuss issues of common interest. The action plans note that the accomplishments of teacher education are a well-kept secret, and they suggest that ATE and AACTE communicate with appropriate media outlets to report best practices, significant accomplishments, meetings, topics of interests to the general public, important research findings, and so forth. ATE and AACTE might begin with a joint statement on the importance of this book as a report of the contributions of the first National Congress on Teacher Education. Teacher education has failed to sing its own praises. It must reverse this behavior, and it has the vehicle in place for beginning to do so. More than a few groups at the congress suggested that the profession consider identifying its own national ambassador. This is an idea worth discussing.

Action Item 6. Moving aggressively forward on the agenda laid out in this and the previous chapter will take courage, initiative, imagination, and funding. Teachers educators can find the first three elements within themselves. They may have to go elsewhere for the fourth. ATE and AACTE appreciate the Department of Education's support and hope to receive similar encouragement for future initiatives. However, teacher education must also reach out to other sectors for support. Many teacher educators are aware of foundations, corporations, businesses, agencies, and individuals that would eagerly or at least willingly support activities to improve teachers' teaching and students' learning, recognizing that doing so would be in their own best interest as well as in that of America and the next generation. As teacher educators and other stakeholders coalesce around themes generated by the congress, they position themselves better to articulate a need for funds. Too frequently, they seek financial support from the same sources, one group unaware of another's interests. They leave the impression that the profession is fragmented. Furthermore, the profession must stop thinking small. It is time to seek millions or several hundred thousands of dollars for reform and improvement.

If the plans for action just identified and those reported in the previous chapter are to succeed, there must be a rethinking of old paradigms. Too often, persons interested in the preparation of teachers have run off in their own directions. They have also tended to overprotect their own turf. I do not recommend mergers of organizations or agencies. However, there must be more meeting of minds and establishing of agendas on items of common interest and commitment. Clearly, the ideas expressed through this congress warrant such collaborative efforts. The tasks before the profession are formidable. Collectively, teacher educators and the other stakeholders can realize this agenda; separately, they probably cannot. The integrity of each participating organization or agency must be maintained, but not at the expense of America's children or the improvement of teacher education. Consequently, the action plans must be coordinated by some sort of collaborative council.

Chapter 9 provides evidence of the energy and the action orientation of the participants. The suggestions in this chapter meet the spirit and the intent of the persons who planned the congress, and they move the agenda forward. As the profession begins to implement this plan, modifications will be necessary. Also, individuals and groups will continue to put forth additional ideas for action. The vehicle for implementing them is in place.

Conclusion

The professional development of teachers does not begin in college and end at commencement. An effective professional learns and matures in ability continually throughout a career. One of the ways in which the success of the first congress will be measured is the degree to which the action that follows promotes an environment that supports continuous learning for the practitioner. Staff development is a priority for action, not a budgetary afterthought. Teaching is a complex career, not a job that any well-intended person can occupy.

Too often, professional meetings become lost in their own rhetoric. Frequently, the persons who assemble forget what brought them together in the first place. With this congress, there is no ambiguity. What must be done is clear. For the new millennium, the definition of teacher must be reconsidered and redefined. There must be better policy and better practice on the respective roles of higher education and schools in the preparation of teachers—that is, how theory and practice are separated and then merged, how collegiate study and clinical experiences are integrated, how preparation moves to induction and gradually to full professional responsibility, and then, if the notion of a continuum in teacher education is valid, how vitality, enthusiasm, and commitment are maintained throughout a career and supported by policy from the structures that govern the profession. The profession must realize that a teacher's strength lies in assisting the learner not only to know more in a more creative environment but also to become a more humane citizen.

The ultimate measurement of the accomplishments of the first National Congress on Teacher Education will be the resulting improvement in the learning of children. Improvement of children's learning was essentially the reason for convening the congress. Children are the teaching profession's motivation, not just its clients. They deserve a society committed to supporting the young. Teacher educators will differ on the many roads available to achieve that goal. However, the stakeholders must agree on what they want to achieve. Anything less is unacceptable. The new millennium offers challenges unparalleled in America's history. Educators must change with the times, perhaps even pioneer change. Whether the deliberations of the congress have meaning and influence will depend on the actions that the participants and their colleagues take. The congress began a revitalization of people to pursue an attainable goal. May that spirit continue.

Reference

Association of Teacher Educators & American Association of Colleges for Teacher Education. (1995). *Teachers for the new millennium: Aligning teacher development, national goals, and high standards for all students* [Proposal to the U.S. Department of Education, Fund for the Improvement of Education]. Reston, VA: Author; Washington, DC: Author.

Appendix: Participants in the National Congress on Teacher Education

The following list of participants in the National Congress on Teacher Education has been compiled from registration records; addresses represent the individual's location at the time of the congress. We apologize to any individual whose name has been omitted or whose address or affiliation is incorrect. Inclusion on the list does not imply endorsement of the ideas or recommendations in this book.

Susan Adler, University of Missouri–Kansas City
Elizabeth Aitken, Christian Educators Association International, Rockville, Maryland
Alejandra A. Ajuria, Educator Preparation Improvement Initiative, Austin, Texas
Gracia A. Alkema, Corwin Press, Inc., Thousand Oaks, California
Parker Anderson, National Association for the Education of Young Children, Washington, D.C.
David M. Andrews, California State University, Fresno
Ted Andrews, Washington State Board of Education, Olympia
Richard I. Arends, Connecticut State University, New Britain
Susan Arisman, Frostburg State University, Maryland
Sylvia Auton, Fairfax Public Schools, Virginia
Michael Bachmann, College of DuPage, Western Springs, Illinois
Sarah W. Bednarz, Texas A&M University, College Station
Karolyn Belcher, TEACH!, New York City
Peggy Blackwell, University of New Mexico, Albuquerque
Charles Bleiker, University of New Mexico, Albuquerque
David Boger, North Carolina A&T University, Greensboro

Fran Bond, Peace Corps, Washington, D.C.
Barbara Brittingham, University of Rhode Island, Kingston
Andrew Brulle, Northern Illinois University, De Kalb
Barbara G. Burch, California State University, Fresno
Sarah B. Burkhalter, Texas Higher Education Coordinating Board, Austin
Kenneth Burrett, Duquesne University, Pittsburgh, Pennsylvania
Eugene J. Campbell, Colorado Department of Education, Denver
Gene V. Campbell, University of Arkansas at Little Rock
Jacqueline Campbell, Detroit Open School, Michigan
Gloria Chernay, Association of Teacher Educators, Reston, Virginia
Doran Christensen, Salisbury State University, Maryland
Rebecca Clemente, Ball State University, Muncie, Indiana
Renee Clift, University of Illinois at Urbana-Champaign
Mary Lynn Collins, Lemoine College, Syracuse, New York
Nancy Cope, North Carolina State University, Raleigh
Dean Corrigan, Texas A&M University, College Station
Fred Curtis, Baylor University, Waco, Texas
William Daly, student, George Mason University, Fairfax, Virginia
Gary DeBolt, State University of New York at Geneseo
Mary E. Diez, Alverno College, Milwaukee, Wisconsin
Billy G. Dixon, Southern Illinois University, Carbondale
Annora Dorsey, U.S. Department of Education, Washington, D.C.
Mildred Dougherty, William Paterson College, Wayne, New Jersey
Terry Dozier, U.S. Department of Education, Washington, D.C.
Edward R. Ducharme, Drake University, Des Moines, Iowa
Mary K. Ducharme, Drake University, Des Moines, Iowa
Rose M. Duhon-Sells, McNeese State University, Lake Charles, Louisiana
Linda DuncanMalone, Ball State University, Muncie, Indiana
Mary Dupuis, Pennsylvania State University, State College
Wilma Durham, Archbishop Carroll High School, Washington, D.C.
Carole Dwyer, Educational Testing Service, Princeton, New Jersey
Roy A. Edelfelt, University of North Carolina at Chapel Hill; North Carolina State University, Raleigh
Daniel Elliott, Christian Educators Association International, Pasadena, California
Thomas Elliott, Virginia Department of Education, Richmond
Dolores Escobar, San Jose State University, California
Christy Faison, Rowan College of New Jersey, Glassboro

Susan Farewell, student, George Mason University, Fairfax, Virginia
Henry Fernandez, Peace Corps, Washington, D.C.
Elizabeth Fideler, Recruiting New Teachers, Inc., Belmont, Massachusetts
Joe Fisher, National-Louis University, Wheeling, Illinois
Linda Fisher, Illinois State University, Normal
Robert E. Floden, Michigan State University, East Lansing
Betty Ford, California University of Pennsylvania
Jackie L. Friedrich, U.S. Department of Education, Washington, D.C.
Mary Fulton, Education Commission of the States, Denver, Colorado
Mary Hatwood Futrell, George Washington University, Washington, D.C.
Anne R. Gayles-Felton, Florida A&M University, Tallahassee
Crystal J. Gips, California State University, Northridge
Susan Gorin, National Association of School Psychologists, Bethesda, Maryland
Robert Gough, education consultant, Surrey, England
Carl A. Grant, University of Wisconsin–Madison
Lynn Gray, San Jose State University, California
Sue Gruskin, U.S. Department of Education, Washington, D.C.
Frederica Haas, Pennsylvania State Department of Education, Harrisburg
Martin J. Haberman, University of Wisconsin–Milwaukee
Janet E. Haffner, Accelerated Academics Academy, Flint, Michigan
Ogden Hamilton, Pi Lambda Theta, Bloomington, Indiana
Vicki Harding, Servicemembers Opportunity Colleges, Washington, D.C.
Pat Harper, National Coalition for Sex Equity in Education, Helena, Montana
Paula Harrema, Mary Lin Elementary School, Atlanta, Georgia
Willis D. Hawley, University of Maryland, College Park
Fay A. Head, North Carolina State University, Raleigh
Brenda H. Heffner, Illinois State Board of Education, Chicago
Menahem Herman, U.S. Department of Education, Washington, D.C.
John Heywood, University of Dublin, Ireland
John Hicks, Slippery Rock University of Pennsylvania
Francisco Hidalgo, Texas A&M University, Kingsville
Maggie Holder, Elizabeth Forward High School, West Homestead, Pennsylvania

Richard Horne, Academy for Educational Development, Washington, D.C.

Robert Houston, University of Houston, Texas

Kenneth Howey, Ohio State University, Columbus

Peggy Hypes, Carson-Newman College, Jefferson City, Tennessee

David Imig, American Association of Colleges for Teacher Education, Washington, D.C.

Peggy Ishler, University of Northern Iowa, Cedar Falls

Ron Jandura, Genoa-Kingston Schools, Illinois

Ronald G. Joekel, Phi Delta Kappa, Bloomington, Indiana

Robbie Johnson, Eastern Michigan University, Ypsilanti

Susan Johnson, Ball State University, Muncie, Indiana

Greg Jordan, student, George Mason University, Fairfax, Virginia

Cheryl Kane, New American Schools, Arlington, Virginia

William Kane, University of New Mexico, Albuquerque

Evelyn Kaplan, Farmington Public Schools, Farmington Hills, Michigan

Leonard Kaplan, Wayne State University, Detroit, Michigan

Dennis J. Kear, Wichita State University, Kansas

Jan S. Kettlewell, University System of Georgia, Atlanta

Joe Kretovics, Western Michigan University, Kalamazoo

Linda Gordon Kuzmack, American Association of University Women, Washington, D.C.

Martharose F. Laffey, National Council for the Social Studies, Washington, D.C.

Sharon Lamson, Central Missouri State University, Warrensburg

Mary Anne Lecos, George Mason University, Fairfax, Virginia

Marsha Levine, National Council for Accreditation of Teacher Education, Washington, D.C.

Ed Little, National Coalition for Sex Equity in Education, Vancouver, Washington

JoAnne Livingston, U.S. Department of Education, Washington, D.C.

Meredith Ludwig, American Association of State Colleges and Universities, Washington, D.C.

Joel Lundak, Peru State College, Nebraska

Kay Luzier, National Parent-Teacher Association, Chicago, Illinois

Ann Lydecker, Bridgewater State College, Massachusetts

Bonnie Lynch, Ball State University, Muncie, Indiana

Robert H. MacDonald, Old Dominion University, Norfolk, Virginia

Gene Maeroff, Carnegie Foundation for the Advancement of Teaching, Princeton, New Jersey
Anne Marino, Howard County Public Schools, Columbia, Maryland
Suzanne Martin, U.S. Department of Education, Washington, D.C.
William Martin, George Mason University, Fairfax, Virginia
Pat Marvell, Barnet Professional Development Centre, London, England
Beverly Mattson, Academy for Educational Development, Washington, D.C.
Patty McAllister, Educational Testing Service, Washington, D.C.
Jane McCarthy, University of Nevada–Las Vegas
Sandra McCormick, International Reading Association, Hilliard, Ohio
James McDonnell, Canisius College, Buffalo, New York
Ken McEwin, Appalachian State University, Boone, North Carolina
Jay McIntire, Council for Exceptional Children, Reston, Virginia
D. John McIntyre, Southern Illinois University, Carbondale
Joane McKay, University of Northern Iowa, Cedar Falls
John G. McLevie, Northern Illinois University, De Kalb
Catherine McNamee, National Catholic Education Association, Washington, D.C.
Bob McNergney, University of Virginia, Charlotte
Hilda Medrano, University of Texas Pan American University, Edinburg
Kathleen Megivern, Association for the Education and Rehabilitation of the Blind and Visually Impaired, Alexandria, Virginia
John B. Merbler, Ball State University, Muncie, Indiana
Frank D. Meyers, University of Nevada–Reno
Ernest Middleton, State University of New York at Oswego
Loren Miller, Cooper School, Fort Dodge, Iowa
Laurajean Milligan, retired, Farmington Hills, Michigan
Joe Milner, Wake Forest University, Winston-Salem, North Carolina
Lynn Montgomery, Anoka-Hennepin Schools, Coon Rapids, Minnesota
Heather Moore, U.S. Department of Education, Washington, D.C.
Judy Munn, Hartley Elementary School, Lincoln, Nebraska
Joyce Murphy, U.S. Department of Education, Washington, D.C.
Charles B. Myers, Vanderbilt University, Nashville, Tennessee
Thomas S. Nagel, San Diego State University, California
Iris Nierenberg, Ball State University, Muncie, Indiana

Priscilla Norton, University of New Mexico, Albuquerque
J. Oakes, Indiana Professional Standards Board, Indianapolis
Karla Oakley, Performance Assessment Instruments, New York City
Bernard Oliver, Washington State University, Pullman
Hans Olsen, University of Houston, Clear Lake, Texas
Leroy Ortiz, University of New Mexico, Albuquerque
Arturo Pacheco, University of Texas–El Paso
Paul Paese, Southwest Texas State University, San Marcos
Annette Palutis, Pennsylvania State Education Association, Harrisburg
Sammie Campbell Parrish, North Carolina Central University, Durham
Barbara Perry-Sheldon, North Carolina Wesleyan College, Rocky
    Mount
Bill Peter, Central Missouri State University, Warrensburg
Carol Ann Pierson, Dakota State University, Madison, South Dakota
Richard Pitcock, American Association of School Personnel Admin-
    istrators, Pittsburgh, Pennsylvania
Wayne Powell, State of New Mexico Office of Rural Health, Albu-
    querque
Lee Ann Prielipp, Washington Education Association, Federal Way
Linda Quinn, University of Nevada–Las Vegas
Marilyn Quinn, Delaware Higher Education Commission, Wilmington
Nancy Quisenberry, Southern Illinois University, Carbondale
Jean Ramage, University of Nebraska at Kearney
Bruce Ramirez, Council for Exceptional Children, Reston, Virginia
Paul Ramsey, Educational Testing Service, Princeton, New Jersey
Charlotte Reed, Indiana University Northwest, Gary
Alan Reiman, North Carolina State University, Raleigh
Diana Rigden, Council for Basic Education, Washington, D.C.
Richard W. Riley, U.S. Department of Education, Washington, D.C.
Martha Roark, Maryland Higher Education Commission, Annapolis
Carrie Robinson, Jersey City State College, New Jersey
Sandra Robinson, University of South Carolina, Columbia
Sharon Porter Robinson, U.S. Department of Education, Office of
    Educational Research and Improvement, Washington, D.C.
Valerie Rockefeller, U.S. Department of Education, Washington, D.C.
Realista Rodriguez, Fairfax County Public Schools, Virginia
Alba Rosenman, Ball State University, Muncie, Indiana
Carole Rothberg, Western Illinois University, Macomb
Herb Salinger, American Association of School Personnel Adminis-
    trators, Sacramento, California

Gloria Santistevan-Feeback, National Education Association, Pueblo, Colorado

Robert Schuck, University of New Orleans, Louisiana

Ana Maria Schuhmann, Kean College of New Jersey, Union

Shirley Schwartz, Council of the Great City Schools, Washington, D.C.

Susan J. Sears, Ohio State University, Columbus

Sylvia Seidel, National Education Association, Center for Innovation, Washington, D.C.

Mary Selke, University of Northern Iowa, Waterloo

Kathlene Shank, Eastern Illinois University, Charleston

Fred R. Sheheen, South Carolina Commission on Higher Education, Columbia

Ken Sheldon, psychologist, Rocky Mount, North Carolina

Julie Sherrill, Ohio State University, Columbus

James Shuman, St. Lawrence University, Canton, New York

Audrey Smith, U.S. Department of Education, Washington, D.C.

Kathryn Smith, Bemidji State University, Minnesota

Larry Smith, Ball State University, Muncie, Indiana

Terry Smith, Bemidji State University, Minnesota

Owen Solomon, U.S. Department of Education, Washington, D.C.

Sam Spaght, Wichita Public Schools, Kansas

George W. Spicely, U.S. Department of Education, Washington, D.C.

Donald Stedman, University of North Carolina at Chapel Hill

Shirley Steele, U.S. Department of Education, Washington, D.C.

James Steffensen, U.S. Department of Education–retired, Alexandria, Virginia

Patricia L. Stock, National Council of Teachers of English, Washington, D.C.

Carol T. Stoel, American Association of Higher Education, Education Trust, Washington, D.C.

Roger Strand, Old Dominion University, Norfolk, Virginia

Neal Supplee, Boeing Computer Services, Seattle, Washington

Thomas J. Switzer, University of Northern Iowa, Cedar Falls

Linda Tafel, National-Louis University, Wheeling, Illinois

Ronda C. Talley, American Psychological Association, Washington, D.C.

Kathe Taylor, Washington State Higher Education Coordinating Board, Olympia

Terri Tingle, Turner Entertainment Networks, Atlanta, Georgia

Janet Towslee, Clayton State College, Morrow, Georgia
Beverly Uhlenberg, University of North Dakota, Grand Forks
Jo Anne Vacca, Kent State University, Ohio
Richard Vacca, International Reading Association, Kent, Ohio
Gene VanStone, Stanley Hall Enrichment Center, Evansville, Indiana
Joseph C. Vaughan, U.S. Department of Education, Washington,
    D.C.
Judith Wain, Minnesota Board of Teaching, St. Paul
David Wallace, The Sequoyah Group, Washington, D.C.
Mary Walsh, Boston College, Chestnut Hill, Massachusetts
Doug Warring, University of St. Thomas, St. Paul, Minnesota
Roy A. Weaver, Ball State University, Muncie, Indiana
Nona Weekes, Bank Street College of Education, New York City
James Whiteman, Fulton County Schools, Wauseon, Ohio
Boyce Williams, National Council for Accreditation of Teacher
    Education, Washington, D.C.
David L. Williams, Jr., Southwest Educational Development
    Laboratories, Austin, Texas
Donna Wissbrun, Eastern Michigan University, Ypsilanti
Edward M. Wolpert, Georgia College, Milledgeville
Paula Wood, Wayne State University, Detroit, Michigan
Tom Wood, University of Texas–El Paso
Donna Zaiger, National Association of School Nurses, Scarborough,
    Maine
Peggi Zelinko, U.S. Department of Education, Washington, D.C.
Stanley D. Zenor, Association for Educational Communication and
    Technology, Washington, D.C.
Nancy L. Zimpher, Ohio State University, Columbus

CORWIN
PRESS

The Corwin Press logo—a raven striding across an open book—represents the happy union of courage and learning. We are a professional-level publisher of books and journals for K–12 educators, and we are committed to creating and providing resources that embody these qualities. Corwin's motto is "Success for All Learners."